DIVING IN

DIVING IN

Bill Ayers and the
Art of Teaching
into the Contradiction

Isabel Nuñez, Crystal T. Laura, and Rick Ayers
EDITORS

Teachers College, Columbia University
New York and London

KH

Published by Teachers College Press, 1234 Amsterdam Avenue, New York, NY 10027

Copyright © 2014 by Teachers College, Columbia University

Library of Congress Cataloging-in-Publication Data

Bill Ayers and the art of teaching into the contradiction / edited by Isabel Nuñez, Crystal T. Laura, and Rick Ayers.
    pages cm
  Includes index.
  ISBN 978-0-8077-5577-8 (pbk. : alk. paper) —
  ISBN 978-0-8077-5578-5 (hardcover : alk. paper) —
  ISBN 978-0-8077-7324-6 (e-book)
    1. Critical pedagogy—United States. 2. Transformative learning—United States. 3. Ayers, William, 1944– I. Nuñez, Isabel (Associate professor), editor of compilation.
  LC196.5.U6B44 2014
  370.11'5--dc23   2014015551

ISBN 978-0-8077-5577-8 (paper)
ISBN 978-0-8077-5578-5 (hardcover)
ISBN 978-0-8077-7324-6 (e-book)

Printed on acid-free paper
Manufactured in the United States of America

21 20 19 18 17 16 15 14   8 7 6 5 4 3 2 1

3/2/16

Contents

Illustration by Ryan Alexander-Tanner

Introduction

Rick Ayers, Crystal T. Laura, and Isabel Nuñez

This volume takes focus and inspiration from the life and work of Bill Ayers. It is not meant to be a tribute book, it is not a venerable academic *Festschrift*, it is not a point of arrival, and it is certainly not a eulogy. Rather it is part of an ongoing conversation and struggle that invites—requires—the insights, reflections, and actions of the largest imaginable community. This book is grounded in the recognition that our identities and destinies are co-constructed in classrooms—and in the many journeys students and teachers take beyond the classroom.

We undertake this project in celebration of the many insights and provocations Bill Ayers has provided over the years. Sometimes his influence was a matter of pushing us to see the world from the point of view of the young; sometimes it was helping us unearth buried knowledge about what is right; and always it was a call to action, to make our values real in the world through our work and struggle.

Perhaps the most generative of Bill's exhortations has been to "write into the contradiction." No student of Bill's is likely to be unfamiliar with this mantra, regardless of the particularities of their own struggles and tensions. After all, there is no one without paradox—and this is something to be celebrated. From Heraclitus we learned that "the opposite is beneficial; from things that differ comes the fairest attunement." Spiritual traditions from Zen to Sufism to the Judeo-Christian mystics have echoed this call for the union of opposites. So has Bill.

In this era of testing and punishing, of anemic standardization, of attacks on communities of the global majority and on teachers and their unions, and of toxic racism in the way schools and larger social forces sort and discipline students, we remind ourselves that there was never a golden age; schools have been repressive, classist, heteronormative, male, and White supremacist—and boring—for centuries. But they are also sites of resistance, creativity, and hope for they are where the project of democracy is worked out on the ground and in the flesh. For students and teachers alike, the norms and expectations of society, imposed through its institutions, regularly blunt or frustrate our deepest values and our desire to seek community and solidarity. In this sense, Ayers's work is radical in that it takes us to the root, the foundational assumptions of the project of democracy. Education is not just about devising ways to transmit a settled body of knowledge into the minds of students. Instead, that knowledge itself and the way knowledge is constructed—by whom and in whose interest—becomes the burning question.

We will not arrive at our answers by traveling a straight road. Questions that bring us this deep must be explored by way of contradictions; they require dialectical reasoning and a journey that wends and winds with many an unexpected stop, each of which shares its own lesson. Bill and his work have inspired countless individuals to set off on this quest. His life is a model of the transformative possibilities when one engages one's context with, as he has described, "one foot in the mud and muck of the world as it is, one foot moving toward a world that could be but is not yet." Coming out of the radical student movement of the 1960s and the call by Students for a Democratic Society (SDS) for "participatory democracy," this work challenges inert and demoralizing formal democracy with a vision of the propulsive power of ordinary people unleashing their imaginations and energies on behalf of a world at peace and in balance, with liberty, joy, and justice for all.

In that spirit, we have pursued this volume as a work-in-progress, a chance for activists, scholars, and educators to consider the challenges and possibilities of our times beyond the well-known and the oft-repeated. We seek conversation, dialogue, and struggle, and our "point-last-seen" is the writing, teaching, speaking, and activism of Bill Ayers.

The ancient Taoist symbol of yin and yang represents the interdependence of opposites, each one resting on and supporting the other. In the modern age, Niels Bohr distinguished "two sorts of truths: profound truths recognized by the fact that the opposite is also a profound truth, in contrast to trivialities where opposites are obviously absurd" (Rozental, 1967, p. 328). In the spirit of diving deeply into both sides of profound truths, we invited contributors to "write into the contradiction," to approach education issues not as settled dogma but as generative zones in a contested space. They have responded with enthusiasm, adding up to a delightful mix that surely will speak to our work today and endure as critical to the social struggles of the years ahead.

References

Rozental, S. (1967). *Niels Bohr: His life and work as seen by his friends and colleagues.* Amsterdam, Netherlands: North-Holland.

Illustration by Ryan Alexander-Tanner

Part I

THE PASSION OF FIRE

There is a reason people refer to the spark of excitement, the first flicker of love, the heat of passion. There are times in every person's life when the body seems too small a vessel for all of the feeling that it needs to contain, when one's emotions are so raw and so powerful that they must erupt as in flame, whether in shouting or in tears—or in delighted squeals. There are times of slow burn, when emotions underlie a relentless drive, when they fuel a determination that will not be stopped. These are the periods when fire energy rules—some of the most transformative times in human life. Fire, after all, involves chemical change, change to substance and material composition.

Bill Ayers is a model of transformative change, both in his personal evolution and in the changes he has helped others to achieve—individually and collectively. His fire energy has burned in anger; he has even, for some, become a caricature of hot-headed action. For far longer, however, his fire energy has fueled the furnace of his tireless work toward others' transformations. Bill's teaching, his writing, and his activism all transmit the warmth of his care for people and his passion for justice. It is no wonder that the essays in this part glow with fire energy.

The first chapter, written by Bill's partner of many decades, Bernardine Dohrn, is called "In My Lifetime, Young People Have Changed the World," and it illustrates how even the youngest of us can put fire energy to transformative use. This historical narrative describes the Birmingham Children's Crusade of the Civil Rights Movement, when thousands of African American youth (some as young as 6) stood up to fight for justice despite arrests, detentions, and violence, ultimately winning a decisive move toward desegregating that city.

The story related by Dohrn of resistance by young people may explain the reactions to one child described by Carl A. Grant, Karla Manning, and Alexandra Allweiss in "Education in Urban Spaces." This chapter analyzes a particular media image from the 2013 school closings in Chicago: an African American child distraught at the impending closure of her school. While the photo would elicit sympathy from some, the authors explain how "othering" discourses of emotional excess—too much fire energy—serve to distance other audiences from this child and her feelings.

Bree Picower, in "Haunted by My Students' Students," provides a stark illustration of exactly such distancing in the attitudes of some preservice teachers toward their future charges. The author seethes with fire energy in recounting how one teacher candidate cannot or will not acknowledge the humanity and blamelessness of a child whose mother entered the United States without documentation.

In "The Personal Is Certainly Political," Patrick Camangian offers reassurance that hegemonic discourses are not all-powerful. Despite the oppressive messages the author heard while growing up—which likely propelled him to a brief stint in jail—he forged an alternative path. In fact, it was in that very jail that the flame of his transformation was sparked. Now he is working to nurture the same kind of change in others.

Bill Ayers himself is presented as another example of this kind of unexpected transformation, by William H. Watkins in "Movement Man, Moral Warrior." How, the author asks, does a White, upper-middle-class young man grow into a fighter for socioeconomic justice, and how can we facilitate such change in others? Acknowledging Bill's unique fire, Watkins suggests that a heightened sense of class consciousness might ignite such a flame for others.

Change feels inevitable when reading Lisa Yun Lee's "Antimonies of Cultural Preservation and Cultural Transformation, or 'Are You a Chinese from Prato?'" Inspired by a disturbing experience of race- and class-based dislocation when traveling abroad in Italy, Lee reflects on a globalizing world, where transnational movements of peoples, languages, and cultural symbols are so rapid as to leave one regularly disoriented. Despite the dizzying pace of change, Lee urges us to consider deeply with whom we share our home fires.

Similar in feeling and ultimate message, Erica R. Meiners and Therese Quinn present a frenetic picture of another kind of movement: social movement building. Elegiac despite its pace, "The New Normal: Meditations on Failure" honors and mourns the many efforts that social justice workers have mounted unsuccessfully. A troubling read in its emotional intensity, the essay nevertheless ends on a note of hope in the power of solidarity, even when what is being shared is sadness.

The final chapter of the part fans that ember of hope into a flame. In "(L)Ayers and Circuits of Provocation and Possibility," Michelle Fine brings us full circle to Dohrn's celebration of the possibilities for resistance, this time at the opposite end of the educational continuum. The academy seems nearly as incongruous as the playground as a site of rebellion, but Fine finds inspiration in the example set by Bill and others for how to live a life of both scholarship and activism, envisioning unbounded alternatives while firmly grounded in the world.

In My Lifetime, Young People Have Changed the World

Children as Social Actors

Bernardine Dohrn

For decades, I've ended speeches and articles with this assertion: *In my lifetime, young people have changed the world.* In Little Rock, in Birmingham, in Soweto, and perhaps also in Tien An Men Square, Palestine, Cairo, the various Occupy encampments around the world, Istanbul, Brazil, it has been the radical impulse to revolt, the spirit of hopefulness, the laser-like insight of adolescents into the hypocrisies of the adult world, the risk-taking impulse of young people willing to break the rules, resisting the immoral taken-for-granted, that has propelled forward major struggles for equality, peace, sustainability, and justice.

Are children whole people, bearers of rights (human and constitutional), and inevitably an active part of their time and place, their culture and community, their race and class, ethnicity and culture, family and community? But are they not also more vulnerable, more easily manipulated and used by adults, more readily drawn to acting in groups, taking risks, and disregarding future consequences, such that they must be—to the extent possible—protected, sheltered, and insulated from hazardous activity and violence? It is this paradox—rights versus protection, actors with agency versus passive victims—these contradictions at the very heart of childhood that lead one to ask: What kind of a person is a child? In the case of children as social actors, these tensions are worthy of diving into. Can both be true? This essay will address some of the enduring complexities of the involvement of young people in direct social justice activities by looking into the Birmingham campaigns of 50 years ago, sometimes called the "children's crusade." Surprisingly, the defiant, direct action of children in the Birmingham struggle to end legal segregation has been less re-explored or remembered than other events of the time, even 50 years later.

Student Nonviolent Coordination Committee (SNCC) forces were dug into Greenwood, MI, voting registration efforts, which seemed stalemated; the Southern Christian Leadership Conference (SCLC) and Dr. King had just departed from a high-profile and "failed" civil rights struggle in Albany, GA, moving SCLC operations to Birmingham where the Reverend Fred Shuttlesworth resided. Planning a full-scale assault on "legal" segregation, SCLC set up their Birmingham headquarters at the Gaston Hotel, convened nightly mass meetings at the Sixteenth Street Baptist Church, and set out to march and bear witness in Kelly Ingram Park across from the church; each became a key site for mobilizations that would lead to downtown.

SCLC settled on a campaign to boycott white-owned and segregated downtown businesses, to mobilize mass demonstrations at City Hall, and to implement a strategy of filling the Birmingham jails. Their Birmingham Manifesto set forth four goals: (1) desegregate public facilities (toilets, water fountains), lunch counters, and department store dressing rooms; (2) hire African American store clerks; (3) implement fair hiring policies in all city departments; and (4) convene a biracial committee to desegregate the schools.

On April 6, Fred Shuttlesworth and 40 civil rights demonstrators (all adults) were arrested and went to jail. A news blackout on the sit-ins and arrests continued, and it became difficult to recruit volunteers willing to be arrested and jailed. SCLC convened citizenship classes for adults and youth in Birmingham, building on Septima Clark and Bernice Robinson's renowned classes developed at Highlander Folk School. These became the forerunners to the brilliant freedom schools, articulated by SNCC organizer Charles Cobb as an independent structure of inquiry, where questions about where African Americans were located, what they made of their circumstances, and what they needed to learn to change their conditions constituted the pedagogy. Bill Ayers has written majestically about the incalculable worth of every child, the Frierean core of the freedom schools, and the kinetic link between liberatory education and social action. For young people, freedom schools opened a powerful path to participation in their own liberation.

Birmingham in 1963 not only was known as the most segregated city in the South, it was the place where the Klan dynamited the homes of those Black people who stood up. Birmingham was also the site of a dual and dueling white power leadership: Public Safety Commissioner Eugene "Bull" Conner's openly confrontational white supremacy, and the "moderate" white business class represented by newly elected Mayor Albert Boutwell. Bull Conner claimed that he had won the mayoral election, and, for this period, there were two city governments of Birmingham: Each met, passed resolutions, used the City Hall parking spaces, and operated in a situation of parallel governance.

Dr. King and Ralph Abernathy went to jail in Birmingham on April 12, Good Friday. Fifty-two other people were arrested by Bull Conner from a march headed to City Hall that had swelled to 1,000. King was held in solitary confinement, with no mattress or sheets, no telephone calls, and, for days, no access to an attorney. On scraps of paper coaxed from an African American jailer and then pages from his lawyer, Martin Luther King wrote his letter of lament to white ministers who were urging caution and religious respectability. Although King's *Letter from a Birmingham Jail* was to become legendary in retrospect, at the time the Birmingham civil rights campaign was denounced by *Time* magazine as "a poorly timed protest" that inflamed tensions when Birmingham was finally making progress, however small, in race relations. Burke Marshall, dispatched by the Kennedy administration to Birmingham, told *The New York Times* that the U.S. government had no authority to take action in Birmingham and privately referred to both King and the movement as a "nuisance." The media characterized both Dr. King and Bull Conner as extremists. *Letter* did not become a rallying cry for justice and equality in Birmingham. It was the subsequent weeks of extraordinary movement activism itself that elevated Dr. King's cry of anguish and anger, well after the fact, into an elegant address of moral victory.

James Bevel was asked by King to preach at the Birmingham mass meeting on Friday night, April 12, just hours after King and Abernathy went to jail. Coming directly from the Greenwood, MI, campaign to register Black voters, Bevel cut loose at a packed church rally, as was his way. Freedom was there for the taking, he declared. All they had to do was to walk: walk to the mass meetings, walk to the courthouse, walk to jail.

Bevel was holding youth workshops on nonviolent direct action with a freedom school curriculum. Birmingham's growing scarcity of adult volunteers willing to go to jail accelerated the work with students. Bevel and Diane Nash, a Nashville movement veteran married to Bevel, began by recruiting the elite student athletes and high-visibility young women, and the workshops went viral. Students began slipping in and out of schools, and showing up at the workshops at younger and younger ages. This was controversial from the beginning, and Birmingham leaders in the African American community who could afford to do so shipped their own children off to distant prep schools or to relatives. Fierce debates emerged within SCLC and among the leading clergy about using children as "battle fodder." Yet the afternoon student workshop attendance was beginning to outnumber the evening mass meetings.

Dr. King, seeking volunteers for the next day's civil disobedience marches, found only students, from high schools and even elementary schools, standing up at the nightly church rallies. At that point, fresh from solitary confinement himself, King explained that the Birmingham jail was no place for children, although he hoped their parents would be inspired by the children's spirit.

On Friday, April 26, a judge ruled that King, Abernathy, their SCLC colleague Wyatt Walker, Shuttlesworth, and seven other Birmingham leaders were guilty of criminal contempt for violating the injunction against marching. He sentenced them to 5 days, the maximum penalty, with the threat of harsher penalties for continuing violations. Shuttlesworth petitioned the city for permission to hold a mass march on Thursday, May 2— but both contending white city councils denied Shuttlesworth's petition. Now anyone who marched would be subject to arrest. And anyone who urged children to participate could be prosecuted for contributing to the delinquency of a minor.

That evening at the nightly church rally, James Bevel announced that the mass march on Thursday would proceed, with or without a parade permit. It would be a special march of high school students, called D-Day. Internally, Bevel argued that any child old enough to belong to a church should be eligible to march to jail. In Baptist practice, any child who could make a conscious acceptance of the Christian faith as a condition of church membership and personal salvation was of age. All such children, his argument went, should be eligible to march to jail. If necessary, they should send young volunteers to jail over the objections of their parents. This too was a way to serve as moral witness. They were not too young to march against segregation.

FBI intelligence, forwarded to the Birmingham police, reported that leaflets were circulating in African American high schools urging all students to leave school at noon on Thursday, May 2. Mass truancy was out of the bag. Bystanders and spectators filled the neighboring streets, and Birmingham police manned the roadblocks from Kelly Ingram Park to downtown. At about 1 P.M. on D-Day, 50 singing, chanting adolescents emerged from the Sixteenth Street Baptist Church. Police moved to contain and then arrest children as young as 6. Children kept coming from the church, marching and singing. Police arrested loads of children, called in school buses to take them to jail, and returned to take more. By 4 P.M., 75 students were jammed into cells built for eight people and 600 of them were in custody.

One thousand adults filled the mass meeting at Shuttlesworth's church by 6 P.M.; the number swelled to 2,000 by the time Shuttlesworth and King arrived. Dr. King reported that 958 children had signed up for jail on D-Day, and assured parents and relatives that the arrested children were learning more than they could in school.

The next day, May 3, Double D-Day, more than 1,500 young people appeared inside the Sixteenth Street Baptist Church, their worried parents and bystanders across the street in the park. The children had emptied the schools. With jail cells overflowing, the city's strategy was no longer mass arrests, but to keep demonstrators away from downtown Birmingham. Law enforcement was gathered, along with school buses, fire equipment, and police vehicles. Students moved forward from the church doors, singing and refusing orders to disperse.

On orders from Bull Conner, Captain Evans signaled the firefighters to turn their hoses on the young people. These were double hoses merging into a single nozzle, water cannons advertised as capable of forcing the mortar from between bricks. The water hit some 10 children who stood their ground, ripping their shirts as they struggled to stay on their feet, throwing them down and back against the wall. New groups of children continued to gather at the other side of the park, utilizing the park confrontation to head for "white" downtown Birmingham. Rocks were thrown from the aroused and angry bystander crowds as young marchers were arrested and loaded onto school buses bound for jail. Conner called for his K-9 corps, and at least three teenagers were bitten and required hospital treatment. A photo of a police dog lunging at the abdomen of a slender, peaceful African American adolescent ran above the fold in *The New York Times* and on the front page of newspapers across the country.

Although more than half of the youthful volunteers still remained in the church, planning to join the witness, 250 had already been arrested. When a police inspector entered the church to negotiate, Dr. King accepted a truce for the day and asked Clarence Jones in New York City to fire off telegrams to the president and attorney general. White Birmingham leaders denounced the use of children as "tools" to threaten lives and property; the juvenile court judge who was overwhelmed with young defendants noted that those who "misled" the children should be jailed. Robert Kennedy stated the White House position that this was a local responsibility to be resolved "in good faith negotiations, and not in the streets." Dr. King and his colleagues privately noted to one another that this outpouring of tender concern for the well-being of Negro children did not extend to their unequal and miserable schools, housing, or family resources.

King refused Washington's pleas to halt the demonstrations. National news reported that 1,000 children had marched to jail in 2 days in Birmingham, and that the city had responded with fire hoses and attacking dogs. Parents, onlookers, and marchers stayed on at the Sixteenth Street Baptist Church. SCLC's Andrew Young cautioned against rock throwing, preaching about the value of remaining a nonviolent movement. Dr. King, received with wild ovations, calmly told the families not to worry about their children. "They are suffering for what they believe." There was an avalanche of volunteers for the next days' marches.

On Saturday, May 5, Wyatt Walker orchestrated groups of dispersed young pedestrians walking near downtown City Hall who suddenly converged with a banner reading, "Love God and Thy Neighbor." Bull Conner personally ordered all 25 arrested. Immediately, a woman and small girl knelt on the steps of City Hall and were arrested. Soon police were arresting "strolling Negroes" in the downtown area, but young people continued to emerge in small groups from two other churches. Police sealed all the church doors shut, shifting the action from prepared nonviolent young activists to the spectator adults in Kelly Ingram Park, some of whom had rocks, knives, and guns. Bevel borrowed a police bullhorn and dispersed the park crowd, unilaterally declaring that Sunday's demonstration was suspended in order to prepare for Monday's march.

Allies arrived from across the country. The Birmingham Black community insisted that King's four conditions were a precondition to ceasing the demonstrations. Privately, the White House and Burke Marshall continued to characterize Dr. King and SCLC as not knowing what they were demonstrating about or what they wanted.

On Monday, May 7, with King back in Birmingham, comedian Dick Gregory and a flock of young people stepped from the Sixteenth Street Baptist Church singing and dancing their way into paddy wagons and buses. And they kept coming in waves, increasing numbers of adults with them, stepping forth to be arrested. The demonstrators were arrested at the rate of 10 each minute, for nearly 2 hours. Both the crowd around the park and the police were losing patience, and when 800 had marched to jail from the church, the demonstrations were halted by SCLC. For the first time, more than 200 demonstrators had been arrested at surprise picket lines in the business districts.

Parents were upset that their arrested children were being held in outdoor pens at the fairgrounds in a rainstorm. When King went to investigate he saw parents throwing food and blankets over the chain link fences to their children. He called Burke Marshall to insist on shelter and federal attention to those young people whom he characterized as "political prisoners." Some 2,500 people were in jail in Birmingham. "Never in the history of this nation have so many people been arrested for the cause of freedom and human dignity," he said. The next day's *New York Times* story by Claude Sitton carried the headline, "Birmingham Jails 1,000 More Negroes."

SCLC organizers had noticed that on Monday, downtown Birmingham was virtually empty of white shoppers, whether in fear of the youth who had reached City Hall or of the "troubles." The freedom strategists decided to saturate the business district with demonstrators, and at 6 A.M. Tuesday morning the youth leaders set out to homes and schools to mobilize their most trusted recruits. As Dr. King gave a press conference, young demonstrators convened in small groups around the business district. SCLC staffers Dorothy Cotton, Isaac Reynolds, and other adults gave direction to small youth groups of 50 or less, while Bevel and Walker ostentatiously showed up at the Sixteenth Street Baptist Church.

At noon, 14 Black children with schoolbooks and lunch bags emerged from the church heading downtown, well before the usual march time. Police rushed to stop them and direct them back to the African American part of town. More "decoy" teams emerged, while the most experienced nonviolent students broke loose, running along the sidewalks from all directions. In moments, there were 600 picket lines in the center of the downtown business district. Police, still concentrated at the church where young people were continuing to step out, were slow to recognize that the demonstrators were actually behind the rear lines. As the police blockade began to divide in two directions, Walker used his walkie-talkie to call for a general charge toward downtown. Youngsters bolted from the church, around the police and past white pedestrians, into the heart of downtown Birmingham, celebrating, weaving in and out of segregated stores, and sitting in. The press estimated that there were 3,000 African Americans, what King called "square blocks of Negroes."

By the end of the day, business leaders thought better of calling for martial law under either Governor Wallace's troops or federal forces. President Kennedy and Attorney General Robert Kennedy privately pressed for settlement. The downtown occupation remained nonviolent, but near riots began near the church. Firefighters used a monitor gun on Rev. Shuttlesworth, who appeared with a line of singing children; the water hose pinned him against the wall of the Sixteenth Street Baptist Church. An ambulance took him to the hospital, but the water hoses continued against further rows of children.

At midnight, the local negotiators went to King, yielding to the reality that any settlement must include him and have his approval. Shuttlesworth and King spoke at a press conference about good-faith negotiations, and President Kennedy began a news conference within the hour, welcoming the progress toward settlement in Birmingham—his first press conference dominated by issues of segregation and racism.

What of the 2,000 movement prisoners still in jail in Birmingham? Perhaps inevitably, at the moment of settlement, Wallace's state troopers began military maneuvers in Kelly Ingram Park and Bull Conner padlocked the church. At a hearing on their convictions from the Good Friday march, King and Abernathy stated that they were unwilling to pay $2,500 bail each, and both were immediately taken off to jail. Now Robert Kennedy needed King out of jail and appealed to Harry Belafonte to raise King's bail. King seized the opportunity to insist that *all* prisoners be released and their charges dropped, or that they be released on their own recognizance, *before* he would be bailed.

It was Thursday, May 9, when King rejected a proposal that the release of the 500 youngest prisoners should be taken as a sign that efforts would be made to release the remaining prisoners in exchange for the settlement. They should never have been arrested, King pointed out. Perhaps the president should raise the $250,000 bail money to release all Birmingham prisoners, many of whom were attempting to go downtown to register to vote. Indeed, Kennedy had raised more than $60 million for the release of the Bay of Pigs prisoners in Cuba just that year. The president and Dr. King agreed to find the $160,000 necessary to bail out all of the prisoners by morning. And they did.

On Friday afternoon, May 10, Fred Shuttlesworth commenced the epic press conference with Dr. King by announcing, "The City of Birmingham has reached an accord with its conscience." King described the settlement terms: integration of the department store dressing rooms by Monday, establishment of a biracial committee in 15 days, integrated public restrooms and water fountains within 30 days, integrated lunch counters and upgraded African American store clerks within 60 days. All movement prisoners were either out of jail or on their way out of jail. King warned that the world would underestimate the enormity of the achievement: "Do not underestimate the power of this movement! These things would not have been granted without your presenting your bodies and your very lives before the dogs and the tanks and the water hoses of this city!" Then he went global: "The United States is concerned about its image. . . . For Mr. Kennedy is battling for the minds and the hearts of men in Asia and Africa—some 1 billion men in the neutralist sector of the world—and they aren't going to respect the United States of America if she deprives men and women of the basic rights of life because of the color of their skin."

Martin Luther King returned to Atlanta on Saturday, May 11, and that night in Birmingham three explosions struck at locations near his family. Thousands gathered, but Dr. King's brother, Rev. A. D. King, and Wyatt Walker slowly dispersed the crowd, singing freedom songs and cajoling folks to go home and not hurt the cause. At this moment, 250 armed Alabama state troopers entered Birmingham at the behest of Gov. Wallace and began an attack with clubs and rifle butts that left six businesses, several houses, and a two-story apartment building burnt to the ground; dozens of cars destroyed; and some 70 Black people taken to the hospital. The goal of the Wallace/Bull Conner forces was to sabotage the Birmingham settlement.

The Kennedy administration resisted federal troop deployment, but remained committed to the settlement. On Sunday and Monday, May 12 and 13, the shaky peace held as supporters from the North flew to Birmingham. It was just under 2 weeks since the first children's march of May 2. One year later, the Civil Rights Act of 1964 was passed by Congress. More civil rights activists would die; Freedom Summer was the next year, Black Power a year beyond that. Voter registration and equal rights were and remain a far longer struggle than almost all imagined.

Today the startling willingness of the African American children of Birmingham to engage in civil disobedience to obtain civil rights continues to demand our analysis and scrutiny. In the uncertainty and complexity of civil strife and disciplined rebellion, shall we see children as agents of their own liberation? Must we give weight to the accusation that SCLC adult leaders "used" children in ways that young people cannot understand or consent to, in ways that endangered them? What do we ponder when contemplating the dynamic role of young people in the Birmingham Civil Rights crucible? Two more recent developments offer additional frameworks within which to think about the multiple and contradictory natures of childhood.

First, the Convention on the Rights of the Child (CRC), passed unanimously by the United Nations in 1989 and ratified by every nation in the world save two (Somalia and the United States), posits children as people under the age of 18 not only in need of protection, but as rights bearers, as people with emerging and developing maturity. Children have individual as well as group rights, including the right to speech and assembly, and the right to be heard in proceedings affecting their circumstances. Young people have the right to choose and practice their religion. The CRC also provides for their right to protection, and for the duty of the state to assist parents and families to protect children's right to health, their right to education, and their right to be free from discrimination. It is fair to say that the CRC recognizes and takes into account the emerging maturity of young people.

Second, the U.S. Supreme Court has held, in a recent series of cases involving the extreme sentencing of young people who are convicted of murders, that children are "categorically less culpable" than adults. Thus, the Court has held that children are constitutionally different, that they were less mature at the time of their crimes than adults, and each must have the opportunity to "attain a mature understanding of his humanity." People under the age of 18 may no longer be subjected to the death penalty, and may not be sentenced to life without possibility of parole without taking into account their youthfulness at the time of the crime, their role in the crime, and their subsequent maturity and growth. Thus, mandatory life sentences that fail to take into account these factors violate the Eighth Amendment and are unconstitutional. This series of cases points to behavioral science research, brain imaging research, and common sense for the conclusion that children are different from adults: less morally culpable and with enhanced prospects for rehabilitation.

Diminished culpability, however, is not the same as lesser competence or capacity. Culpability is popularly misunderstood, and the conversation about adolescent development research frequently becomes an imprecise discourse that easily collapses into language of lesser adolescent competence. Anyone who works with young people or knows teenagers, or remembers his or her own youth, can identify adolescent brilliance, insight, inventiveness, clarity, imagination, and creativity.

Other instances, beyond the scope of this essay, of characterizing adolescents (primarily adolescents of color) as incompetent or in need of surveillance, control, and regulation abound in contemporary U.S. law and practice. Examples include efforts to regulate child access to the Internet; to criminalize behavior by young people such as bullying; to exclude students from constitutional rights to speech, and freedom from unwarranted search and seizure; and to punish youthful misbehavior in schools with zero-tolerance policies that deprive children of an education.

Because the issues surrounding children as social actors have complex ethical ramifications and must be considered in a context-specific framework, they are worth deeper contemplation. These concerns should be discussed by and among young people of all ages. Sixteen-year-old Pakistani Malala Yousufzal, speaking to the United Nations in the fall of 2013, directed us to the human rights activism of young girls: "So here I stand, one girl among many. I speak not for myself, but so those without a voice can be heard. Those who have fought for their rights. Their right to live in peace. Their right to be treated with dignity. Their right to equality of opportunity. Their right to be educated. . . . One child, one teacher, one book, and one pen can change the world." Young people are meaning-makers and world changers.

Education in Urban Spaces

Media Images and Neoliberal Discourses

Carl A. Grant, Karla Manning, and Alexandra Allweiss

AP Photo/M. Spencer Green © 2013 The Associated Press

As we set out to write this piece, there was an image from The Associated Press that we could not get out of our heads. This image of 8th-grader Deviyea was taken by M. Spencer Green on March 21, 2013, for an article discussing the Chicago Teachers Union (CTU) opposition to 54 public schools set to be closed. The pain in Deviyea's expression is clear as she listens to CTU President Karen Lewis tell of plans to close her school. The caption reads:

> Deviyea Dean, an eighth grader at Mahalia Jackson Elementary
> School in Chicago, listens as Chicago Teachers Union President Karen

Lewis speaks outside the soon-to-be shuttered school . . . The city of Chicago began informing teachers . . . [of] a contentious plan that opponents say will disproportionately affect minority students . . .

Looking across the images of Chicago Public Schools (CPS) students responding to the school closings led us to a common concern for the children in the pictures and also raised questions about the structural forces that gave rise to these images. These questions and concerns led us to ask the question: "What do media images that come from school closings in Chicago tell us about neoliberal discourses and education in urban spaces?"[1] Our question was not rhetorical. We were motivated to explore the purpose and the social, historical, and political contexts of these photos. To this end, the chapter is divided into three parts. The first looks at neoliberal ideologies, school reform policies, and media images. The second explores the history of racial housing segregation and school reforms in Chicago. The final part analyzes the image of Deviyea and explores how the media portrays and defines education in urban spaces. Collectively, these three discussions help us answer the question that frames this chapter.

Background

People of all colors and the media in general discuss education in urban spaces most often in narrow and sometimes troublesome ways. Conversations—wherever they take place—and reports in the media, from pundits or in newsprint, that address education in urban spaces often feature a narrative of the schools' "problems": violence, poverty, teacher strikes, family structure, student mobility, and low test scores. Although conversations around "urban education" have become commonplace, when everyday people and media pundits are asked to offer a comprehensive definition of education in urban spaces—"urban education"—they struggle because there is no common definition (Grant & Allweiss, in press; Milner & Lomotey, 2014). Instead, code words are used, and the children in urban spaces, most of whom are Black or Brown (especially in Chicago), have their education reduced to "failures" and shortcomings.

In much of the media, the narratives and images discussing the education of children in urban spaces often are narrowly focused, produced, and directed to sensationalize and capture audience attention, rather than to show public accountability. The media often essentialize notions of "suburban" and "urban" education in ways that position the two as opposites and tell people in urban spaces that their children are very different from children in the suburbs. We noticed this framing on an episode (May 30, 2013) of *World News with Diane Sawyer* profiling Strawberry Mansion, which the show described as one of America's most dangerous schools and in the queue to be shut down. While the show attempted to show individual students' successes and struggles, the narratives and images used throughout the episode reinforced negative stereotypes of high schools in urban spaces—that is, that largely low-income, Black, and/or Latino/a students are innately less "successful" and that high schools in urban spaces are more dangerous and violent than high schools in suburban spaces, where mostly middle-class, White, and/or Asian populations are enrolled.

Images and Ideology

To explore the meaning of images is to recognize that they are produced within dynamics of social power and ideology. Images are an important means through which ideologies and values are produced and "onto which ideologies are projected" (Sturken & Cartwright, 2009, p. 22). Within a political system of neoliberalism, globalization, and digitized technologies, the role of media images is significant in that it works to promote values, ideologies, and ways of reasoning about a particular phenomenon (McChesney, 2004). Essentially, media images serve to transmit ideologies and values about public institutions, including the public school system (Margolis, 2004). In the discussion of education in urban spaces, photographs have been used to establish racial and cultural identities (Ryan, 1997) within the context of neoliberal racialized discourses. Fujioka (2005) posits that media images of "minoritized" people influence public opinion on racial policies and that negative media portrayals of African Americans contribute to White viewers' negative perceptions of Blacks in general (pp. 450–451). Placed within specific conventions of sociocultural (Mirzoeff, 2009), historical, and classed aesthetic tastes (Bourdieu, 1984), along with the ability for images to be reproduced and circulated (Benjamin, 1969), the meanings of images are thus generated. Brown and Kraehe (2010) state:

> Visual texts connote a range of meanings as viewers draw from their personal/ cultural prior knowledge, experiences, memories, and feelings as points of congruence or disjuncture with the text's images. At the same time, meanings are not arbitrary. They exist within a sociopolitical hierarchy that places ideological limitations on potential commonsense, legitimate readings. (p. 77)

Within the mass media, Goldstein (2011) argues that images are given particular meanings and values through what is presented in the image, along with framing of the story, its headline, and other visual and textual information.

Significant to this project is to understand the structure within which journalists are operating: a focus on maximizing profits and the increasing corporatization of the media (McChesney, 2004). Dan Rather has stated, "The news stops with making bucks" (as quoted in Mitchell, 2008). Similarly, Ben Bagdikian (2000), former editor of *The Washington Post*, said in speaking about six corporations owning all of the U.S. news media outlets, "When we consider some of the most spectacular mergers in the media industry, we confront a more subtle but profound power. It is the power to socialize, to influence the values and behavior of individuals and of whole societies."

Neoliberal Ideologies, School Reform Policies, and Media Images

The increased corporatization of public outlets is a hallmark of neoliberal ideologies. In the 1970s, neoliberalism emerged as the dominant ideology out of the crisis of capitalism. Neoliberalism is focused on the "market" and the consolidation of capitalism globally. Neoliberal theory is based on the "utopian" assumption that "individual freedoms are guaranteed by freedom of the market" (Harvey, 2005, p. 7). In this context, access to the market is framed as a "right," democracy as "choice in the marketplace and freedom as personal freedom to consume" (Lipman, 2011, p. 10). Harvey (2005) argues that

> we can . . . interpret neoliberalization either as a *utopian* project to realize a theoretical design for the reorganization of international capitalism or as a *political* project to re-establish the conditions for capital accumulation and to restore the power of the economic elites . . . the second of these objectives has in practice dominated. . . . The theoretical utopian of the neoliberalist argument has, I conclude, primarily worked as a system of justification and legitimation for whatever needed to be done to achieve this goal. (p. 19, emphasis in original)

With this has come a rolling back of the welfare state, the privatization of public goods, and a move from government to governance. This framework is based on "rational" individualism and competition. Lipman (2011) states, "Neoliberalism has been the defining social paradigm of the past 30 years. . . . It has developed as a new social imaginary, a common sense about how we think about society and our place in it" (p. 6).

Schools and education are a central part of this "social paradigm." Within the neoliberal model, education is seen as an individual good and an investment in human capital development, which as a public good should be privatized. The guiding assumption is that "improvement comes when schools are put into competition with one another, like businesses, in a so-called free market" (Ayers, Kumashiro, Meiners, Quinn, & Stovall, 2010, p. 125). This framework is necessarily raced, classed, and gendered, since, as Apple (2006) states, "marketized systems in education often *expressly* have their conscious and unconscious raison d'être in a fear of 'the Other'" (p. 61, emphasis in original).

It is within this framework and context that city/urban educational spaces have become a battleground over access to opportunity, equity, and power. Under neoliberal frameworks "urban" communities are pathologized and "urban" education is framed as a "problem." With the focus on individuals and communities (rather than on structures), such factors as low test scores, poverty, "broken" family structures, lack of motivation and discipline, poor teacher quality, and so on, are framed as individual "failures" and "problems to be solved." This deficit narrative includes a framing in the media of students of color as the "problem." The subsequent responses to this "problem" include high-stakes testing, school closings, privatization of public schools, and the elimination of teachers' unions (Lipman, 2011).

Through a myriad of visual imagery that seeks to present the students in urban spaces as violent, fearful, and out of control, neoliberal educational and media discourses present a framework in which "many people have come to accept the idea that the closing of schools is a reform strategy" (Ravitch, 2013). Through subtle biases and the construction of naturalized inequalities (McChesney, 2001), the neoliberal agenda is advanced through the media and its images that portray ideas of responsibility, self-control, order, structure, articulation, cleanliness, intelligence, and a state of serenity as social ideals.

This new "common sense" is positioned and defined as normal by constructing its opposite as irrational and "abnormal." The visualization of education in urban spaces that operates in neoliberal discourses thus employs a variety of visual codes and conventions that portray the opposites of the rational individual—irrationality, disorderly conduct, excessive emotions, violence, irresponsibility, and a lack of self-control and discipline. In this neoliberal frame, those who do not represent what is seen as positive are viewed as barriers. "Urban education" discourses have been framed through particular fears of the "urban student" (Popkewitz, 2008)—which are partially constructed through these codes in visual imagery. This issue of framing is significant in political and popular media discourses in that it "shape[s] the public's perception of a situation or group of people" (Baldridge, 2012, p. 3). Because of this framing, Latinos and African Americans, along with "urban education," are constructed as problematic and in need of a saving solution.

In Chicago, these "saving solutions" have been framed through neoliberal school reforms that have led to the closing of public schools, predominantly in poor communities of color, that have been labeled as "failing." In their place 110 privately operated charter schools and contract schools have been opened as of April 2, 2013 (Bellware, 2013). However, these policies tend to look at these responses as "solutions" to the communities' "problems" in the here-and-now without a careful exploration of their historical and structural context. In Chicago—and other communities affected by these neoliberal education reforms—deep histories of exclusion, marginalization, exploitation, and resistance influence the way these policies play out and are experienced.

Looking Back: Racial Housing Segregation and School Reforms

Looking through media images of school closings in Chicago and the way they were framed, we saw an overall lack of historical contextualization. We have argued above that neoliberal ideologies and policies are based in ahistorical understandings of current educational issues and a singular focus on the market for solutions. Thus, this brief overview of racial history and policies in Chicago aims to speak back to this framing and expand the conversations around Chicago's school closings. The history leads to a better understanding of the context and multiple meanings of the images that frame this chapter as well as why the education reform policies target predominantly African American students (88%) in Chicago.

Segregation in Chicago began well before the Great Migration (1910–1930). Chicago's Black Belt was established in 1837 and became home to a number of free Blacks and those who escaped slavery. The Black Belt (later known as Bronzeville) was a strip of land on Chicago's South Side where Blacks were permitted to live. While Chicago passed a number of anti-segregation lawsuits, including one in 1874 that stated children could not be banned "on account of color from the public schools," schools remained segregated. The schools in Black communities were overcrowded. Many schools ran "double shifts" with students attending school for only a half day, and they lacked access to sufficient resources and unbiased materials (Grant & Grant, 2013). Even though there were spaces for Black students in "undercrowded" non-Black schools, restricted housing covenants prevented students from moving into those schools (Knupfer, 2006). Additionally, banks and savings associations initiated a practice of "redlining" that used race as a determinant for how homes would be financed (Pattillo, 2007).

In 1948, the Supreme Court ruled that housing segregation and restricted housing covenants were unconstitutional; however, this had little effect. While some Blacks were able to move into White communities, in 1955, the construction of high-rise housing projects led by the Chicago Housing Authority (CHA) and Chicago's mayor, Richard Daley, continued to reinforce racial segregation. Crawford states, "Old Man Daley saw the value of high-rises being about keeping blacks hemmed in" (quoted in Bernstein, 2008, p. 6). And Wille argues that race and class intersected in the construction of the huge high-rises that the CHA built, which ultimately created "a wall between black and white, between poor communities and affluent communities" (quoted in Bernstein, 2008, p. 6). This period also coincided with the construction of Chicago's highway system, which served to further isolate African American communities and facilitate White flight from the increasingly Black inner-city to Chicago's suburbs. This history of restricted housing policies and the construction of high-rises and highways served to shape the spatial composition and social imaginary of the city of Chicago. Similar histories of redlining and "urban removal" have shaped the histories of Latinos in Chicago and the spaces in which they live.

In 1988, the Chicago School Reform Act was passed, which established elected Local School Councils (LSCs)—community-run school governance groups that arose out of the African American and Latino movement for quality education and bilingual education (Lipman, 2011). However, the LSCs did not have the resources or support to change historically "underresourced and underserved" schools (Lipman, 2011, p. 39).

In 1995, Mayor Daley took complete mayoral control of CPS. The mayor had the power to select the school board and appoint the CEO (previously the superintendent). Lipman (2011) states this "began a corporate regime at CPS" (pp. 40–41). Mayoral control, however, did not improve the academic and structural conditions of schools serving poor Black and Brown communities, which continued to be underresourced and did not show improvements in performance on standardized tests. In response, the Commercial Club of Chicago published *Left Behind* in 2003 to show CPS's "failures" under the standards set forth by No Child Left Behind and to argue for greater "accountability" measures. Lipman (2011) states, "The

Club's solution was to inject competition through the market. They blamed LSCs and the teachers' union for obstructing reform" (p. 42). In 2004, Renaissance 2010 was announced by Mayor Daley, which called for closing approximately 70 public schools and opening 100 new schools, mostly charter or contract schools (privately run, but publicly funded).

The policy to close schools coincided with the 2000 CHA housing initiative—the Plan for Transformation—which called for the demolition of thousands of high-rise public housing units, but without the requirement for a one-to-one replacement (Lipman, 2011). These policies show the move to the city's divestment from public and social services and the increasingly firm hold of the neoliberal project in Chicago.

Thus, current school closings and the negative characterization of Chicago schools in urban spaces cannot be separated from the histories of social exclusion and previous policies in Chicago. We concur with Aristotle's statement, "If you would understand anything, observe its beginning and its development." It is essential to understand current neoliberal policies within the historical contexts of the places and spaces where they are occuring. In addition, this understanding provides a deeper context for the image that frames this chapter and our final point of discussion. This context generally is hidden in media accounts, allowing for the continuance of raced and classed discourses of individual "failures" without a critical understanding of the structures in which they are situated.

Media Portrayals and the "Defining" Images of Urban Education

Now, we use a photographic image to examine the ways media images of students in urban spaces can be used to define urban education within the larger discourse of neoliberal policies and a history of racism. Through a visual news framing analysis (D'Angelo & Kuypers, 2010), we consider a representative image[2] based on our review of many images in Chicago newspapers about school closings. We explore how its meaning is produced within the larger social, cultural, and structural environments. While we do not analyze the process of frame building (and thus how these images are made), we do discuss the effects of the framing of the student and how she may contribute to the larger political economy of urban education. A news frame refers to the "central organizing idea or storyline that provides meaning to an unfolding strip of events" (Gamson & Modigliani, 1987, quoted in Rodriguez & Dimitrova, 2011).

We draw on Rodriguez and Dimitrova's (2011) framework for visual news frame analysis. They used this framework to analyze news images in *The New York Times* of four poor Sudanese women with their children.

Rodriguez and Dimitrova suggest that the camera angles, along with the positioning of their bodies and their saddened faces, worked to decontextualize these women from their environment. The accompanying story perpetuated this decontexualization by neglecting an analysis of capitalism and poverty—that is, the structures—that affect these women.

We also use a visual news frame analysis to explore how neoliberal discourses are constructed within visual and written texts found in the media. In this sense, visual images act as framing devices, because they have the capacity to convey ideological messages. We seek to unravel the multilayered meanings of the image of Deviyea and discourses that work in tandem with its circulation. Visual frames have worked and continue to work to *construct* representations of students in urban spaces.

The Image: Deviyea's Gaze

In this image, we see the face of young Deviyea Dean, an African American 8th-grader at Mahalia Jackson Elementary School in Chicago, which is among the schools slated to close. Deviyea's face fills the majority of the frame. Her hair hangs to her nose but does not cover her eyes or hide her brown face. The lower part of her face is hidden by one of her arms, clothed in a black jacket.

The attention-grabbing feature in this image is Deviyea's dark eyes looking away from the camera. Her gaze is intense and could be described as an oppositional gaze, one that is staring down neoliberal policies, structures, and plans that are affecting her education. bell hooks (1992) speaks of such a gaze:

> Even in the worst circumstances of domination, the ability to manipulate one's gaze in the face of structures of domination that would contain it, opens up the possibility of agency . . . spaces of agency exist for black people wherein we can both interrogate the gaze of the Other but also look back . . . the "gaze" has been and is a site of resistance for colonized black people globally. (p. 116)

Deviyea's eyes mirror the resistance that has a long history on the South and West Sides of Chicago.

However, within a context of neoliberalism and race, meaning making of her gaze could be shifted and (re)interpreted in multiple ways. Alternatively, the gaze may be seen as an emotional representation of anger, pain, and disparity. Sontag (2004) argues that such visual representation of pain in photography also could allow viewers to distance themselves from the subject in the image. Sontag posits that the saturation of photographs of pain and suffering acts to desensitize viewers to the "pain of others" and facilitate a distance between them and the subject. This image of Deviyea, according to Sontag's thesis, could cause some viewers to adopt an "othering" stance toward the image; instead of being empathetic and supportive of Deviyea, the viewer may see her as a distant, emotional Other.

As discussed above, within the discourse of neoliberalism, emotions are framed as irrational and out of control, calling for neoliberal reforms to make the Other more rational and to bring "them" under control. Iyengar (1991) argues that the way journalists and media corporations frame their news influences public perceptions of politics and other events, issues, and people. Such framing within neoliberal discourses reinforces problematic and contested understandings of education in urban spaces, which in turn influence the way teachers, administrators, policymakers, and society view "urban" students. These frames seek to "define problems, diagnose causes, make moral judgments, and suggest remedies" (Entman & Rojecki, 2000, p. 49). When Deviyea's image is read through the lens of neoliberalism and current discourses around education in urban spaces, it may serve to reinforce neoliberal educational solutions such as school closures and the privatization of education for "those" students. In addition, whether through agency or pain, Deviyea's image speaks to the varied discourses that are embedded within urban school and neoliberal policies, and positions urban education within a complex and often shifting state of existence.

Concluding Thoughts

While a deep understanding of place has been central to the construction of this chapter, Chicago is not alone in the shift toward neoliberal educational policies taking place in cities across the United States. With mayoral control and the closing of schools in urban spaces being taken up in more cities, we can expect to see more media stories and photos of students like Deviyea. Ayers et al. (2010) argue that "Chicago . . . can be considered not singular at all, but rather a somewhat representative site of the complex and abiding crisis experienced by people everywhere, particularly in poor areas and in communities of color" (p. 5). We argue that media stories and photos should be observed through a lens that critiques neoliberal policy, racism, and the history of the urban spaces in which these policies are playing out. We call for readers to critically interrogate the multiple ways the framing of media images contributes to discussions of education in urban spaces.

Notes

1. We purposely employ the phrase "education in urban spaces" instead of "urban education" because we have not found in the literature a comprehensive definition of "urban education." Urban education has become a sliding signifier for a number of negatives and/or educational deficits, such as poverty, low student performance, disinterested parents, school violence, and/or some combination of these ideas and other issues. That said, we recognize that education in urban spaces also has its inherent tensions as the word *urban* also is used as a shifting signifier. Nevertheless, we hope that shifting the terminology serves as a call for attention to these issues and an invitation for others to think critically about how *urban* is used in discussions of education.

2. Due to space constraints, we explore only one image in depth; however, we discovered many other images that speak to our argument and which were taken into account within this discussion.

References

Apple, M. W. (2006). *Educating the "right" way: Markets, standards, god, and inequality* (2nd ed.). New York, NY: Routledge.

Ayers, W., Kumashiro, K., Meiners, E., Quinn, T., & Stovall, D. (2010). *Teaching toward democracy: Educators as agents of change.* Boulder, CO: Paradigm.

Bagdikian, B. (2000, June). Merger mania and creativity: What is achieved and what is lost. Presentation at the WAN World Meeting in Hanover, Germany. Retrieved from http://archive.today/NFNnw

Baldridge, B. (2012). *(Re)Imagining Black youth: Negotiating the social, political, and institutional dimensions of urban community-based educational spaces* (Doctoral dissertation). Retrieved from ProQuest (3507381)

Bellware, K. (2013, April 2). Chicago charter school demand: New analysis shows demand for charters in district "overstated." *Huffington Post.* Retrieved from www.huffingtonpost.com/2013/04/02/chicago-charter-school-de_n_2999889.html

Benjamin, W. (1969). The work of art in the age of mechanical reproduction. In J. Evans & S. Hall (Eds.), *Visual culture: The reader* (pp. 72–79). London: SAGE.

Bernstein, D. (2008, September 10). Daley vs. Daley. *Chicago Magazine.* Retrieved from www.chicagomag.com/Chicago-Magazine/September-2008/

Bourdieu, P. (1984). *Distinction: A social critique of the judgment of taste.* New York, NY: Routledge.

Brown, K., & Kraehe, A. (2010). When you've only got one class, one chance: Acquiring sociocultural knowledge using eclectic case pedagogy. *Teaching Education, 21*(3), 73–89.

D'Angelo, P., & Kuypers, J. (2010). Introduction: Doing news frame analysis. In P. D'Angelo & J. Kuypers (Eds.), *Doing news frame analysis: Empirical and theoretical perspectives* (pp. 1–13). New York, NY: Routledge.

Entman, R. M., & Rojecki, A. (2000). *The Black image in the White mind: Media and race in America.* Chicago, IL: University of Chicago Press.

Fujioka, Y. (2005). Black media images as a perceived threat to African American ethnic identity: Coping responses, perceived public perception, and attitudes towards affirmative action. *Journal of Broadcasting & Electronic Media, 49*(4), 450–467.

Goldstein, R. (2011). Imaging the frame: Media representations of teachers, their unions, NCLB, and education reform. *Education Policy, 25*(4), 543–576.

Grant, C. A., & Allweiss, A. (in press). Education in urban spaces: Social justice pushing against a rhetoric of neoliberalism. *Texas Education Review.*

Grant, C. A., & Grant, S. J. (2013). *The moment: Barack Obama, Jeremiah Wright, and the firestorm at Trinity United Church of Christ.* Lanham, MD: Rowman & Littlefield.

Harvey, D. (2005). *A brief history of neoliberalism.* New York, NY: Oxford University Press.

hooks, b. (1992). *Black looks: Race and representation.* Boston, MA: South End Press.

Iyengar, S. (1991). *Is anyone responsible? How television frames political issues.* Chicago, IL: University of Chicago Press.

Knupfer, A. M. (2006). *The Chicago Black Renaissance and women's activism.* Urbana, IL: University of Illinois Press.

Lipman, P. (2011). *The new political economy of urban education: Neoliberalism, race, and the right to the city.* New York, NY: Routledge.

Margolis, E. (2004). Looking at discipline, looking at labour: Photographic representations of Indian boarding schools. *Visual Studies, 19*(1), 72–96.

McChesney, R. (2001). Global media, neoliberalism, and imperialism. *Monthly Review, 52,* 1–19.

McChesney, R. (2004). *The problem of the media: U.S. communication politics in the twenty-first century.* New York, NY: Monthly Review Press.

Milner, H. R., IV, & Lomotey, K. (2014). *Handbook on urban education.* New York, NY: Routledge.

Mirzoeff, N. (2009). *An introduction to visual culture* (2nd ed.). New York, NY: Routledge.

Mitchell, G. (2008, June 8). Dan Rather admits failure on Iraq—and hits corporate media. *HuffPost Media.* http://www.huffingtonpost.com/greg-mitchell/dan-rather-admits-press-f_b_105896.html

Pattillo, M. (2007). *Black on the block: The politics of race and class in the city.* Chicago, IL: University of Chicago Press.

Popkewitz, T. (2008). *Cosmopolitanism and the age of school reform: Science, education, and making society by making the child.* New York, NY: Routledge.

Ravitch, D. (2013). Chicago to shutter 50 public schools: Is historic mass closure an experiment in privatization? [Interview with Amy Goodman and Aaron Mate on *Democracy Now!*]. Retrieved from www.democracynow.org/2013/5/28/chicago_to_shutter_50_public_schools

Rodriguez, L., & Dimitrova, D. V. (2011). The levels of visual framing. *Journal of Visual Literacy, 30*(1), 48–65.

Ryan, J. R. (1997). *Picturing empire: Photography and the visualization of the British Empire*. Chicago, IL: University of Chicago Press.

Sontag, S. (2004, May 23). Regarding the torture of others. *The New York Times*. Retrieved from www.nytimes.com/2004/05/23/magazine/regarding -the-torture-of-others.html?pagewanted=all&src=pm

Sturken, M., & Cartwright, L. (2009). *Practices of looking: An introduction to visual culture* (2nd ed.). New York, NY: Oxford University Press.

Haunted by My Students' Students

Bree Picower

As a teacher educator, I am haunted by the children who will sit "criss-cross apple sauce" in front of my student teachers. I know as an educator myself that I aspire to be the dedicated and caring teacher written about in the literature who makes a difference in the lives of my students. Yet, when I hear the deficit conceptualizations that my student teachers too often use to talk about their future students (Picower, 2009), I struggle with the contradiction of trying to apply those holistic approaches to my own students. I realize it is a race against time—how many of their stereotypes can be challenged before they are released into schools to teach the children they see as sons and daughters of "illegals," "freeloaders," or people who "'just don't care" about their children's educations? More often than not, because student teacher attitudes are so riddled with assumptions and because there is so little opportunity to meaningfully challenge them, I find that our teacher education programs are not designed to address ideological needs such as these that our students present.

These are the anxiety-producing doubts that I push to the back of my mind as I go about my daily routines teaching courses and supervising student teachers. To engage such thoughts forces me to ask myself tough questions about my chosen work. Am I just wasting my time? Am I teaching the wrong people? What purpose is there in working with preservice teachers who at best will make minimal changes that still may not situate them to see the strength and genius of their future students? What role am I playing in reproducing a system that continues to benefit young (mainly White and/or privileged) teachers at the expense of low-income students of color? Couldn't my time be spent more strategically elsewhere?

"A Kind and Just" Teacher

Bill Ayers wrote about the juvenile justice system and its self-titled role as "kind and just parents" for children in its charge. He states, "I meant the phrase 'a kind and just parent' to bristle with irony: here was this lofty, sentimental ideal laid low by a dysfunctional system and a society out of control" (Ayers, 1997, p. xviii). In working through the system, however, he encountered dedicated individuals who lived up to these ideals and he implored readers to listen and learn from them. In this tradition, I consider the characteristics of a "kind and just" teacher—characteristics of a teacher who values students and teaches toward democratic ideals even within a system riddled with the contradictions of liberation and reproduction. I reflect on these ideals of a kind and just teacher in terms of what I hope to instill in my students but also as an educator myself. Three themes in Ayers's descriptions of teachers stand out as key foundational ideals on which successful teaching might be built. Kind and just teachers must be self-reflective, critical thinkers; must honor the humanity of their students; and must recognize that students are experts in their own lives.

Kind and just teachers must be self-reflective and critical, asking, "Who in the world am I? How did I get here and where am I going? . . . What's my story, and how is it like or unlike the stories of others?" As kind and just teachers, we must reflect on our lives, questioning our belief systems and what influences have shaped our ways of seeing the world. Ayers (2010) claims that "if teachers are never self-critical, they will lose their capacity for renewal and growth. They will become self-justifying and dogmatic" (p. 144). For future teachers, the capacity for self-reflection and critical thinking is the foundation on which other teaching skills are built.

Like Ayers's kind and just parents, kind and just educators recognize who their students are and value where they come from. We must honor the humanity of our students and recognize the value and knowledge they carry into the classroom. As Ayers (2004) contends, "Making a commitment to the humanity of our students is in the first place an act of faith—we don't require our students to prove their three-dimensionality to us in situations that diminish and contain them, but rather we accept their humanity as the 'evidence of things not seen'" (p. 43). As educators, we must not make assumptions about who our students are, or group or label them based on preconceived deficit constructions. Ayers (2004) sees focusing on the humanity of our students as an act of "resistance to the machinery of labeling that characterizes the modern predicament in all areas and has become endemic and relentless in the realm of schools, re-sistance to the reduction of humanity into categories" (p. 43). By resisting the tendency to label, we focus on who our students actually are and move closer to democratic ideals by "invit[ing] people on a journey to become more thoughtful and more capable, more powerful and courageous, more exquisitely alive in their projects and their pursuits" (Ayers, Kumashiro, Meiners, Quinn, & Stovall, 2010, p. 14).

Part of recognizing the humanity of our students includes valuing the knowledge and ideas they bring with them. Ayers et al. (2010) insist: "Every student is an expert on his or her own life. . . . Conscientious teachers ask themselves all the time what it is that they need to know in order to be successful with this kid, or with this one, or this one" (p. 33). Educators must honor students' emotions and feelings and examine students' contexts and circumstances that shape their experiences. This allows teachers to support students to "think freely about all the issues that affect their lives, to imagine wild and colorful alternatives, and then to step up boldly toward their dreams" (Ayers et al., 2010, pp. 27–28).

By honoring the humanity of our students, recognizing what they bring to the table, and reflecting on our own way of seeing the world, teachers lay the prerequisite groundwork for developing caring relation-ships, developing an engaging and culturally relevant curriculum, and ad-vocating for their students both inside and outside of the classroom.

"Kind and Just" Students?

While I wholeheartedly agree with these ideals, particularly when I think about teaching children, they don't always translate as cleanly to the adult learners I work with who plan on being teachers themselves. I find myself challenged to be a kind and just professor of students who spew jingoistic and racist conceptualizations of children of color, low-income children, and immigrant students. How can I insist that they are experts in their own lives when their "expertise" includes a belief that, for instance, White people are the victims of racism?

The key breakdown when trying to apply the three ideals of kind and just teaching to my own students happens whenever these students are unwilling to entertain the first ideal: to self-reflect or develop a crit-ical analysis toward teaching and their future students. In keeping with Ayers's philosophy, I must recognize who my students are and how where they come from shapes their ideology toward their future students. Just as I couldn't blame my former 6th-graders for not knowing how to do long division because they hadn't been taught a foundation of double-digit subtraction in 5th grade, I cannot blame my preservice education students for not having been exposed to a way to critically analyze dominant deficit ideologies about diversity. Knowing that many of my students may come from racially homogeneous communities in which they have had little exposure to diversity, and that the media often served as their main educator, I cannot necessarily blame them for the hegemonic understandings they hold about people different from themselves. In both of these instances, it is my responsibility as the teacher to take a step back to provide the necessary foundation from which to build the knowledge and skills for the tasks at hand.

In this vein, Ayers suggests a relationship between the teacher and the student that shapes how one might approach the kind of teaching that asks students to self-reflect and develop a critical analysis. As Ayers (2010) expressed it, "The fundamental message of the teacher is this: You must change your life. Whoever you are, wherever you've been, whatever you've done, the teacher invites you to a second chance, another round, perhaps a different conclusion. . . . The teacher beckons you to change your path" (p. 141). Many of my students are excited to change their path and think critically about assumptions they may be making about their future students, their families, and their communities. However, when preservice teachers are unwilling to consider "perhaps a different conclusion" (Ayers, 2010, p. 141), I as their teacher struggle to hold up my end of the bargain of honoring their humanity. Where is the humanity in being unwilling to transform conceptualizations of kindergarteners as laundry lists of problems associated with their race, class, or family status?

So while I can't blame my preservice teachers for their incoming beliefs, I can be concerned about their unwillingness to examine them, particularly as this ability to self-reflect is in and of itself one of the three ideal characteristics of a kind and just teacher. In situations in which preservice teachers approach the development of these ideals from a place of resistance rather than openness, the development of the other characteristics of valuing their students' humanity or seeing them as experts in their own lives is virtually impossible.

In class, I showed *Fear and Learning at Hoover Elementary* (Simón, 1997), a film designed to demonstrate to my students the complexities of the lives of immigrant children, in order to help my students develop empathy for children caught in the cross hairs of national citizenship policies. Before watching the film, one of my students, Becky, expressed disdain for immigrants, complaining that "illegals" are "lazy" for not learning the language; she also shared some theories about how they are damaging the economy by being on welfare and stealing educational services.

After watching the film, which follows Mayra, a 3rd-grade girl from El Salvador, at a school in Los Angeles, many of my students thought critically about their role as future teachers and expressed discomfort with the idea of ever having to reveal a child's immigration status. Becky's beliefs remained unchecked; she declared that she thought it would be best if Mayra's mother was deported because she broke the law by coming to the United States. Another student tentatively asked what would then happen to Mayra, who was born in the United States, because there was no one here to care for her. Becky avowed that it actually would be for the best because Mayra would be taught a valuable lesson about what happens to people who break the law. Because Becky was unwilling to critically analyze her understanding of undocumented people as criminals, she was unable to see the humanity of 7-year-old Mayra and her family. I find it hard to imagine that she could value what this child would bring to her classroom. Beyond a lack of empathy, Becky has the potential to inflict damage on Mayra based on the way she judges the child's family, the way she may talk about the child, and the potential that she very well could "out" the family's lack of documentation, resulting in the separation of mother and child.

I wish Becky's response was an unusual one, but as many other teacher educators can attest, we hear such uncritical deficit constructions of children and their families on a regular basis. Sadly, more students silently think such thoughts than are willing to proudly announce them as Becky did. Often, preservice teachers who are more moderate in their thinking have the capacity to develop a critical analysis, but it often takes repeated exposure and multiple attempts to help them challenge the beliefs they have spent much of their life developing. The problem lies in lack of time available in the typical once-a-week course in a 3- to 4-semester teacher education program; there simply isn't time to lay the foundation necessary to develop the critical-thinking skills needed to analyze what students will be presented with as they enter the field. The lack of critical analysis will block them from developing the other ideals, setting these future teachers up to do damage to, rather than honor, the humanity of their students.

Systemic Problem

So where is the mechanism for interruption? Students such as Becky can and do pass my course. Did they learn how to develop lesson plans? Did they adapt their lesson plan to students with special needs? Did they respond to readings on Blackboard? Yes, yes, and yes. These are the graded components of the course. It is much harder, and often quite tricky, to grade students' dispositions or political beliefs. Should they not pass the course because they believe, like at least half of our citizens, that undocumented immigrants should be deported? As students like Becky and her more silent contemporaries succeed in our courses, pass the Praxis, and take jobs at charter schools that value test scores and scripted curriculum over critical thinking, there are few systemic opportunities to mitigate the potential damage that such teachers can inflict on their future students. These three ideals of critical thinking, valuing students' humanity, and recognizing that students are experts in their lives may be the building blocks of being a kind and just teacher—but they are not valued systemically. They are unassessed, so demonstrating proficiency in them is not part of the graduation requirement. Thus, I am haunted by the students of my students as I, and the rest of my institution, have failed to provide these children either a kind or a just teacher.

It appears that trying to interrupt the flow of uncritical "Beckys" into classrooms is increasingly challenging. The stranglehold of new national standards such as the Common Core and external evaluations such as EdTPA and the Council for the Accreditation of Educator Preparation place no value on the characteristics of kind and just teaching, and yet our institutions are held accountable to them. However, for those of us who are committed to our students' students, we must find ways to unite and push back against the lack of humanistic criteria within these outside evaluation systems.

As Ayers et al. (2010) say, "There is a far greater purpose and a much more fundamental goal driving teaching in a democracy than loyalty to the state . . . we are geared toward empowering free people to think freely about all the issues that affect their lives, to imagine wild and colorful alternatives, and then to step up boldly toward their dreams" (pp. 27–28). To fulfill this mission of preparing kind and just teachers, we must find ways to evaluate and hold our students accountable to humanistic ideals before we send them to the field. We must actively participate in struggles to end policies and practices that stand in the way of preparing caring educators, if we hope to live up to the ideals of being kind and just teacher educators.

References

Ayers, W. (1997). *A kind and just parent: The children of juvenile court.* Boston, MA: Beacon Press.

Ayers, W. (2004). *Teaching toward freedom: Moral commitment and ethical action in the classroom.* Boston, MA: Beacon Press.

Ayers, W. (2010). *To teach: The journey of a teacher* (3rd ed.). New York, NY: Teachers College Press.

Ayers, W., Kumashiro, K., Meiners, E., Quinn, T., & Stovall, D. (2010). *Teaching toward democracy: Educators as agents of change.* Boulder, CO: Paradigm.

Picower, B. (2009). The unexamined Whiteness of teaching: How White teachers maintain and enact dominant racial ideologies. *Race and Ethnicity in Education, 12*(2), 197–215.

Simón, L. (Producer & Director). (1997). *Fear and learning at Hoover Elementary* [Documentary]. Los Angeles, CA: PBS.

The Personal Is Certainly Political

Our Past Must Inform Our Purpose as Educators in the Present

Patrick Camangian

I love seeing our people fighting to get theirs
Fighting cuz this concrete jungle is war
I don't love the struggle, but what we're struggling for

—Kiwi, "Love Continued," 2003

Meeting with my academic counselor, dean of students, principal, and mother after my involvement in a gang fight across the street from campus marked the end of my high school enrollment in 1989. The principal summed up the school's sentiments by stating, "You're not cut out for a high school like this." I agreed, dropped out, and never really earned my high school diploma. I earned a high school equivalency in 1992. Eight years later I came across Freire's *Pedagogy of the Oppressed* (1970) and Peter McLaren's *Life in Schools* (1994). These texts opened my eyes to a world I had been introduced to only recently and helped me to realize that schooling experiences like mine are symptomatic of larger institutional practices that silence historically dominated cultures, ignore oppressive social conditions, and push masses of students out of the educational system.

Three years prior, I had the privilege of sharing narratives with an older, more reflexive African American ex-gang member in the 9500 block of Los Angeles Men's Central County Prison. Critically reflecting on his military service in the Philippines made for relevant and engaging dialogue between this O.G. (original gangster) and me as he introduced me to the concept and historical reality of colonialism, drew connections between my history as an Americanized Pilipino, his as a Black man, and the history of indigenous and other Third World people who have been dispossessed of their resources and found themselves struggling collectively as a result of this historical relationship to Europe. In my current use of colonialism, I want to acknowledge the different historical contexts, material outcomes, and experiences of colonialism while focusing on the ways "all colonized people have much in common" (Memmi, 1965/1991, p. ix). Yes, I say this while also claiming settler privilege so as to not be "deceptively embracive and vague . . . [as] a move towards innocence" (Tuck & Yang, 2012, p. 17), as I acknowledge that "[u]ntil stolen land is relinquished, critical consciousness does not translate into action that disrupts settler colonialism" (p. 19).

One line has stood out to me for years as the O.G. pointed out the predominance of Black and Brown men in the prison: "We're doing exactly what *they* want us to do." This conversation served to further clarify that the interconnectedness of oppressed people's struggles is a product of worldwide social injustice that is strengthened by massive self-hate, irrelevant schooling structures that overlook transformative potentials in schools, and a criminal (in)justice system that serves to buttress a burgeoning prison state in the United States. After 1 week in the dormitory, I was transferred to a four-bed jail cell that was occupied by six men. I slept on the floor next to another man who I assumed was also new to the cell.

I do not offer this narrative to suggest by any means that I was some tough street kid whose legitimacy is grounded in my experiences in a gang, or in jail. I often joke when I tell this story in public that I was, instead, what many would consider a *Scared Straight!* reject. Still, this was my experience, and this experience served as the foundation for my work as an educator for the rest of my life. In the Fanonian (1967) sense, "I am my own foundations. . . . It is through the effort to recapture the self and to scrutinize the self, it is through the lasting tension of [our] freedom that [people] will be able to create the ideal conditions of existence for a human world" (p. 231). Still, rather than offer this up as some special story to gain some esteem from others, I tell this story as a mirror for others to reflect on their own lived experience—how their experiences shape who they are today—and to be clear with how our identities as people shape our political purpose as professionals. See your story in mine, and as I theorize the commitments and contradictions in a radical teaching life through my own lived experience, please do so simultaneously with yours.

During one of my first nights in the jail cell, I began to reflect on the O.G.'s message and use it as a lens to reflect on the journey that led me to county prison. My life started to make more sense as I began to see all the self-hate, social vice, and divide-and-conquer as a social phenomenon of one segment of historically dominated people doing exactly what this system of oppression wanted us to do.

The O.G.'s narrative evoked a consciousness in me that was first stimulated by N.W.A.'s (1988) "Fuck the Police" and KRS-One's (1989) "You Must Learn." Scaffolding his eloquent deconstruction of Western imperialism to hip-hop's scathing critique of society, I understood the motivating power of counterhegemonic discursive spaces for youth of color shortly after. It was during this time that I decided that, given the opportunity, I would be the type of teacher I wish I'd had prior to leaving school. Fortunately, I was granted that opportunity, and after 6½ years in community college I finished the credits needed to transfer to California State University, Los Angeles, with the support of the Gang Violence Bridging Project and Educational Opportunity Program. I learned exactly what I needed to learn from a person I was not supposed to learn it from and learned in a place that I was not supposed to learn in. I often wonder, to this day, what my life would have been like had I actually been introduced to this analysis and exposed to that type of wisdom during my time in school.

Just like many students of color in urban schools throughout the country, my struggles could be traced largely to the failed relationships that too often define interactions between students of marginalized cultures and their teachers. The "street life" captivated me in ways that teachers and traditional school curriculum did not. Schooling did not develop my capacity as an agent of learning. Meanwhile, my "homies" understood the conditions of our reality and offered practical, albeit misguided, solutions to our problems. The streets were teaching me to survive. School was, as Bill Ayers always says, putting me to sleep, anesthetizing me, when what I needed was to open my eyes, wake up, and become keenly aware of all that was really happening to me and to the people around me. I experienced irrelevant classroom curriculum and poorly trained, impersonal, and culturally nonresponsive teachers. My sense of academic marginalization ultimately resulted in my dropping out of high school. A few generations later, we can see the same substandard state of urban schooling and similar self-defeating, often reactionary responses from students.

This phenomenon speaks to a larger body of experiences for historically dispossessed youth in urban communities around the country. Urban school curricula and governing policies are community irrelevant and culturally hostile. They fall short of providing critical spaces where young people of color can deconstruct racialized identities and historically oppressive relationships. By not engaging in school, students do not develop the skills necessary to matriculate through the highest levels of American universities or participate in a market-driven economy.

Recognizing the consequences of this reality for my own life, and my fortune at having avoided the school-to-prison pipeline more seriously, I continue to resist social injustice, researching ways to develop the type of knowledge of self, solidarity, and self-determination I wish I had when I was supposed to be in school. In this sense, my work as an educator is both personally cathartic and of urgent relevance to the masses of youth who experience the culturally alienating effects of schools, part of a protracted struggle to end U.S. imperialism, colonialism, and all forms of social misery finally and forever.

However, as it currently is playing out, I have no confidence in the educational community to solve problems facing historically dispossessed people in the context of our contemporary social conditions. I say this without any hesitation. This is not a conclusion I have come to easily. My work in schools, and as an early-career scholar, informs my lack of confidence. If we understand education in U.S. schools as indoctrination (Apple, 1993), it is clear that educational policies like No Child Left Behind and Race to the Top are designed to undermine the identity of people of color and to replace that identity with a lens through which to view the world that is at odds with the existence and history of oppressed people. If we are to serve the needs of dispossessed communities, educators must name this problem clearly because it is an educational contradiction that oppressed people throughout the world have confronted historically.

What we have, too often, is an educational system that does not reflect the needs of oppressed communities because we, as educators, have not seen ourselves as servants to those who experience society on the margins. Instead, we come across as servants of oppressive philosophies and a social system that is hostile to those living life on the margins. This is a real contradiction that progressive, critical, and socially transformative educators are confronted with. We have endless discussions about education reform, but, for the most part, dispossessed communities do not find themselves included in these conversations. So, those seeking social transformation the most remain defenseless in hostile situations. To help solve the problems facing oppressed communities, more educators must serve the articulated needs of the people we claim to be serving.

The United States is a predator state, founded on the vicious genocide of indigenous people, the enslavement of Africans, the feudal exploitation of Asians, and the stealing of labor and resources from civilizations all over the world (Marx, 1867/1954). As described by Fanon (1963/2004), "Capitalism, in its expansionist phase, regarded the colonies as a source of raw materials which once processed could be unloaded on the European market. After a phase of accumulation of capital. . . . [t]he colonies have become a market" (p. 26). As a result, all of these thriving communities have become impoverished because they have been dispossessed of their material resources. According to Marx and Engels (1976), our consciousness is formed through social and economic relationships. This means that the way we think is usually based on the types of relationships we have with people, and the types of relationships we have with money, or capital.

Not to simplify the complexities of the colonial phenomenon as it relates to education, but a simple way of understanding colonialism in this context is by imagining me as a representative of colonial society, and you as representatives of colonized people. And let us say that my great-great-grandparents' great-great-grandparents' great-great-grandparents were extremely poor, and your great-great-grandparents' great-great-grandparents' great-great-grandparents were substantially wealthy. To alleviate our poverty, my family decided to send explorers to your family's house, steal everything of value, and claim it as ours. The descendants of my family get to benefit from the inheritance stolen from your ancestors, and hundreds of years later, it is my family that is collectively controlling the wealth, and it is your family that is collectively poor. Despite this wealth actually coming from your family, your descendants are struggling for an education that will allow you to get only microscopic access to your family's resources. In the same way, it is now European society that is sitting on and alienating us from resources that are inherently ours, and we are working extremely hard to get very small pieces of what ought to be ours in the first place. This is the essence of colonialism. So, if our consciousness is formed through our social and economic relationships, then our consciousness is formed through our relationship with colonialism.

The education we historically have gotten in the United States, as a result, has been set up in ways that keep dispossessed people alienated from resources that are inherently theirs. It is an education that has kept them alienated from their own land, kept them alienated from their own indigenous ways of knowing, kept them alienated from knowing who they are as a people, and kept them divided and conquered from the people they should be united with the most.

So what should we do? More of us must teach and research in the interests of oppressed communities—not by simply exploring ways for them to more effectively access culturally irrelevant curriculum so that they can conform to a system that has been born of their oppression and exploitation. At the same time, it would be a contradiction if those of us who have graduated from universities in order to teach in the first place do not teach our children the academic literacies that afforded us the privilege of earning our college degrees. It is important for those of us who educate on the side of the oppressed to struggle for a more holistic interpretation of the world because, for too long, dispossessed communities have not been allowed to explain the world as they understood it. This requires, in the Freirean (1970) sense, a philosophy that is different from the ideology of the oppressor. The oppressed must have an approach to educating their own—an education that can explain the situation they find themselves in, and can inform how they must move forward to transform their relationships to White supremacy and colonialism in their collective consciousness and communities.

The oppressor has a different purpose. It is in the oppressor's interest to maintain its hegemony, and it is in the interests of the oppressed to understand and transform it. In order to understand the world as it is, we have to access information that will help us to understand the root causes of oppression and create the necessary conditions to resist and transform it. Instead, schools privilege hegemonic ideologies through "official knowledge" (Apple, 1993) and "hidden curriculum" (Giroux & Purpel, 1983). Disinvestment from cultural alienation and community irrelevance in school often is internalized, rationalized, and reproduced as the only viable form of agency against a hostile schooling culture (Kohl, 1994).

Why is that? That is the question we have to pose for the young people we teach, the young people we love, and their teachers, if we are going to come up with a relevant answer. Research suggests that educational success for marginalized students of color might best be connected to transformative resistance (Akom, 2003; Solorzano & Delgado-Bernal, 2001). Thus, the communities we serve need to be able to envision a future beyond the seemingly normalized oppression that they have to suffer through, and it is our responsibility to help provide an education that allows them to do just that. This future must not simply be about "non-Native peoples [being] promised the ability to join in the colonial project of settling indigenous lands . . . [as much as] strategic alliances with each other based on where we are situated within the larger political economy" (Smith, 2006, p. 69). This will allow us to make sure that justice for some does not come at the expense, or dispossession and necessary disappearance, of others—in this case, native people seeking native sovereignty.

Now that more of us, as scholars, are capturing our voices, our experiences, and our needs, we are in a much better position to tell too-often-untold stories. More among us have to assume the responsibility for doing this type of work. It is irresponsible to leave this for others to deal with. It is those of us who recognize this contradiction that must come up with a basic research agenda, pedagogical pathway, and genuine analysis. This is a profound responsibility that we have as educators.

As educators committed to the struggle for historically informed justice, we have a different responsibility, and, for us, education plays a different role. The existing system, at best, teaches us to conform to a system of oppression, while a justice-oriented education must teach us to transform it. In this way, we have to consider how the education we know is necessary actually can awaken critical consciousness and touch students' hearts. This is why culture is important, not simply as a form of entertainment. Culture must not be simply a diversionary medium. We must incorporate culture in our education not for incorporation's sake, but as a vehicle for people to effectively communicate, bridge across differences, and unite for a common cause. The use of the people's culture in this way "frees human consciousness, thought, and imagination for new potentialities" (Bakhtin, 1965, p. 49).

An important lesson here is that our purpose as people can be driven by serving in ways that we wish we had been served as young people in the communities and streets that we came from. This is not to draw binary lines between those who are privileged and those who are not. Radical change happens wherever the radical change agent makes it happen. Most of us exist with privilege along the intersections of our various identities, but what is important is not the privilege we have, but what we do with that privilege. We all have different hopes and different dreams, and will end up heading in different directions with our work; we must, however, "check our aspirations against the aspirations of other communities to ensure that our model of liberation does not become the model of oppression for others" (Smith, 2006, p. 69). Whatever happens, it is important that we never forget where we come from and, more important, why we do this work in the first place—to join with the ranks of others who are struggling with and for those who have the least. Forgetting this as we move years into our profession, and too often become comfortable with our distance from immediate struggle, is exactly what *they* want us to do. It is important that we do not forget this. This has to drive our work. If we take pride in who we are and the greatness of the people and struggles that drive our purpose, then we can take pride in being a part of something larger than ourselves. Not only must we not forget where we have come from, but we also must let that show in how we approach our work.

The trendiness of our research agendas and the inaccessibility of our terminology will not get our communities as far as the power of our message and the vision of our ideas as educators connected to a movement larger than the forces that keep us isolated in our classrooms and universities. On a personal level, the struggles that devastate us the most can guide us the most if we search our souls to find our purpose and be the kind of educators our communities need us to be. We must imagine what we would like to see for our communities, our social movements, and ourselves, and ask: what are we willing to sacrifice to get this? When we find our answers, we must live our life as educators being true to those answers. We have to join others so we have a united front, across differences, to grow into a militant social movement. This is how we must deal with the commitments and contradictions in our radical teaching lives. Start with self, build with others, define ourselves in our own interests, and, in the Gandhian sense, be the change we want to see in the world—collectively. This struggle will not be easy, but as my homeboy Kiwi—cited at the beginning of this chapter—from my high school days said in a song he wrote many years later, "[we] don't love the struggle, but what we're struggling for."

Being in the classroom in South Los Angeles and East Oakland as an English teacher for the past 15 years, I continue to develop an ongoing understanding of the impact of colonial oppression on the lives of dispossessed youth in contexts like these. It would be inauthentic to pretend that every one of my students became socially conscious, unlearned their self-hate, and united with others engaged in this struggle for self-determination. A large number of students continued to struggle with the realities of their everyday lives. Some simply joined the working masses, while others struggled to find work, and a few even tried their hands at the underground economy. Many pursued a college education and found it a useful pathway for their career trajectory, and others did not make the connection between their college degrees and the direction they wanted to go with their lives. For the most part, however, students were able to capture their voices, strengthen their cultural and intercultural bonds with one another, and imagine (in academically disciplined ways) a life beyond the one that society was trying to narrate for them. Long after I taught many of my students, we continue to connect on the basis of having spent meaningful time together. I do not look on this experience as a shortcoming. Instead, I am reminded of the words of Salud Algabre, the only woman leader of the 1935 Sakdalista peasant uprising against U.S. imperialism and the neocolonial government of the Philippines, who once said, "No uprising fails. Each one is a step in the right direction" (Sturtevant, 1976, p. 296). Similarly, no effort to engage in radical teaching is a failure. Each experience is a step in the right direction, and, as such, we must learn from these efforts and be sure to build with others to advance our struggle.

With this chapter, I just wanted to share my story and observations. There are many other educators much smarter than I, and collectively we are more powerful than we are individually. I do not proclaim to know much. I simply am attempting to agitate, arouse, and incite others to think more actively about being in the trenches with the people whose voices are under-represented in our work. We must understand that it is not enough to teach for teaching's sake—this is business as usual. Ultimately, our responsibility is to end, finally and forever, oppressive education, and oppression altogether. As a result of this chapter, I hope to have meaningful discussions with others concerned with putting into practice some things we can do as educators moving forward. Whatever we do practically in the short term has to be informed by a collective recognition of our long-term interests as educators, and activists, aiming to end oppression, colonialism in all its forms, and U.S. imperialism altogether.

References

Akom, A. (2003). Reexamining resistance as oppositional behavior: The Nation of Islam and the creation of a Black achievement ideology. *Sociology of Education, 76*, 305–325.

Apple, M. W. (1993). *Official knowledge: Democratic education in a conservative age.* New York, NY: Routledge.

Bakhtin, M. M. (1965). *Rabelais and his world* (H. Iswolsky, Trans.). Cambridge, MA: MIT Press.

Fanon, F. (1967). *Black skin, White masks.* New York, NY: Grove Press.

Fanon, F. (2004). *Wretched of the earth.* New York, NY: Grove Press. (Original work published 1963)

Freire, P. (1970). *Pedagogy of the oppressed.* New York, NY: Continuum.

Giroux, H., & Purpel, D. (Eds.). (1983). *The hidden curriculum and moral education: Deception or discovery.* Berkeley, CA: McCutchan.

Kohl, H. (1994). *"I won't learn from you": And other thoughts on creative maladjustment.* New York, NY: Norton & Norton.

Kiwi. (2003). Love continued. On *Writes of passage* [Self-released album].

KRS-ONE. (1989). You must learn. On Boogie Down Productions's *Ghetto music: The blueprint of hip hop.* New York, NY: Jive/RCA Records.

Marx, K. (1954). *Capital* (Vol. 1). London, England: Lawrence & Wishart. (Original work published 1867)

Marx, K., & Engels, F. (1976). *The German ideology* (3rd. rev. ed.). Moscow, Russia: Progress.

McLaren, P. (1994). *Life in schools: An introduction to critical pedagogy in the foundations of education* (2nd ed.). New York, NY: Longman.

Memmi, A. (1991) *The colonizer and the colonized.* Boston, MA: Beacon Press. (Original work published 1965)

N.W.A. (1988). Fuck the police. On *Straight outta Compton.* Compton, CA: Ruthless Records.

Smith, A. (2006). Heteropatriarchy and the three pillars of white supremacy. In *INCITE! Women of Color Against Violence's The color of violence: The INCITE anthology* (pp. 66–73). Cambridge, MA: South End Press.

Solorzano, D., & Delgado-Bernal, D. (2001). Examining transformational resistance through a critical race and Latcrit theory framework: Chicana and Chicano students in an urban context. *Urban Education, 36*(3), 308–342.

Sturtevant, D. (1976). *Popular uprisings in the Philippines, 1840–1940.* New York, NY: Cornell University Press.

Tuck, E., & Yang, K. W. (2012). Decolonization is not a metaphor. *Decolonization: Indigeneity, Education & Society, 1*(1), 1–40.

Bill Ayers

Movement Man, Moral Warrior

William H. Watkins

I have been asked to think about the long and illustrious career of Professor William Ayers. We have worked as faculty mates, editorial board members, committee members, and brothers in the struggle for many years. Bill has been an influential, even towering figure in our building. He has been a reliable source of encouragement and healing.

I would like to share my reflections in three interconnected parts. First, I attempt to situate Bill within the movement. This is a high-risk proposition wrought with subjectivity and lacking any permission. Second, Bill has always referred to me as a hardliner and I have always believed we could all benefit from a deeper understanding of the irreconcilability of economic classes in American society. Since we are both lifelong learners, I have included a brief lesson to provoke discussion. I dusted off an old essay by Mao Tse-tung that might be relevant as we Americans stumble over social and economic class issues. Finally, part three looks at Bill's legacy as seen through my eyes.

Movement Man

Like all of us humanoids, Bill Ayers is a complex being. What drives him? What drives his life's work? What is his legacy? Does he see himself as others do? What compels a child of privilege to step forward in righteous indignation and protest? How did Bill Ayers become a movement person? What kind of movement person is he?

Unfamiliar with his formative years, I attempt to comment on the mature Ayers. However and whenever it evolved, Bill seems driven by a fierce moral compass that has sensitized him to the plight of the oppressed, the conquered, the marginalized, the enslaved, and the "othered." Fairness and justice mark his compass.

Because Bill rejects any orthodoxy that leads to dogma, he has not taken great pain to ideologically and politically define himself. He has played with the term *anarchist*; however, I believe it was driven more by dissociation than adherence. Labeling is a dangerous game, although it does convey one's view about another. Some ideological descriptors I might attempt to apply to Bill include populist, perhaps Fabian, and perhaps most accurately, radical democrat.

Bill is outraged at the abuses and usurpation of avaricious imperialism, although he has not taken up the Leninist solution. Bill is skeptical that the proletarian state can deliver on its promises. For Bill, fairness and justice transcend the battle for state power. Bill's commitment to the ethics of caring and morality has become a political end in itself.

Bill has a praxis and seriously attends to it. He fans the flames of discontent. He is a movement man. His movement is for social change. His movement is for social justice. His movement is for morality.

What is the Left movement? Is it about revolution? Is it about reform? Is it about the eradication of capitalism? Is it about confronting racism? Sexism? I have always been fascinated by who joins the movement. What are they looking for? What are they finding? How far are they willing to go? How long do they stay? Is everyone welcome? The answers vary as we all occupy positions along the political spectrum. While all these questions are far too vexing and involved for this essay, perhaps we can examine a few relevant issues.

I have spent over 20 years in conversation with Bill Ayers about the movement. Perhaps this is a good time to talk not only about Bill but also about the "movement," which is at least as complex as Bill. As for myself, also a movement person, I am most interested in consciousness and class. More specifically, I'd like to know how consciousness is birthed and shaped. Do people simply wake up one morning and declare indignation? Do they see a movie about India and develop sympathy for the outcasts? Do they go to college and learn about imperialism and conquest? Does their religion engender altruism and charity? I have heard people testify that reading the *Autobiography of Malcolm X* (1965/1992) radicalized them.

While those questions are difficult to answer, other matters are more clearly addressed in the theory and history of social movements and revolution. The nature of economic and social class seems to be one of great misunderstanding in the American context. Perhaps this sketch may be useful.

Clarifying Class: Some History and Examples

Frontier America housed unequal wealth and a landed gentry, but never possessed a formal hereditary aristocracy. Buffered by great oceans on either side, America experienced a growth and development absent frequent invasion. The early 20th-century seizure of Spain's colonial possessions alongside the industrial juggernaut catapulted America to world power. It moved from internal colonizer to international colonizer. Class station was clear in early industrial America; however, a middle class was rapidly under formation. America's white- and blue-collar proletariat emerged within the context of the pronounced division between mental and manual labor. How are class divisions taught and learned in American schooling and social thought?

Americans don't learn much about socioeconomic class. We are taught that we are all Americans. Each can rise based on merits, not bloodline. Owing to America's unprecedented prosperity, the merit argument has many followers. That prosperity also supported the construction of an unprecedented middle class. The Civil Rights Movement of the late 1960s further expanded the Black and Latino middle class. Class in America is greatly misunderstood. People often think they are capitalists because they work, bank, own an iPad, try to advance, and consume. America badly needs a serious class analysis rooted in history and evolved in the ever-changing economic dynamics of the nation.

Prior to the 1949 revolution in China, Chairman Mao Tse-tung (1926) wrote an essay that proved to be a game changer. Entitled "Analysis of the Classes in Chinese Society," it helped clear up many misconceptions of who was situated where. For the unfamiliar, I present a thumbnail summary of Mao's insightful work. Perhaps readers will find useful themes here.

If revolution was to be the overthrow of one class by another, it was crucial to identify who the classes were and how they stood in relationship to one another. Mao wrote:

To distinguish real friends from real enemies, we must make a general analysis of the economic status of the various classes in Chinese society and of their respective attitudes towards the revolution.

The landlord class and the comprador class. In economically backward and semi-colonial China the landlord class and the comprador class are wholly appendages of the international bourgeoisie . . . the most backward and most reactionary. . . . Their existence is utterly incompatible with the aims of the Chinese revolution.

The middle bourgeoisie. This class represents the capitalist relations of production. This national bourgeoisie wants to eliminate foreign capital so that it may control indigenous profits. They favor revolution against imperialism and the warlords but wish to maintain capitalist relations.

The petty bourgeoisie. Included in this category are the owner-peasants, the master handicraftsmen, the lower levels of the intellectuals—students, primary and secondary school teachers, lower government functionaries, office clerks, small lawyers and the small traders. . . . As for the movement against the imperialists and the warlords, they merely doubt whether it can succeed (on the ground that the foreigners and the warlords seem so powerful), hesitate to join it and prefer to be neutral, but they never oppose the revolution. . . . When they come to settle their accounts at the end of each year, they are shocked, exclaiming, "What? Another deficit!" As such people have seen better days and are now going downhill with every passing year, their debts mounting and their life becoming more and more miserable, they "shudder at the thought of the future." They are in great mental distress because there is such a contrast between their past and their present. Such people are quite important for the revolutionary movement; they form a mass of no small proportions and are the left-wing of the petty bourgeoisie.

The semi-proletariat. What is here called the semi-proletariat consists of five categories: (1) the overwhelming majority of the semi-owner peasants, (2) the poor peasants, (3) the small handicraftsmen, (4) the shop assistants, and (5) the peddlers. The overwhelming majority of the semi-owner peasants together with the poor peasants constitute a very large part of the rural masses. . . . They borrow at exorbitant rates of interest and buy grain at high prices; their plight is naturally harder than that of the owner-peasants who need no help from others, but they are better off than the poor peasants. For the poor peasants own no land. . . .

The proletariat. The modern industrial proletariat numbers about two million. It is not large because China is economically backward. These two million industrial workers are mainly employed in five industries—railways, mining, maritime transport, textiles and shipbuilding—and a great number are enslaved in enterprises owned by foreign capitalists. Though not very numerous, the industrial proletariat represents China's new productive forces, is the most progressive class in modern China and has become the leading force in the revolutionary movement. . . . They have been deprived of all means of production, have nothing left but their hands, have no hope of ever becoming rich and, moreover, are subjected to the most ruthless treatment by the imperialists, the warlords and the bourgeoisie. That is why they are particularly good fighters. The coolies in the cities are also a force meriting attention.

Apart from all these, there is the fairly large *lumpen*-proletariat, made up of peasants who have lost their land and handicraftsmen who cannot get work. They lead the most precarious existence of all. In every part of the country they have their secret societies, which were originally their mutual-aid organizations for political and economic struggle. Brave fighters but apt to be destructive, they can become a revolutionary force if given proper guidance.

Mao sums up:

> It can be seen that our enemies are all those in league with imperialism—the warlords, the bureaucrats, the comprador class, the big landlord class and the reactionary section of the intelligentsia attached to them. The leading force in our revolution is the industrial proletariat. Our closest friends are the entire semi-proletariat and petty bourgeoisie. As for the vacillating middle bourgeoisie, their right-wing may become our enemy and their left-wing may become our friend—but we must be constantly on our guard and not let them create confusion within our ranks. (pp. 15–28)

Now dated, this is nevertheless a great history lesson. What can we take away from Mao's writings and our own nation's experiences? All students and proponents of social change must have a broad framework of who might be invested in the existing structure and who has nothing to lose. Who has the most to lose? Who might likely fight? Who perhaps may not fight?

Accomplished social theorists, among them Karl Marx (Marx & Engels, 1969), Karl Mannheim (1952), Antonio Gramsci (1988, 1992), and many others, have explored economic classes and the sources of consciousness. In the 1920s movement people coined the term "Wall Street." More recently, "Occupy" people gave us the notion of the "1%." Perhaps soon Americans will have their own well-theorized class analysis rooted in our history and practices.

While Mao's analysis turned out to be insightful, perhaps even prescient, it was not the end of the story. Station in life is not a foolproof predicator of consciousness. Consciousness turns out to be a squiggly and elusive thing. People regularly betray their class background. In America, the poorest of the poor often side with the richest of the rich. Additionally, skin color loyalty cannot be overlooked in this highly racialized society. While the debate will likely continue, at the end of the day all who oppose tyranny, exploitation, and oppression are, and should be, welcome in the movement.

Bill's Legacy: Teacher and Preacher

Bill has attached himself, intellectually and personally, to the greatest and most respected teachers of our time. For Bill, learning is perhaps the ultimate human endeavor. Learning is a freeing experience and everyone should be free. He views school as contested space where ideas and ideologies battle. Hence, the classroom can be a magical place where agency and actualization are cultivated. Teaching is Bill's chosen trade and political practice. He has developed an ethic of teaching that defines his legacy. Several propositions are included in this ethic:

- Teaching as a craft. Teaching is sacred. It should not be undertaken by the pretender, the casual, the sophist, or the charlatan. Teachers must understand that their special role is not because they know so much but because so much is at stake.
- Teaching as liberation. Passivity, ignorance, and complacency are bondage; teaching should be liberatory. It contributes to the freeing experience and is perhaps the greatest gift of the teacher. The good teacher encourages the free exchange of ideas and the emancipation of expression.
- Teaching for reflection. Unlearned people waste lots of time reliving the past. Growth and progress demand that we all be able to engage in both affirmation and negation. The reflective process should be one of contemplation and discovery. We should recognize that we are all in a state of being and becoming.
- Teaching for exploring the world. We should all be participants not spectators in the events of our lifetime. We must bring the world into our classroom and take our students out into the world.
- Teaching for social justice. While *critical thinking* has almost become a trite expression, equity is perhaps the most important concept of our time. Democracy demands we critique every established order for abuses, usurpations, and oppression.
- Fostering imagination and hope. Imagination separates us humans from the animal kingdom. We dream of a better existence. Being dreamers, we know a better world is possible.
- Teaching for action. Enlightenment without practice is wasted. Rounded people don't simply study the world, they endeavor to change it.

I submit that these concepts are central to Bill Ayers's ethic of teaching and perhaps his credo for life and living. This is my take on the man I call colleague, co-worker, comrade, and friend.

References

Gramsci, A. (1988). *The Antonio Gramsci reader: Selected writings 1916–1935*. New York, NY: Schocken Books.

Gramsci, A. (1992). *Selections from the prison notebooks*. New York, NY: Columbia University Press.

Mannheim, K. (1952). *Essays on the sociology of knowledge*. New York, NY: Oxford University Press.

Mao Tse-tung. (1926). Analysis of the classes in Chinese society. In *Selected works of Mao Tse-tung* (Vol. 1). Beijing, China: Foreign Languages Press.

Marx, K., & Engels, F. (1969). Karl *Marx and Frederick Engels: Selected works* (Vol. 1). Moscow, Russia: Progress Publishers.

X, M. (with Haley, A.). (1992). *The autobiography of Malcolm X*. New York, NY: Ballantine Books. (Original work published 1965)

6

Antinomies of Cultural Preservation and Cultural Transformation, or "Are You a Chinese from Prato?"

Lisa Yun Lee

This past summer, after an extended day of art viewing in Florence that included time at the Uffizi Gallery, the Accademia, and the Palazzo Vecchio, I entered a cab to get back to my hotel on the outskirts of town. I was startled when the driver gruffly asked me, even before I could say a word, "*Sei una cinese di Prato?*" (Are you a Chinese from Prato?) I replied in English, "Sorry, I'm from Chicago. I don't speak any Italian." He then apologized and said: "That is good. You are not one of those Chinese who are destroying our Italian culture and our way of life."

Vincenzo introduced himself to me and went on to explain how Chinese immigrants had "taken over" the nearby Tuscan city of Prato. Employed in the textile industry and leather factories to make belts, purses, and shoes that traditionally have been produced by Italian artisans, the Chinese provide the necessary labor to quickly and cheaply produce goods for voracious consumers around the globe who prefer products *Made in Italy*. He passionately described how the Chinese ruin the high-quality craftsmanship that is essential to Italian identity, and bamboozle indiscriminate buyers who actually are purchasing products "Made by Chinese in Italy." He interrupted his comments every so often to say, "No offense, of course," as he looked back at me through the rearview mirror. And as we pulled up to my hotel, Vincenzo seemed genuinely saddened by what he described as the Chinese immigrants' refusal to learn the Italian language, and the fact that "they don't even eat Italian food!"

The experience of this cab ride provided both comic and painful moments that reveal a set of antinomies around the ideas of cultural preservation and cultural transformation that I explore in this essay. I interrogate these moments to raise questions about cultural purity and appropriation, the expansiveness of globalization, and the resurgence of national identity with an emphasis on local economies; and to examine cultural privilege and access in regard to race, class, and gender. These tensions provide the necessary friction to move us toward a more progressive understanding of culture, one that is not implicated in the continued exclusion and oppression of marginalized people in our societies. Insisting on the preservation of specific ways of life and practices as a means of resisting the homogenization of life, even as we recognize the necessity of radically altering our practices, is part of the work of creating a more just world.

"Fast Fashion" and "Slow Food"

There are up to 45,000 Chinese immigrants in Prato, a city of around 189,000 inhabitants. The exact number is difficult to calculate since so many of these laborers are undocumented. Almost all of these immigrants work in 3,500 factory workshops that undergird the fashion industry. It might seem easy to consider the Chinese in this Tuscan city as one homogeneous group, but in fact there have been several different periods of migration and immigration, and the situation is much more complex. The first group of Chinese immigrants came in the early 1990s to work for well-known designers like Salvatore Ferragamo and Gucci. Many of these immigrants were already living in Europe and employed by fashion houses like Christian Dior in Paris, but chose to migrate south, perhaps in search of better weather and less expensive housing. More recently, Chinese businesspeople have opened their own factories built on cheap labor and plagiarized designs. These owners control the entire supply chain—from the buying of textiles in China, shipping to factories, production, and selling to the retailer. A new group of immigrants, mostly from Wenzhou, in the Province of Zhejiang, came over to labor in mostly unregulated sweatshops. Women and men work in small rooms, often with their children: sewing and mending, stitching, cutting, and measuring. They work for as long as 24 hours straight and in conditions that are considered illegal by European labor laws (Johanson, Smyth, & French, 2009). These practices enable the thriving industry referred to in Italy as "Pronto Moda," or fast fashion.

Vincenzo's anxiety about Chinese workers lowering the standards of craftsmanship and robbing Italians of their cultural identity reveals how contested our understanding of culture is. Dick Hebdige (1979) laid this out so well in his influential and still relevant work *Subculture: The Meaning of Style*. Hebdige describes two divergent and conflicting notions of "culture" at play throughout history. On the one hand, there is culture understood as rooted in aesthetic supremacy. This is a normative, classical, and conservative understanding of culture—one that supports an established canon of what is excellent and what is desirable and pleasing. In this definition, culture is backward looking and consists of art forms, institutions, and practices that have been deemed worthy and valuable. In the other understanding, culture is not a thing that can be possessed or accessed, nor is it simply a set of practices. This definition is forward looking and moves away from immutable and fixed understandings of what is considered excellent to an emphasis on culture as sets of relationships between people in different social contexts in "everyday life." Constantly in flux, culture is being created all the time and consists of a dynamic set and sum of all relationships woven through all social practices. This oft-cited passage by T. S. Eliot in *Notes Towards a Definition of Culture* (1969) describes this complex notion in the most straightforward of terms and bears reading and re-reading:

> Culture includes all the characteristic activities and interests of a people: Derby Day, Henley Regatta, Cowes, the Twelfth of August, a cup final, the dog races, the pin table, a dart board, Wensleydale cheese, boiled cabbage cut into sections, beetroot in vinegar, nineteenth century Gothic churches and the music of Elgar. (p. 50)

In this seemingly dissonant amalgam of events, foods, art, music, and rituals, the distinctions between so-called "high" and "low" culture are obliterated. The extraordinary and the ordinary mix and mingle, and the porousness of these boundaries is made obvious. Culture is not inherited or passed down, nor is it static, but emergent—that is, something that is made and remade through a set of intellectual, artistic, and daily practices.

While it seems obvious to me that this second definition of culture more adequately captures the expansiveness of our lived experiences and the way our lives are woven together, it is the first definition of culture that is the most prevalent. For example, most of our academic, arts, and cultural institutions operate as if there is an established canon of what is excellent or what is aesthetically pleasing, and their responsibility is to act as the protectors, transmitters, and gatekeepers to this culture. Access is presented within a system of patronage, where there is an elite group that out of noblesse oblige or a sense of social responsibility allows culture to be more or less accessible to others.

Vincenzo's sadness in what he perceives as the lack of engagement in Italian culture—in learning the language or eating the food—reveals his investment in the first definition of culture as described by Hebdige. It is also evident, by his comment about consumers being duped into buying "Made by Chinese in Italy" products, that full social inclusion, whether by participating in cultural life through language, palate, or immigration status, actually would not be enough to identify a Chinese immigrant with his notion of what it means to be Italian. While I felt apologetic for my inability to speak Italian, and for most Americans and their monolingual lives, Vincenzo was perfectly happy to converse in English and seemed to accept English as an international language. Interestingly, he did not display any anxieties about the dominance of English, and its massive demand worldwide, similar to those about the dominance of and demand for Chinese labor. English as a Second Language is a worldwide industry exported vigorously by the United States and Britain, and peddled whole-sale around the globe, along with the myth that studying English is what one needs for success in life.

Arjun Appadurai (1996) has beautifully complicated the strange interaction between the global and local within taxi cabs, describing these sites as "diasporic public spheres." While in Chicago and in a cab, I am almost always struck by the truth of his description. What is this strange space inside the cab, where a driver from Pakistan listening to recorded sermons from thousands of miles away whisks one through modernist downtown Chicago from the Art Institute off Michigan Avenue to the National Museum of Mexican Art in Pilsen? In Florence, it was my turn to occupy this diasporic space. While my identity as an English-speaking American was foregrounded, my Asian identity was never completely absent, acknowledged with every, "No offense, of course."

As I paid for my ride and hopped out of the cab, I resisted the urge to contribute to the pervasive myth that pasta was imported from China by Marco Polo (Kummer, 1986), but I did inform Vincenzo that the Chinese have been eating noodles since at least 3000 B.C.E. It is not unusual that anxieties around cultural inclusivity and exclusivity would end on a note about food. Ideas of cultural authenticity and purity assert themselves pervasively through the hierarchies of taste and gastronomical differences. Most infamous is Samuel Gompers's 1902 treatise coauthored with Herman Gutstadt entitled "Meat vs. Rice: American Manhood Against Asiatic Coolieism." Gompers was the stalwart, charismatic president of the American Federation of Labor (AFL). He vehemently opposed the inclusion of Asian workers in the AFL membership and believed their presence adversely affected the fortunes of the American male laborer. Gompers advanced his xenophobia through a culinary argument in this treatise and by testifying in front of Congress in favor of Chinese Exclusion Laws, contrasting the strength of White men as hearty meat eaters, and effeminizing Chinese immigrant labor as weak rice eaters. The idea that "You are what you eat" became a rallying call for anti-immigration sentiment.

To further complicate matters, Prato is the center for both "Pronto Moda" and Italy's Slow Food Movement. Slow Food originated as a protest against the proposed opening of a McDonald's near the Spanish Steps in Rome and against the corporatization and globalization of our food systems and their effects. Its three tenets of good, clean, and fair food incorporate the importance of pleasure and deliciousness with nutrition and environmentalism, and with issues of access and just labor practices. Slow Food also advocates for regional specificity and local traditions, but as a means of resisting hegemony and the homogenization of life.

And while challenging the authenticity of Italian goods made in Italy by Chinese, one might as well wonder whether Chinese food made by Chinese in Italy is Chinese or Italian? In the United States, there are more Chinese restaurants than McDonald's, Wendy's, and Burger King restaurants combined (Lee, 2008). "Where can I get some *real* Chinese food in Chicago?" is one of the most common questions I am asked. The idea, however, of authenticity in terms of foods and desire for cultural discreteness has been debunked over and again. In *Everybody Was Kung Fu Fighting*, Vijay Prashad (2001) asks us to recognize our "mulatto history":

> Can we, for example, think of "Indian" food (that imputed essence of the Indian sub-continent) without the tomato, the first fruit harvested by the Mayans, and the base for most curries? Are not the Maya, then, part of contemporary "Indian" culture? (p. 61)

Prashad's argument asks us to stop pretending that our histories are not already overlapping. Giving up the myth of cultural purity and authenticity allows us to give voice to our intertwined cultural histories and struggles. For example, by relinquishing any claims on the authenticity of the tomato as one of the elements of Italian cuisine, what kind of shared struggles might a cab driver in Florence be able to find with a garment worker in the textile industry in Prato?

Am I a Chinese from Prato?

On my final day in Tuscany, I felt compelled to travel to Prato, which is only a short 25-minute train ride from Florence. I was the daughter of immigrants who traveled to the United States in the 1950s from Taiwan. My parents achieved some degree of social mobility, moving from a working-class to a middle-class lifestyle in Poughkeepsie, NY. I grew up speaking Chinese at home and with friends from the Mandarin school I attended on weekends. I ate Chinese food for dinner every night and will always remember the first egg salad sandwich I ate at Michael Fried's house when I was 7 years old, which introduced me to the magical, creamy, exotic taste of mayonnaise. Up to that point, the only eggs I had ever eaten were boiled in soy sauce.

Arriving in Prato, I was surprised to see soy sauce eggs for sale in the train station! It was uncanny to see so many Chinese people lingering in the streets and in the shops, waiting for buses and living their lives in this Italian city. The experience was overwhelming and I felt a sort of dizzy euphoria. There is something called *hyperkulturemia*, otherwise known as Stendhal syndrome, which is a psychosomatic response characterized by symptoms including the feeling of faintness, heart palpitations, and dizziness, all brought on by the enormous awe one experiences when viewing an array of supremely beautiful art in Florence. It is named after the 19th-century French author Stendhal (1959), who described a visit to the tombs of Machiavelli, Michelangelo, and Galileo, and his viewing of Giotto's frescoes in the Basilica Santa Croce in this way:

> I was in a sort of ecstasy, from the idea of being in Florence, close to the great men whose tombs I had seen. Absorbed in the contemplation of sublime beauty . . . I reached the point where one encounters celestial sensations. . . . Everything spoke so vividly to my soul. Ah, if I could only forget. I had palpitations of the heart, what in Berlin they call "nerves." Life was drained from me. I walked with the fear of falling. (p. 89)

According to the Italian psychiatrist Graziella Magherini (1989), who coined the term "Stendhal syndrome" in 1979, locals are immune to the beauty of the city in this way, and only tourists and visitors are susceptible. She observed, described, and documented more than 100 cases of breathlessness, panic attacks, fainting to the floor—all as a result of encounters with the city's cultural treasures. I felt this same kind of breathlessness in Prato. The landscape is a culturally miscegenated cacophony of street signs in Mandarin, English, and Italian. The Chinatown, which is known as St. Beijing, stretches from the far western side of town to Porta Pistoiese, the historic center. The youth switch with ease between speaking Italian among themselves and Mandarin to their parents.

The knowledge of the oppressive labor conditions that inform the very existence of St. Beijing, and the fact that this once Left-leaning town is now staunchly governed by Right-wing conservatives with anti-immigration stances (promising to protect Italian culture from the incursion of the Chinese at any cost), cast a long shadow on the sunny streets. I remember an audio piece that I asked Bill Ayers to make for the Jane Addams Hull-House Museum while I was the director there. In this fierce and eloquent audio essay, which you can hear on the museum's website, Ayers draws the distinction between working in service to someone versus being in solidarity with them. The former is a stance of charity toward the needy, and the latter is one of political identification with the marginalized and the oppressed. At this moment, I am "a Chinese from Prato."

References

Appadurai, A. (1996). *Modernity at large: Cultural dimensions of globalization.* Minneapolis: University of Minnesota Press.

Eliot, T. S. (1969). *Notes towards a definition of culture.* London, England: Harcourt.

Gompers, S., & Gutstadt, H. (1902). *Meat vs. rice: American manhood against Asiatic coolieism.* Washington, DC: American Federation of Labor.

Hebdige, D. (1979). *Subculture: The meaning of style.* London, England: Methuen.

Johanson, G., Smyth, R., & French, R. (2009). *Living outside the walls: The Chinese in Prato.* Cambridge, MA: New Castle.

Kummer, C. (1986, July). Pasta. *The Atlantic,* p. 21.

Lee, J. 8. (2008). *The fortune cookie chronicles.* New York, NY: Hachette.

Magherini, G. (1989). *La sindrome di Stendhal* [The Stendhal syndrome]. Florence, Italy: Ponte Alle Grazie.

Prashad, V. (2001). *Everybody was kung fu fighting.* Boston, MA: Beacon Press.

Stendhal (R. Coe, Trans.). (1959). *Naples and Florence: A journey from Milan to Reggio.* London, England: Calder.

7

The New Normal

Meditations on Failure

Erica R. Meiners and Therese Quinn

How does it feel to be a problem?

—W.E.B. Du Bois, *The Souls of Black Folk*, 1903

1. In our landscape of social and political movements these days, failure feels like an inescapable soundtrack. People and projects are littered by the side of the road and their histories are narrated for us: *This tactic failed; this campaign failed; this strategy failed; this relationship failed; this program failed; this organization failed. We failed*, in other words.

The year 2013 fell hard. Despite strong opposition and ongoing organizing and protest by parents, students, teachers, and community members, the mass school closures in Chicago's poor Black and Brown communities appear to be unstoppable. The Social Justice High School, achieved through a hunger strike by mothers and grandmothers in the city's Latino Little Village community, has been forced from the promise of its name. Despite years of amazing organizing and no shortage of need, New York's Queers for Economic Justice faced emptying coffers and shuttered their doors, as did the amazing Chicago-based Young Women's Empowerment Project. Also in Chi-town, 3,000 school workers were pink-slipped in the early summer and the teachers' union is bleeding numbers; it's the smallest it has been in decades. And Trayvon Martin is still dead.

One in three Americans lives below the federal poverty level and the United States still has the largest prison population on the planet. CeCe McDonald is still behind bars, as is Chelsea Manning, ousted from the position of Grand Marshall of San Francisco's 2013 Pride Parade by its board. Edward Snowden is hiding in Russia, and the planet is hotter today than it was last year and the year before. At home in Illinois, we celebrated the hard-fought closure—vehemently opposed by the American Federation of State, County, and Municipal Employees labor union—of the Dwight maximum security prison for women, only to find it probably will reopen to house people in the federal system. Our politicians are lying; they've been caught, hand in the till, putting family on the payroll, taking selfies on the job, boldly obfuscating. And Trayvon Martin is still dead.

We started this essay directly after the acquittal of George Zimmerman, the man who shot 17-year-old Trayvon Martin for being suspicious (meaning young, male, and Black) as he walked through a Florida gated community. It is not just Martin's terrible death that we are feeling; the bodies stack up. Chicago, our home city, has had a bloody year. The police and politicians like to remind us that fewer people have been murdered this year than last, as if that news will ease anyone's pain. Trayvon Martin is still dead, and another dark brother lost his life yesterday, didn't he?

Like too many times before, against this tide of blood and pain many people struggle to foreground and resist state violence. Alongside others, we create art, organizations, and uprisings that aim to build the world we need. Over years and hours these gatherings, meet-ups, cooperatives, schools, and groups flare, illuminate, explode, and fade. Some days we imagine that just over our left shoulders there is a crazy Day of the Dead–style field teeming with the phantoms of alliances and confederacies, plans and people, relationships and projects, all bedecked in marigolds and skull garlands, hanging out together in the streaming sunshine. We loved each of these entities (some desperately) that were cultivated with sweat and blood and time. They are a part of us and now, quietly or with a deadly flare, they are no more; their ends are sealed by consultants or screaming matches, cooptation or fiscal starvation, bullets or bars, *interpersonal issues* or burn-out, obsolescence or exhaustion.

Despite our narratives of this landscape, we know, of course, that failure is a construct, an artifact of time and place. We are the people who tell others, over the charred embers, how we are building strong communities of struggle along the way, about how the lenses of failure and success are the unhelpful framings of another paradigm. What is important is that we continue.

We have lost a certain shame associated with our collapses, and over the years our affective commitments shift in relation to social justice work, campaigns, projects. When the campaign spins out, the organization shutters, the project collapses, or the person is sentenced, experience demonstrates that this particular or specific moment, as deep as the feelings of anger or betrayal or sadness may be, is part of a longer, wider, deeper trajectory. This perspective has been enormously helpful and sustaining, especially when the losses feel crushing and the exhaustion or pain cannot be understood as temporal or generative. The possibilities of radical potential, of becomings and openings, and the change that results from *collective* praxis keep us going. Some days, committing to imagination and engagement seems like the only path away from despair. This, a comrade identified, is "slow work," always collective and at the same time exquisitely lonely.

And we do believe this: Success and failure are valuations of an economy that always ensures we are losers; yet, at the same time, we don't *fully* believe this. Sometimes the losses are too real, too present. It feels, inescapably, like failure when we lose the case, she dies, the draconian bill becomes law, all the Black teachers get fired, the new immigration prison is built, the military takes over another public high school, he is executed, the carceral state starts to use our words and our experiences of harm against us, she loses custody of her kids because of her repeated history of incarceration, and on and on. In these moments, the slow work view, the *other* paradigm outside of the success and failure binary, is hard to access. There are so many losses, some days. And Trayvon Martin is still dead.

2. Universities, in particular, are contested and contradictory sites for justice work. They are places where the metrics of success and failure are produced and reinforced. And through many lenses, the project of postsecondary education in the United States is an imploding carcass, a *bizarro* world of precariously balanced dreams and despairs.

For example, the Pell Grant, a federal subsidy that historically has supported many individuals to access college, now covers less than 32% of the cost of a year of undergraduate tuition. Earning a degree means amassing debt—according to the Institute for College Access and Success Project on Student Debt, the average borrower will receive her degree along with a debt load of $26,600—without, in a time of dwindling salaries and part-time jobs, any guarantee of eventually paying it off. Across the United States there is now an estimated trillion dollars of student debt, which many economists expect will lead to the equivalent of the recent housing collapse.

As the steady squeeze of "austerity" further shrinks tenure-stream faculty lines—less than 25% of all postsecondary classes are now taught by tenure-stream faculty—most public state universities run on tuition dollars, not state contributions, and are bolstered by the suppressed wage labor of students on campus who do the critical work of teaching core

courses and running academic departments, libraries, residences, food services, and more. As our graduate employees' unions point out, the university works because they do.

Today, higher education cultures are shaped less by faculty senates,
unions, or even politicians, than by student loan companies, multinational
food service corporations like Sodexo, military and big pharmaceutical
research dollars, real estate developers, and so on. Public community colleges, the postsecondary institutions where the overwhelming majority of
people receive an education, have eviscerated their liberal arts courses and
expanded technical job–training programs despite the disappearance of
almost all forms of labor except retail and service work. A privileged few,
under the punishing logic of meritocracy, access a sparkling range of curricular options at resource-endowed private and public restrictive-enrollment research universities where the tuition bills exceed what the federal
government thinks two families of four should be able to live on for a year.
It is painfully common to hear many, including some of our co-workers at
public institutions, describe elite, wealth-hoarding, tax-avoidant private
colleges and universities as "good" schools that offer "good" educations,
when these narrations affirm and naturalize a landscape that is not simply
wildly unjust, but a rigged enterprise from stem to stern.

In 2010, to reframe California's budget crisis, student organizers
created the facetious entity the University of California Movement for
Efficient Privatization (acronym UCMeP, tag line "Privatize Now, Ask
Questions Later"), which proposed a synergistic merger between universities and prisons, producing a UNISON. As a UNISON highlights, prisons
and universities are both involved in the business of managing and shaping people's life pathways: state-sanctioned futures for those who are the
"best of" and those who are, well, just not the "best of."

The system is not broken. It is working exactly as designed.

And yet despite the bleakness of this snapshot, universities are also
sites offering the potential for radical possibilities. Historically and today, campuses can work to bring people together to name, resist, and
challenge the conditions of their labor and postsecondary educations,
and wider oppressive political and social systems including military draft
and rape culture, apartheid, sweatshop labor, immigration policies, and
more. For example, an early Occupy-inspired action was to "occupy student debt" visually through images and texts describing the devastating
effects of debt loads posted on Tumblr and shared on Facebook; examples can be viewed at: dropstudentdebt.tumblr.com and www.facebook.
com/OccupyStudentDebt.

After student debt protesters were pepper-sprayed out of town squares and parks nationwide, participants regrouped to initiate Student Debt Crisis (studentdebtcrisis.org), which organized via Twitter and other modes of social media. These testimonies tackled the presumptive personal shame of debt, pointing out its systemic and group effects.

Cyber-based and on-the-ground student uprisings—from Puerto Rico and Chile, to Montreal and Finland, and elsewhere—push back and organize against escalating tuition rates, skyrocketing student loan debt, and campus working conditions. Simultaneously, the working and learning contexts of universities, both public and private, open access and exclusionary, cannot be separated from our bankrupt infrastructure: full prisons and record high deportations; increasing poverty; our perma-temp, 28-hour-per-week jobs and misleadingly named "right to work" legislation; our shortening life expectancies, warming planet, and permanent war economy. Those targeted and harmed by punishing state practices and the situations created through negligence or destabilization are not arbitrary—poor, Black and Latino, First Nations, queer, disabled, old and young—rather, they are people who are shut out of our nominally democratic and public institutions.

Within the university spaces and moments of resistance are what we look for, where we do our work, and what we examine more closely; these are the impulses toward justice attended by our creative and paid labor. Across postsecondary education sites, and in particular within restrictive-enrollment private and public universities, social justice is tentatively embraced. For example, we track the uneven but noticeable development of funded "social justice" institutes, the use of this language in tenure-track faculty position descriptions, the incorporation of "social justice" into the mission statements of universities, departments, and programs, and a few granting imperatives. We initially welcomed these initiatives and are still supportive of and engaged with practices on our own campuses that both require and recycle this language: A critique of "social justice" can be published and added as a line in our CVs. Yet, we anxiously note also how universities absorb and assimilate the social justice movement's terms, and even its oppositional frames, into their working status quo. For us, the university does seem to be a particularly tough place to keep one's eyes-on-the-prize. Despite a trend toward social justice programs, initiatives, majors and minors, and hires, the phrase *social justice* often feels evacuated of meaning, and at the same time, sponge-like, absorptive—capable of representing almost anything. It can even be deployed in conflict with the aims of radical social movements.

For example, frameworks for analyzing difference and power, such as social justice and intersectionality, circulate in universities where capitalism is the lifeblood and a discourse of liberal multiculturalism seeks to manage and assimilate particular forms of difference, not redistribute resources. Tuition escalates, cutting off access to many, and African American and Ethnic Studies programs and centers are defunded, and yet campus "Diversity Days" proliferate. Relatedly, the push for civic engagement at universities often initiates calls for scholars to work with community partners. This impetus has resulted in conference presentations and publications, for example, where professors stake claims to authenticity capital from their relationships with students, teachers, parents, poor people, "real" organizers, and so on. In these instances, *diversity, social justice,* and *community partnerships* become decoration and window-dressing, with resource-sharing, solidarity, and the awkward and often slow give-and-take of coalitional work sidelined. Social justice rings hollow as academics mint forms of scholarship, described in ever more obscure and copyrighted terms, when the house we work in—the university—is excluded from investigation and critique, and in particular when our laboring practices become normed within, not resistant to, structures that oppress.

University ties to regressive paradigms are hardly new. The framework that insists "violent offenders" must pay a debt to society has underwritten aspects of feminist and lesbian, gay, bisexual, and transgendered (LGBT) social movements that rely heavily on criminalization of individuals as a solution to a structural problem. Highly visible anti-violence and hate crimes movements, often ideologically linked to Women's Studies and LGBT Studies, continue to augment and naturalize the carceral state while masking some central sources of violence and harm. Carceral feminism describes a trajectory of scholarship that advances "feminist" goals using incarceration and prisons as forms of punishment and as a mythic "deterrent." Cooptation is an inadequate explanatory frame for the work of carceral feminist scholarship, or for the "embedded anthropologists" collecting data alongside U.S. military forces in Iraq and Afghanistan, or for how military dollars have dominated and reshaped the field of physics in alignment with the U.S. military's priorities; rather, these linkages between our scholarly fields and oppressive regimes and structures—including capitalism and White supremacy—are embedded and naturalized within the grammar of our institutions and our attainments.

Of course: People are trained and funded and hired and recognized and tenured to do this work.

The system isn't broken. It is working exactly as designed.

While increasingly wary of the university's alluring offers to designate social justice experts and objectives, we try to adapt and to use these institutional frames to seek support for our work. Yet what is the check *on us*? What are *we* not seeing? What are we legitimating? When social justice is the defanged equivalent of multiculturalism or diversity in our worksites, will it matter that we have taken a stand for or against its academic forms? Are we there already?

Yet, these often troubling relationships between scholars and their higher education bases are dynamic, and the very same sites produce possibilities for the circulation of radical pedagogies and theoretical interventions. The contemporary sociopolitical contexts on campuses have supported decidedly queer configurations, or to use words of Stefano Harney and Fred Moten (2013), "maroon"—renegade—groupings in the "undercommons." Harney and Moten imagine

> maroon communities of composition teachers, mentorless graduate students, adjunct Marxist historians, out or queer management professors, state college ethnic studies departments, closed-down film programs, visa-expired Yemeni student newspaper editors, historically black college sociologists, and feminist engineers. And what will the university say of them? It will say they are unprofessional. This is not an arbitrary charge. It is the charge against the more than professional. How do those who exceed the profession, who exceed and by exceeding escape, how do those maroons problematize themselves, problematize the university, force the university to consider them a problem, a danger? (p. 30)

Universities are ripe for a queer kind of political engagement, and consequently are also sites targeted for hyper-regulation.

Given this landscape and these contradictions, our starting point is a position of both undecidedness about the current values of the university, and simultaneously a commitment to think, to make, to act—with others—regardless of our ambivalence. It is this point of tension that Marge Piercy evokes in her poem, "To Be of Use" (1973/1982), when she describes loving those who "jump into work head first/without dallying in the shallows" (p. 106). Our location is fraught and failure attendant, but we have committed to the dive. Ethnic Studies scholar and worker Dylan Rodriguez identified in a 2012 issue of *American Quarterly* that he is in a "stand-off position"—not sure whether the university is recuperable from its (he uses *its*, we say *our*) genocidal and proto-genocidal legacies. Our analysis started from this location, *a stand-off*, eyes wide open to our genocidal and proto-genocidal tendencies, and we wrap with an acknowledgment of our obligation and willingness to engage, with no guarantees about outcome.

3. In the *Queer Art of Failure*, cultural studies critic Judith (Jack) Halberstam (2011) aims to dislodge the pervasive progress narrative central to contemporary understandings of U.S. life. Beyond attempting to dispose of the "success/failure" binary, Halberstam argues to inhabit and to explore failure, as we have attempted here:

> Under certain circumstances, failing, losing, forgetting, unmaking, undoing, unbecoming, not knowing may in fact offer more creative, more cooperative, more surprising ways of being in the world. (p. 2)

It is not hard to see what the trouble with success might be for Halberstam and for queers or others whose bodies and life paths are incompatible with *normal life*. For many *failing* at what normative culture has marked as success seems not only more attractive and promising, but the only possible path. Why not celebrate that?

And this is not just a queer tactic. What passes as normal is wickedly narrowing and shuts many out while also shoring up, and naturalizing, oppressive forms of state violence. For example, the normal body is a productive worker. Someone who *earns her keep, pays her way, purchases her own house and car, contributes to society, works hard, keeps her head down*. Someone who *has a career* and *finds meaning in her job*. In academic terms, someone who is *doing her work*. In arts terms, someone who is *making work*. To not be a worker is to not be normal; it is scandalous, unthinkable, a shame.

Failure to be a laboring body, through disability or perhaps a conscious affective disinvestment, makes one not only unproductive, but potentially ungovernable. As the theorist Frank Wilderson (2003) pointedly questioned in relation to Black people in the U.S. empire, this positionality poses a radical critique of *the normal* produced by capitalism.

> What does it mean to be positioned not as a positive term in the struggle for anti-capitalist hegemony, i.e., a worker, but to be positioned in excess of hegemony, to be a catalyst that disarticulates the rubric of hegemony, to be a scandal to its assumptive, foundational logic, to threaten civil society's discursive integrity? (p. 23)

In what ways are our investments in production, success, and progress reproducing racialized, gendered, and ableist norms? What if, to build from Wilderson's position, instead of arguing for the rights of workers, one organized from the standpoint that work should not define people, and that laboring is not a norm? What might it mean to inhabit failure at this political moment in universities? Or is this, again, a recuperable, coopt-able, and already-failed, yet theorizable, political gesture, available only to the select and the privileged? How do we argue against particular forms and valuations of labor while engaged in practices that we love?

Tethered to flawed and dynamic people and struggles, including ourselves, this is life in the long arc. We take heart remembering dreamers like Don West, the communist poet who cofounded the Highlander School with Myles Horton. Refusing to sideline or cover his politics, West led an itinerant life, teaching, writing, and organizing with others in every place he lived. Or Ida B. Wells-Barnett, who used research and documentation as a tool to erode the terrorist practices White supremacist groups used against Blacks, Jews, unruly women, and others who rejected the social norms of hatred and oppression. And the many who continue to come together in the urgent moment to fabulously and ferociously insist on beautiful and flourishing lives for us all. These are the people that have refused the tyranny of pragmatism and demanded more.

We are particularly enlivened by and see ourselves as part of a contemporary constellation of radical anti-racist, feminist, anti-capitalist queer and disability thinkers, doers, and artists with ties to a wide range of racial, economic, and norm-critical justice organizations that interrupt the socially and politically narrowing moves of, for example, a mainstream gay and lesbian movement that defines success as "gay marriage." While marriage brings with it a host of benefits for same-sex couples, this access is offered at a moment when fewer individuals receive *any* state support or protection. Throughout this essay we have named markers of our decaying public sphere, including attacks on labor and public education. Select lesbians and gays are being invited to make a deal: Norm up, and you can get bigger tax refunds, and probably a toaster, too. We have been offered a trade, and yet there is a cost: Leaders of LGBT groups linked with mainline politics, including the Human Rights Campaign, made the choice to focus their attention and resources on marriage, rather than a host of other more urgent concerns and goals—fully funded pre-K through higher public education, universal health care, and paid family leave, to name just a few vital national needs. It is at these precise moments, when those formerly outside the dominant paradigm are promised access to power and privilege, that critical engagement and analysis are needed, and the thinkers within radical queer groups and related justice-seeking organizations can provide important interventions.

While to some it might seem odd that for this volume we have focused on failures and this political moment, and on analyzing and critiquing social justice work within universities, we cannot think of anything more fitting. Writing into the contradictions of our time, not to solve problems or fix people or places, but to render contexts visible, to create communities of thought and possible action, and to recognize one another as colleagues and partners in struggle (however temporarily), is a strategy we have come to appreciate and a skill we have acquired through our collaborations with comrades, and in particular, Bill Ayers. These beloved labors begin with accepting the flawed and partial, and then recalibrating and starting again; this requires and produces a kind of generosity for our surroundings, our companions in struggle, and ourselves.

4. Lovingly, we fail; with pleasure and gratitude, we inhabit this space together.

References

Du Bois, W. E. B. (1989). *The souls of Black folk*. New York, NY: Bantam Classic. (Original work published 1903)

Halberstam, J. (2011). *The queer art of failure*. Durham, NC: Duke University Press.

Harney, S., & Moten, F. (Eds.). (2013). *The undercommons: Fugitive planning and Black study*. Brooklyn, NY: Autonomedia.

Piercy, M. (1982). To be of use. In *Circles on the water* (p. 106). New York, NY: Knopf. (Original work published 1973)

Rodríguez, D. (2012). Beyond "police brutality": Racist state violence and the University of California. *American Quarterly, 64*(2), 18–27.

Wilderson, F., III. (2003). The prison slave as hegemony's (silent) scandal. *Social Justice, 30*(2), 18-27.

8

(L)*Ayers* and Circuits of Provocation and Possibility

A Story Not About Bill

Michelle Fine

In 1899, after learning about the lynching of Sam Hose, W.E.B. Du Bois left the academy to pursue a life of journalism and action. Walking through Atlanta with a newspaper editor colleague, Du Bois was startled to view Hose's burned knuckles in a storefront display. In his own words, Du Bois could no longer "be a calm, cool, and detached scientist while Negroes were lynched, murdered, and starved." He realized that "the cure wasn't simply telling people the truth, it was inducing them to act on the truth" (Lewis, 1994, p. 162).

For more than 30 years, Bill Ayers (never alone) has sculpted, designed, protected, and liberated intellectual, political, and ethical space within and beyond the University of Illinois at Chicago, refusing detachment, insisting on action, cultivating democracy, telling the truth, and inducing others to tell the truth. That he did, and how he did, lifts up an opportunity to interrogate the debt of public universities to host, incite, and harvest rich projects of social justice, radical recognition, and wild redistribution; to open spaces for speaking and imagining the unspeakable among allies and strangers; and to provoke currents of radical possibility.

As the academy privatizes, a crucial strategic question for the Left asks whose university, whose curriculum, whose debt, and whose political project? We might gather, around this essay, to think about how we ensure that the membranes of public life remain porous, in and around universities, for conversations worth having, open to those long betrayed by educational institutions; and for projects written in the fugitive, the subaltern, and the subjunctive to expand, in the language of C. W. Mills,

the sociological imagination and to activate, as embodied by the life of Bill
Ayers, circuits of radical provocation and possibility.

It is perhaps no surprise that Bill's poppa, Thomas G. Ayers, was, at
one point, chairman and CEO of Commonwealth Edison; Bill seems to
carry the family gift for cultivating electricity, this time through circuits of
politics, power, and possibility.

Occupying the Public (University)

Across the past few years, we have witnessed a dramatic fiscal and
ideological makeover of the public sphere, a grotesque shredding of
budgets for public education and social services while millionaires and
corporations enjoy tax breaks. Across the country, public officials have
chosen to transfer the economic pain onto the already-burdened poor and
working class, in drag as austerity, as if the economic crisis were natural
and inevitable, as if we were truly engaged in shared sacrifice. On every
measure of social life, inequality gaps are swelling. British epidemiologists
Richard Wilkinson and Kate Pickett document how these gaps jeopardize
our collective human security in terms of health, infant mortality, crime,
fear, violence, civic participation, voting, and sense of shared fates. Former Secretary of Labor Robert Reich keeps reminding us that the wealthi-
est 1% own at least 25% of privately held wealth, while law professor and
scholar Michelle Alexander, in her 2010 book *The New Jim Crow: Mass
Incarceration in the Age of Colorblindness,* tells us that there are more
Black men in prison today than were enslaved in 1850, and the *Chron-
icle of Higher Education* continues to report that financial assistance to
higher education is in jeopardy for low-income youth, youth of color, and
youth with precarious documents. On the front of educational policy for
democracy, national and local policies have been corporatized, gentrified,
privatized. But the drumbeats of organizing for educational justice can be
heard across the country in and beyond the academy. Chicago is no small
mother-source of the resistance. Indeed, there is no finer example of activ-
ist-scholars claiming the university to be a radically diverse meeting space/
pub of the mind/sauna for the ethical soul/kitchen table/radically disrupt-
ed checkpoint, than in the work of so many friends in Chicago—Bill, Kar-
en Lewis, Pauline Lipman, Dave Stovall, Bernadine Dohrn, Charles Payne,
the entire Klonsky family, and scores of others I am surely leaving out.

For these educators, the project of public education, higher (university), and even higher (in the spiritual sense, K–12) has always involved
carving out and squatting within self-consciously safe and provocative
spaces for thinking through crisis, pain, and solidarities. They recognize

that the university—as a tax-exempt institution that shapes, distorts, leeches on, and can enhance and enchant urban life—bears a responsibility to resist the policies and cleanse the capillaries of elitist exclusion so that resources, movements, ideas, and bodies can flow across the university/community membrane.

I worry that Du Bois, Jane Addams, Myles Horton, and so many others chose to leave the academy to pursue projects of social justice. I so appreciate these Chicagoans' commitment to squat in the academy, embodying a collective responsibility to insist on democratic practice, critical engagement with students and the broader public, deep participation; to interrogate the "crises" the Right-wing and mainstream media dole out to us, with their privatized solutions; and to commute across the borders and also offer academic offices/classrooms/auditoriums as living rooms, with the warmth of bad lighting as if it were a fireplace, for varied publics to gather to critique what is and mobilize for what must be.

Contesting "Crisis"

At the dawn of the 1900s, W.E.B. Du Bois published *The Crisis,* a magazine committed to chronicling the ongoing exploitation of the African American community. Brilliant man, he understood that our country would not likely attend or respond to the cumulative structural neglect and miseducation of Black children until a profit could be made or until the people would revolt. One hundred years later, the perverse braiding of poor people's pain with corporate profit is becoming an American tradition, evident in predatory lending, housing foreclosures, the proliferation of for-profit charters, and the money being made from the prison industrial complex.

The media circulates caricatures of K–12 educators, especially those with tenure and experience, by distributing popular images of rubber rooms, incompetence, greed, and educators with criminal records. Some conservative media tried—unsuccessfully—to unsettle the reputations of Francis Fox Piven and Bill Ayers, Judith Butler and Omar Barghouti, in addition to scores of other critical scholars of participatory democracy, educational justice, Palestinian rights, Chicano studies, and labor studies. Periodic Twitters bemoan fat pensions and the "tragedy" of public universities. These media stories occlude the sustained conditions of poverty and discrimination, highlight public-sector "failure," selectively report "data" on privatized success, and serve as ideological lubricant for aggressive budget cuts, policies of privatization and relentless power (and land) grabs, and raw, rabid nips at censorship.

A new regime of power brokers—Republicans indeed, but Democrats too, philanthropists and venture capitalists—have self-appointed as the architects of the dazzling new market economy of education, funding their own studies, handpicking their racially/gender diverse Benetton photo-op models to speak the gospel, making movies, tailoring headlines, declaring crisis, ignoring sustained structural violence, and subsidizing a reconfigured "common sense." As the logic goes, the public sector and our unions are inefficient, corrupt, greedy, and in need of radical reform, takeover. Leeching onto the pain of cumulative structural disinvestment in poor communities, this message resonates for some with justified outrage over generations of miseducation in low-income communities. But while corporations and market logic promise to save poor people from the inefficiency of the public, crucial political questions of participatory democracy, racial and ethnic justice, schools and universities as a resource in community life, the autonomy of knowledge, questions of community/youth/educator power, and accountability (to whom?) gently slip off the policy table and media headlines, into a neoliberal wastebasket as schools in poor communities are closed and more police are sent in to "keep the community safe"—both acts of structural violence in drag as accountability.

Let us be clear—there is no evacuation of public monies into poor communities; more accurately, we are witnessing a grotesque reallocation of resources targeted at testing children, evaluating teachers, closing schools, scanning, stopping and frisking, ticketing and arresting, and tattooing "disposable" onto the backs of low-income children of color. With a bit of military recruitment tossed in so youth in poverty have "opportunities." But the flames of resistance emerge globally, and in the halls of the University of Illinois at Chicago, from CORE and community groups in Chicago, and then link delicately to eruptions of solidarity in Detroit, Newark, Philadelphia, Denver, Austin, Los Angeles—sometimes surprising allies pop up in the midst of struggle.

When busloads of Professional Staff Congress (PSC) members traveled to Albany, NY, on March 23, 2011, to protest the budget cuts to CUNY, a small group of faculty, students, and administrators agreed to engage in civil disobedience and be arrested, to demonstrate the breadth and depth of this fiscal injustice. As the state troopers gently placed handcuffs on the aging PSC members, a few whispered, "Thanks for doing this for public workers. You know, we can't." In Albany as in Madison; Chicago; Detroit; Washington, DC; and so on, we witness the emergence of a stunning, tentative but swelling alliance among college students and educators, and police officers, firefighters, housing activists, K–12 educators, social service advocates, public health workers, and other public employees. Indeed, Chuck Canterbury, National President of the Fraternal Order of Police, spoke for his colleagues in Madison, asking, "Who are these evil teachers who teach your children, these evil policemen who protect them, these evil firemen who pull them from burning buildings? When did we all become evil?"

Scaffolding Bridges of Solidarity in Times of Precarity

Since I am not talking about Bill, I will note only that in the (L)*Ayers* of provocation and possibility that are his legacy, we find not only spaces of activism, resistance, and provocation, but also funny, sweet, and complicated scenes of stretching across, searching for common ground, and seeking solidarity with low-income communities, of course, and also with elites in the city of Chicago—Obama for goodness' sake, the media, Annenberg, and so on. This perhaps under-recognized (L)*Ayer* of educational praxis involves building delicate bridges with the wisdom of how to avoid getting burned, captured, or coopted. If we were talking about Bill, we would learn a great deal about his lifelong dance of solidarity in times and contexts of precarity. But instead we turn to nature.

Let me borrow an image from biology writer Janine M. Beynus (2002), who has lectured around the globe on mighty oak trees that survive natural disaster. Beynus pulls social problems up by their roots and asks, "How would nature solve this?" Standing tall, almost unbowed, she tells us, oak trees grow in communities, expansive, bold, and comfortably taking up lots of space. While they appear autonomous and free-standing, the truth is that they are held up by a thick, entwined maze of roots, deep and wide. These intimate underground snuggles lean on one another for strength, even, and especially, in times of natural disaster.

Those of us teaching and learning and laboring, laughing and crying and going mad in public institutions, know the sweet comfort and knotty entanglements of entwined roots, and we know in our bellies the intimate pain of inequality gaps sketched into the faces of our students. We know that we are weakened by segregated neighborhoods and schools, with some of us locked in gated communities, others behind bars, and increasing numbers deported. And we know how jazzed we can get in our wildly diverse classrooms as students or faculty when we meet strangers in pulsating public spaces like parks, libraries, basketball courts, and subways; as we listen to National Public Radio, bike in public parks, visit the library, zoo, and botanical gardens; even as we sit in funky juries or subways with strangers we might not ever know; as we breathe in the luscious sounds and visions of museums and public concerts.

We recognize that as the nation has walked away from, or coopted, notions like diversity, community, access, choice, and civil rights, we have a responsibility and a yearning to build what Gloria Anzaldúa has called nos-otras (we "others")—a movement strengthened by attention to power and difference, or, in the language of Maria Elena Torre, a contact zone riddled with electrifying power lines of history, conflict, and possibility. We sit in a precarious moment where social movements must be deeply grounded in place and across place, fueled by what John Dewey (1934) called "aesthetic" experiences that inspire sensual imagination for what might be, which he contrasted with "anesthetic" experiences that deaden "heart, mind and soul."

Holding these spaces open is not enough; we must be deliberate about the vast moral community that sits at the kitchen table of educational justice and democratic participation. For wisdom we turn to the memoir of another Chicago ancestor. In 1902, Jane Addams published *Democracy and Social Ethics*, in which she wrote about the dangerous and pernicious effects of the longstanding American tradition of structurally excluding the working man, and woman, the poor, homeless, and immigrants from the moral community of the deserving:

> It is because of a lack of democracy that we do not really incorporate him in the hopes and advantages of society, and give him that place which is his by simple right. We have learned to say that the good must be extended to all of society before it can be held secure by any one person or any one class; but we have not yet learned to add to that statement that unless all men and all classes contribute to a good, we cannot even be sure that it is worth having. In spite of many attempts we do not really act upon either statement. (p. 220)

The university is an increasingly gentrified space, where SAT scores serve as passports and debt as souvenir. Online avatars will deliver remediation and PhD courses; adjunct faculty will serve as migrant labor; community college classrooms will be stuffed with bodies long betrayed by public schooling. As we resist all the ways in which higher education is becoming a Whitened gated community, Ayers asks us to re-member the brilliant ghosts of democratic educators who came before—those who dared to disrupt, to teach, to touch, to mobilize; those whose words, wisdom, and passions were routinely buried alive.

Epilogue: On Bill and E-PRAXIS

When I read/listen to Right-wing media, or even the mainstream, or the Democrats, about Bill, I realize they too are not writing about Bill. They have invented a strategically perverse caricature of a national counter-hero and have chosen to ignore/distort/white-out his commitments to national and international movements for democracy, public education, juvenile justice, deep accountability, and building communities that lean toward those who have paid the greatest price of injustice. One can argue with Bill—I have, in the spirit of friendship and solidarity—but that too is what is remarkable about the man, the capacity and willingness to engage across commitments and contentions. But perhaps most missing from the media's public dis'play of Bill is something I can't end this piece without commenting on: Bill's endless capacity to be a loving friend (to Maxine Greene and so many others), teacher, father, son, partner, brother, and grandpa.

To be rooted in place, politics, community, and family; to be engaged with one's institution, community, city, state, nation, and beyond; to have the intellect and integrity to work across feuding gang territory in the policy stratosphere—these are the qualities that render Bill Ayers eminently eligible to be named E-PRAXIS: the Emeritus Professor of Radical Access, Xceptional Insurgence, and Sustainability.

Thanks, Bill, for modeling big shoes to fill and for carving deep paths so that the next generation may walk/march/dance on shoulders even as they blaze open new tributaries in the struggle for educational justice.

Glad you stayed in the family business.

References

Addams, J. (1902). *Democracy and social ethics*. Chicago, IL: Tradition Books.

Alexander, M. (2010). *The new Jim Crow: Mass incarceration in the age of colorblindness*. New York, NY: The New Press.

Beynus, J. (2002). *Biomimicry: Innovation inspired by nature*. New York, NY: Morrow.

Dewey, J. (1934). *Art as experience*. New York, NY: Putnam.

Lewis, D. L. (1994). *W.E.B. Du Bois, 1868–1919: Biography of a race*. New York, NY: Owl Books.

Illustration by Ryan Alexander-Tanner

Part II

THE FLOW OF WATER

Fire and passion do not rule us exclusively; there are other forces at work in the human personality. When the flames subside and the breathing slows, a growing sense of peace is often a sign that water energy has become ascendant. Water is soothing and smoothing, cooling and calming, always moving toward the lowest point, the place where we as people can discover what we have in common. Water is receptive and accepting, flowing easily into and out of diverse perspectives and spaces.

Bill Ayers exudes water energy, calming anxiety and soothing worry by his very presence. He has an uncanny capacity for empathy, for accepting people for who they are and where they are in the present moment. Whether he is speaking to an individual, a classroom full of students, an auditorium crowd, or a television audience, Bill's voice and tone, mannerisms and gestures, put people at ease. He is adept at inviting others to join him in the refreshing coolness of water energy, and the authors in this part have done just that.

Alice Kim's "On Freedom Dreams" begins this part by describing what is possible with the openness and receptivity of a child's sense of wonder. She recounts a childhood visit to Korea and the sense of boundless potential that her many new experiences there occasioned. That sense of wonder stayed with her in her later collaborations with death row inmates, allowing her to flow to the moments of joy in what was surely emotionally difficult work.

In "Giving Childhood a Chance to Flourish," Hubert M. Dyasi makes an explicit case for nourishing and protecting this sense of childhood wonder in the teaching of science. In addition to the respect and validation this demonstrates for childhood itself, the author points to the positive effect this is likely to have on students' engagement with and learning of scientific material. In fact, a sense of receptive awe is at the heart of the project of science in the history of humankind.

While Dyasi looks to the school to protect the youthful sense of wonder, Avi D. Lessing in "A Story in Parts" looks to a child's family members, the earliest teachers. A teacher himself, the author here focuses instead on his own learning of how to live. In a series of vignettes, Lessing illustrates the mentorship of his father and his own apprenticeship in the lifelong project of approaching the world with awe and amazement.

In "Powered by Hope," Joel Westheimer turns our attention to the teacher, and how experiences in schools might provide mentorship in living. He describes the importance of moving in water energy for educators, recalling how his own initial desire for control as a young teacher eventually was taken over by a willingness to go with the flow of the already-present currents in the classroom. Letting his students lead him, Westheimer discovers, is a much more effective way of getting somewhere meaningful for everyone.

In "What Doctoral Studies and Dissertations Can Be," Bill Ayers's longtime colleague William H. Schubert shows how the two of them brought that very approach to teaching to their work with PhD students. In the Curriculum Studies program at the University of Illinois at Chicago, coursework and research were self-designed and self-discovered—as appropriate for a terminal degree in curriculum. Presented as a drama, the chapter uses a composite character to represent the many doctoral students that both Bills have mentored and inspired in their many years of work together.

Ming Fang He, in "Diving into Life and Writing into Contradiction," reveals what can result when doctoral studies are self-directed and personally meaningful. She describes the dissertation work of several of her own doctoral students, all of whom are motivated in their inquiries by their own lives and experiences, and all of whom connect their work to the larger struggle for social justice. Not only is this flow between the personal, the political, and the scholarly beneficial to each of her students, but it helps enrich understanding for those who read their work and this essay.

Craig Kridel takes a broader view in "Child-Centered Schools and Society-Centered Schools." In this chapter, he uses water energy to find common ground in many of the most enduring debates in education. A historian, the author looks to the past for ways to reconcile seeming contradictions in educational philosophy and practice. He even brings us back to the value in testing (right, as it is, in the word *evaluation*), excerpting examples of meaningful exam questions that might (like water) soften the roughest anti-testing edges.

The last chapter in this part presents a character who himself flows through contradictions with the help of cold, brewed beverages. Fred Klonsky introduces us to "Tony at the Red Line Tap," a man of many experiences, a multitude of cousins, and much consumption of beer. Sitting on one of a pair of barstools, the narrator learns the history of social class in Chicago and, most of all, to go with the flow.

9

On Freedom Dreams

Alice Kim

When I was 10 years old, I went on a whirlwind trip to Korea. On this 3-week-long sojourn to my parents' homeland—the first and only time I ever visited Korea and our last family vacation—I felt estranged from everything Korean. I got motion sickness on the 14-hour nonstop flight to Seoul and only vaguely remember getting off the plane at Kimpo airport and being greeted by a throng of relatives whom I had never met before. This was Mom and Dad's first trip back to Korea since they emigrated to the United States 2 decades before, and on our arrival our relatives fawned over all of us. In America, I was tall for my age, and in Korea, this meant that I stuck out as foreigner as I towered over all my aunts. Yet, I remember the ease with which I seemed to fit in with my large extended family.

For 2 weeks, we stayed with Big Aunt and Big Uncle in their American-style house, but I would learn that most Koreans lived in small box-like apartments without indoor toilets or showers with hot water. My uncle was a news anchor, the Phil Donahue of Korea, or at least that's how he described himself, and on this trip we benefited from his status. The entrance to their house was at the end of an alley where little kids played, old grandmothers squatted for hours as their watchful gaze took in the happenings on the street, and men and women of all ages stood next to carts filled with tube socks or dried fish heads or roasted chestnuts for sale.

On this trip, I bathed in a big plastic tub with a hose, tasted a spicy soup with morsels of coagulated cow's blood (which I refused to eat once I learned what it was), insisted on eating McDonald's only to be disappointed by the fishy taste of my Big Mac, visited a mountainside owned by my Dad's family where all our ancestors were buried, and rode through Seoul's busy streets on the back of my cousin's motorcycle. Growing up I was a shy kid, but I don't remember feeling timid around my newfound extended family. And one day, I went onto the balcony overlooking the alley and I sang the chorus of the song "Tomorrow" from the hit musical *Annie*, which I recently had seen. I sang unabashedly, loudly and with glee. When I looked out into the alley, all the kids, grandmothers, and men and women standing by their carts stopped what they were doing and listened to me. At that moment, anything seemed possible.

I'm grateful for this small but precious memory. I was just a kid singing a song from a musical I liked, but for me it was a magical moment of inspiration and spontaneity. It was a moment filled with hope and possibility. Back then, when I was 10 years old, I had no idea what was in store for me. That in college, I would choose a life of activism, that the people who would become my chosen family would share a commitment to social justice and conspiring with others to make a better future for all of us.

For nearly 15 years, I worked with death row prisoners, not as a lawyer but as an activist and an organizer. These years were transformative for me. I came to know men on death row and their family members—people I otherwise would likely never have met if it weren't for our common interest in ending the death penalty. I came to know men like Anthony Porter, who came within 48 hours of being executed when he won a stay of execution, and within a year students in a journalism class at Northwestern University uncovered the real killer; Nathson Fields, a former leader in the El Rukn gang who was innocent of the crime for which he was convicted—the judge in his case was corrupt and is now doing time for taking bribes; and Madison Hobley, who was on death row for over 20 years, wrongfully convicted for murdering his own wife and child. I first met these men behind Plexiglas at Cook County Jail. Since then, they have all been freed after years on death row.

I also remember my first visit to Pontiac Correctional Facility in 1998 when I visited Ronnie Kitchen and Stanley Howard. The prison was as sterile and inhospitable as you could imagine: cold concrete walls and linoleum floors, the smell of the Styrofoam cups we drank water out of, the clanking of the chains that were wrapped around prisoners' waists to tether them to the visiting tables. But the other image that stays with me is of the wide smiles and warm embraces of both Ronnie and Stanley despite the inhumanity that exuded from every inch of the prison.

My work as an organizer against the death penalty has been filled with both joy and despair. I've witnessed exonerated death row prisoners putting their arms around their mothers for the first time as they walked out of prison, their wrists finally unbound from the chains to which they had become all too accustomed. I've also experienced the maddening executions of Shaka Sankofa, Stanley Tookie Williams, and Troy Davis, who were put to death despite overwhelming evidence of their innocence and massive international campaigns to save their lives, campaigns that I had thrown myself into. On the eve of Troy Davis's execution, September 21, 2011, I gathered with hundreds of others at the Federal Building hoping against hope for a last-minute stay. I remember wondering what Troy was doing and thinking at that exact moment about how torturous the last minutes of his life must have been for him. He refused to place a last-meal request, a morbid death row tradition in which prisoners are afforded their desired last-wish meal before execution. And he refused the institution's meal tray comprising cheeseburgers, oven brown potatoes, baked beans, coleslaw, cookies, and grape beverage (the details of this meal was an odd focus of the media at the time of his execution).

At one point, when the execution was delayed for several hours, we thought Troy's life might have been spared. But this short reprieve was misleading. In the end, the State of Georgia chose to disregard overwhelming evidence of Troy's innocence and proceeded with the execution later that same evening. In the days following, I was listless and hopeless. In Illinois, we had successfully abolished the death penalty that same year, but in Georgia it was alive and well, and Troy was dead. Although I had never met Troy in person, I knew him through his sister, Martina Correia, his staunchest advocate. A few years earlier, when Martina was in town for a conference, a group of us gathered for a dinner in her honor at my place. Troy happened to call and Martina put him on speakerphone so that we all got to talk to him. It was another magical moment. My little sisters in the movement, FM Supreme and Deja Taylor (both poets and rappers), were in the house, and they spit a piece for him. This inspired Troy to spit a poem he had written back to us.

That night was filled with so much promise. These moments, the dinner with Troy's sister, the exchange of poems over the phone, the protest at the Federal Building, become part of our collective memory. And I learned that even in the face of death, what we do matters. We need to honor and remember these magical moments—and we need to infuse our community work, our social justice work, with creative spontaneity and hope. We need to be the kid on the balcony singing her heart out. In the face of tragedy and injustice—as we resist the inhumanity around us—we must insist on dreaming. In a book called *Freedom Dreams,* Robin Kelley (2002) said: "Without new visions, we don't know what to build, only what to knock down." I couldn't agree more. It's not enough to know what we're against; we need to know what it is that we're for. And to know what we're for, we need to unleash our radical imaginations, unapologetically.

Another world is possible, and to achieve it, we need to see ourselves as map-makers, change-makers, history-makers, each in our own right, creating visions that reflect hope and possibility, visions of the world we want to live in. When I allow myself to dream, I see:

- social workers roving our blocks instead of police
- help centers replacing blue lights and cameras on our inner-city streets
- affordable organic eateries in place of every McDonald's
- I-go cars and bikes for everyone
- international transportation escorts instead of the National Guard at our borders
- intragenerational learning spaces with state-of-the-art new media technologies and cooperative housing facilities in place of supermax prisons

Malcolm London, a 20-year-old Chicago poet who is a teaching artist with Young Chicago Authors, takes this further. Also an activist against school closings and standardized tests, recently he was featured in a 1-hour PBS special called *TED Talks Education* (Blake & Anderson, 2013). On the show, he said this: "We live in a world where we have limitations set upon us, but we have to live as though there are no limitations." What a simple and insightful observation. I have taken inspiration from a group of young people who are doing exactly this: living in a world with great limitations—but living as though there are none. That is what young immigrants who organized the Undocumented and Unafraid campaign are doing every day.

With boundless courage and imagination, undocumented youth collectively challenged the boundaries of citizenship and insisted on their human rights by "coming out of the shadows"—as they themselves have put it. As these activists began to disclose their status publicly, putting their lives on the line, their stories captured the attention of the national media and people all across the nation and the world. Their own experiences, their activism, their tenacity, and their radical imagination fueled what has become a national campaign that shifted the immigration debate and put immigration reform on the table. And most important, because of their audacity to dream, to insist that their lives mattered, to live without the limitation of an imposed immigration status, undocumented youth are no longer invisible today. Their efforts are reminiscent of the 1960s when African American college students staged sit-ins at lunch counters across the country—refusing to accept the limitations of Jim Crow segregation and ultimately not only changing the course of history but changing themselves.

It would be far too easy to accept a culture of cynicism. Yet, as Bill Ayers (2004) has often reminded us,

> Each of us is planted in the mud and the muck of daily existence, thrust into a world not of our choosing . . . each of us is also endowed with a mind able to reflect on that reality, to choose who to be in light of the cold facts and the merely given. We each have a spirit capable of joining that mind and soaring overhead, poised to transgress boundaries, destroy obstacles, and transform ourselves and our world. (p. xiv)

He wrote this in the context of teaching, as an educator faced with the challenge and the joys of teaching toward freedom, yet it is apt and fitting for all of us who want to change the world. The way to a new future is to be relentlessly curious, to take risks, to embrace struggle and the poetics of resistance, to be that kid on the balcony singing her heart out, and to always remember to dream.

References

Ayers, W. (2004). *Teaching toward freedom: Moral commitment and ethical action in the classroom.* Boston, MA: Beacon Press.

Kelley, R. (2002). *Freedom dreams: The Black radical imagination.* Boston, MA: Beacon Press.

Blake, J., & Anderson, J. (Executive producers). (2013). *TED talks education* [Television program]. New York, NY: WNET & TED Conferences.

10

Giving Childhood a Chance to Flourish

Hubert M. Dyasi

In 1981, a science educator in New Zealand asked 10-year-olds, 13-year-olds, and 15-year-olds whether a tree is a plant. At all three ages she found children who thought that a tree was not a plant. Reporting on this study, the world-renowned British scholar Wynne Harlen (2000) quotes a 10-year-old, who told the researcher, "No, it was a plant when it was little, but when it grows up it wasn't, when it became a tree it wasn't" (p. 8). Harlen further reported that almost half the children interviewed "considered that a carrot and a cabbage were not plants; they were vegetables. Over half did not consider a seed to be plant material even at the age of fifteen, following considerable exposure to science" (pp. 8–9). The 10-year-old's idea about a tree not being a plant suggests the child's focus is only on appearance, and the responses to questions about a carrot and cabbage might have been influenced by everyday usage of these words.

Cultural norms do exert a great influence on children elsewhere, too. Allieu Kamara (1971) carried out a study among the Temne of Sierra Leone in which he showed pairs of children in their early teens two equal balls of rice cake and ascertained that they understood that the balls were equal. He then flattened each into a pancake and asked one member of a pair this question: "If you were to give your friend one of these cakes and you take the other, would each of you have the same amount?" In most cases, the children said the other would have more or less. These apparently strange responses did not surprise Kamara because he knew that in Temne culture rice cakes are a delicacy and children share them unequally, with an older child getting a larger share. In his study, a child said the partner would get more if the partner was older, but get less if the partner was younger. The children's responses to Kamara's question about conservation of matter were determined more by cultural propriety than by mathematical considerations. The "wrong" responses were cultural effects.

These examples demonstrate that children look at the world from specific frames of reference. If these frames of reference are not engaged in school, children may "learn [science concepts] for purposes of a test but revert to their preconceptions outside the classroom" (National Research Council, 1999, p. 2). An education that claims to be at once excellent and democratic must honor children's frames of reference or it undermines itself and children's wholesome development.

So, what has that got to do with Bill Ayers? A lot.

A Continuous Focus on the Child

Ayers is tall among scholars who have thought and reflected deeply, acted decisively, and written clearly, powerfully, and persuasively about learner-focused and morally responsible democratic education. Drawing from his vast educational knowledge and experience, he has offered invaluable suggestions to teachers as they work with children in schools. In *Teaching Toward Democracy: Educators as Agents of Change* (Ayers, Kumashiro, Meiners, Quinn, & Stovall, 2010), for instance, one of Ayers's pieces of advice to teachers is:

Take the elegant but straight-forward idea that every human being is a three-dimensional creature much like yourself, a person with hopes and dreams and aspirations and skills and experiences, each with a body and a mind and a spirit that must somehow be valued, respected, and represented in your classroom, and somehow taken into account in your teaching. If you take this as a value you intend to carry in your pocket into the classroom—if it's something you want to take as an iron-clad commitment to live out every day *no matter what*, and to embed, then, deep within the classroom structure, culture, and environment—it challenges you to find concrete ways to reject and resist actions that treat students as objects, any gesture that erases or obliterates or ignores or silences any other human being. (p. 19, emphasis in original)

Ayers's rejection of the notion of treating children as objects and/or of regarding them as less than full human beings is a clear invitation to teachers to be inquirers—into their students, into their own situations as educators, and into their own teaching. In his words:

This is one of the great challenges of teaching: you will find that every student you encounter is an unruly spark of meaning-making energy on a voyage of discovery and surprise, that is, you will learn that each is unique, like you, each a dynamic work-in-progress, unfinished, contingent, leaning forward. If you decide to embrace that diversity (as opposed to spending gobs and stacks of energy denying and suppressing it) your classroom will of necessity become a work-in-progress as well, unfinished, ever-changing, and contingent. . . . Each year is different, each child presents new opportunities and different challenges, and each group has its own dynamics and personalities. You need to make the classroom your own, for sure, and simultaneously you need to give the classroom away. Never an easy thing to do. (p. 22)

He repeats this call in another book where he implores teachers to be inquiring learners, intensely interested in knowing their students and their complex human milieus.

Teaching for social justice demands a dialectical stance: one eye firmly fixed on the students—Who are they? What are their hopes, dreams, and aspirations? Their passions and commitments? What skills, abilities, and capacities does each bring to the classroom?—and the other eye looking unblinkingly at the concentric circles of context—historical flow, cultural surround, economic reality. (Ayers, Hunt, & Quinn, 1998, p. xvii)

The exhortation to regard students as "work-in-progress" and each as "an unruly spark of meaning-making energy on a voyage of discovery and surprise" evokes and resonates with science as learning, continually expanding horizons of human knowledge and understanding, while forever refining existing scientific knowledge of the world. Childhood has an admirable way of coping with impermanence or unending change, and a way of refining what has already been achieved while simultaneously dealing with surprises and rude awakenings. Yet school curricula, standards, and testing regimes seem to regard students as flawed, standardized beings who must be continuously remolded and repaired, and to present science as a finished product.

The Legitimacy of Childhood

Think of childhood as a way of being, full of wonder and of wonderings and of "aha moments." From infancy, humans pay attention, not always necessarily to the things adults select for their attention, but that is often an essential ingredient of actualizing diversified human possibility. Without curiosity children cannot learn what they come to know and do as infants, as children, and as grown-ups. That is how they come to distinguish between the familiar and the unfamiliar; that is how they come to talk, to walk, to use a variety of tools, to use the bathroom, to play well with others, to learn all that they learn at home and at school. It is a necessary condition for coming to know the world and to interpret it logically.

Childhood is a huge bundle of reality and possibility in which, as Ayers points out, are embedded capacities, "hopes and dreams and aspirations and skills and experiences" of individual children that must be acknowledged, valued, respected, and allowed to bloom; they make possible a way of experiencing and looking at the world as it is, a way of being in the moment, as it were. All these human attributes are manifest in action and in paying attention. In her book *The Logic of Action: Young Children at Work*, which was first published in 1969, Frances P. Hawkins noted that action is the universal language of human infants; it is the first language of the human species. There are many, many instances in childhood that convey its syntax and vocabulary. When a baby has had enough to eat, it turns its head away from the food; when it sees a face, it follows the face with its eyes. Because it is our first language, action is also the best medium through which to communicate. Of course, we do learn and become exceptionally fluent in other ways of communication, but they remain translations from our first language. It is very hard to completely break away from our first language, and schools that ignore this reality imperil children's full and joyful development.

Attempts to Honor Childhood Through Science Education

While Ayers was exhorting teachers to recognize and respect children's attributes and contexts in their classrooms, sections of the elementary science education community were independently developing science teaching and learning materials that took into serious consideration important aspects of childhood. Admittedly, some materials appeared aimed not at explicitly enriching childhood but at portraying children's education as preparation for a future adult life during which they would contribute to the advancement of the country's economic, social, military, and other kinds of leadership in the world. Yet childhood is a distinct, full, and legitimate stage in its own right in the life cycle of human growth, with unique and general characteristics that demand attention in education. Thus at every level of human development, education is life and not a preparation for life.

A Case Study: The Elementary Science Study

A science education program that purposefully respected important aspects of childhood was the Elementary Science Study (ESS). Inaugurated in 1959, it was described by David Hawkins, its first director, as a study of

> the transformation which science undergoes when minds which are young and fresh are brought into the arena of scientific experience. The experience clusters around phenomena of nature which we value because, as the history of science so far has taught us, they are potent, instinct with form, with the food of the eye and the imagination and the mind. (Hawkins, 1970, Foreword).

ESS represented science education *reform* at the elementary school level rather than science education *improvement*. Reform requires a re-thinking of the bases of science education, while improvement presumes that the bases are good and only need tweaking here and there. The essence of the reform at the K–5 level of education was a view of childhood as self-contained, combined with a view that some important features of the practice and understanding of science have a family resemblance to the culture of childhood. Hawkins elaborated on the effects of this reform:

> So offered to children, "science" is not an indigestible textbook regime, though it opens books to them. It is not a standardized array of "processes" weighed out and calibrated in units of performance, though it opens the way to discipline of method. It is not a hierarchy of eminent "concepts" abstracted from currently fashionable synopses; *it is watchful and respectful, rather, of the conceptual powers of children, active or latent,* when these are invited into play and observed responsively. (Hawkins, 1970, Foreword, emphasis added)

Referring to science for children, Philip Morrison, a professor of physics at the Massachusetts Institute of Technology (MIT) and a leading scientist in ESS, maintained that "science is not itself the world; it is one reaction to the world. It is on this view of science, and on the view of man which underlies it, that we choose to rest the structure of our growing curriculum" (Morrison, 1970, p. 99).

In the ESS approach and view of science, children directly manipulated phenomena of nature, some from the living world, others from the inanimate worlds, and still others from the atmosphere and the sky. The justification for this practice was that the "problems and puzzles of science, real, concrete, and varied," rightfully belong in the elementary school (Morrison, 1970, p. 100). Children's experiences with each phenomenon were described in self-contained modules or units. Units were not combined to form a sequential curriculum, which was a drastic departure from the textbook approach and syllabi characteristic of school curricula.

The ESS Education Strategy

Earlier I cited Ayers's call to teachers: "You need to make the classroom your own, for sure, and simultaneously you need to give the classroom away. Never an easy thing to do." Even as he gave the advice he was fully aware of obstacles in the path to bringing change in schools. He said:

> This is easy enough to say, this simple injunction, but excruciatingly difficult to enact in the daily lives of schools or classrooms, especially places where labeling students, sorting them into hierarchies, and managing their behaviors have become the commonplace markers of good teaching. How will you deal with this? What alternative markers will represent and illuminate your valuing of students' lives? (Ayers et al., 2010, p. 19)

To deal with this problematic situation, ESS developed a strategy that has had a huge impact on science education: creation of a powerful partnership of teachers, scientists, school principals, and parents and their children to cultivate in classrooms a firm belief and practice in engaging children in firsthand study of phenomena of nature before giving them a name and/or embarking on an intellectual, theoretical analysis. It is not that the name and theoretical analysis are not important, but rather it is a matter of which comes first; in some ways it is also a recapitulation of the history of the development of science knowledge itself as well as acknowledgment of how humans learn. Components of the strategy include selecting phenomena of interest, raising questions about them that can be answered by collecting data and turning them into evidence, reasoning and establishing relationships among superficially disparate data, and making scientific sense and ideas that are supported by the evidence. From these learning experiences, children build a rich repertoire of science "facts" or a data base from which to build ever more broadly applicable science ideas. These activities, therefore, are directly related to science inquiry and practices and to the understanding of science ideas. Consequently, a child creates a habit of mind that always seeks to establish how we know what we say we know, to recognize patterns in nature, and consequently to build or use evidence-based intellectual models to accurately explain and predict observations of the natural and made world. The strategy—working with elementary school children to bring about transformations in the view of science for childhood and using ordinary experiences with phenomena of nature to enrich children's science education development—was a radical departure from elementary science teaching of that time. The strategy unfortunately was labeled as "hands-on" learning. Unfortunate because it combined "hands-on" with curiosity and intense intellectual activity of making judgments about what to observe and what observations are of scientific consequence and why.

Partnership implies a coherent coming together of entities playing different active roles to achieve a common purpose. Classroom teachers, for example, are more than mere facilitators of children's learning experiences; among many functions, they play an active role in accurately understanding children's strengths, motivations, and accomplishments; participating directly in children's science inquiries in learning situations; providing feedback and guidance; and suggesting science ideas arising from the inquiries, all grounded in their knowledge of how children learn.

The ESS impact on the teachers, scientists, and children associated with its design and development was succinctly summarized by Hawkins (1970) as follows:

> Those of us who knew children before science have now seen the former (and ourselves as well) in a new light—as inventors, as analysts and inventors, as homelovers, lovers of the world of nature. Those of us who knew science first and children later have an altered and more childlike view of science—more humane, more playful, more available, and even at its most "elementary," full of unexpected delights. (Foreword)

In a personal communication, Rick Ayers has perceptively summarized the conflict between science education as represented by the Elementary Science Study and the current state of education in this country:

> ESS is a call for holistic and deep science education. But the education establishment, the No Child Left Behind (and other education) plans are simply "improvement"—are indeed about preparation for adult careers in the military-industrial complex rather than discovering new ways of seeing the world. Also science education today is devoid of ethical consideration. So we are still in

a conflict, a dialectical process, between different ways of regarding knowledge, human development, and purposes of science.

Sign of the Future?

It will be a wonderful educational world when public policy officials and leaders of school districts understand that educational approaches like ESS are the best way to cultivate future citizens, and excellent teachers, scientists, economists, jurists, engineers, physicians, nurses, technicians, and other skilled professionals. There are indications from the cognitive sciences research world that the educational situation should change in that direction. The National Research Council (1999), for example, published a study entitled *How People Learn: Bridging Research and Practice,* which suggests applications of research findings in the context of classroom case studies of teaching science based on the principles of how people learn and on respecting students' conceptions. It reports three key findings from the research:

1. Students come to the classroom with preconceptions about how the world works. If their initial understanding is not engaged, they may fail to grasp new concepts and information presented in the classroom, or they may learn them for the purposes of a test but revert to their preconceptions outside the classroom.
2. To develop competence in an area of learning, students must have both a deep foundation of factual knowledge and a strong conceptual framework.
3. Strategies can be taught that allow students to monitor their understanding and progress in problem solving.

If followed in practice, these findings would have a significant impact on teaching. Regarding the first one, for example, the authors write that it "requires that teachers be prepared to draw out their students' existing understandings and help to shape them into an understanding that reflects the concepts and knowledge in the particular discipline of study" (p. 2). These findings validate Bill Ayers's advice to teachers, which, as pointed out earlier in this essay, he developed and for which he has always made a strong, principled stand throughout his long career. Teachers alone, however, cannot create classrooms that humanely apply the findings. It will take the kind of partnership used by the Elementary Science Study to bring about classroom transformations recommended in this essay.

References

Ayers, W., Hunt, J. A., & Quinn, T. (Eds.). (1998). *Teaching for social justice: A democracy and education reader*. New York, NY: New Press.

Ayers, W., Kumashiro, K., Meiners, E., Quinn, T., & Stovall, D. (2010). *Teaching toward democracy: Educators as agents of change*. Boulder, CO: Paradigm.

Harlen, W. (2000). *Respecting children's own ideas*. New York, NY: The City College Workshop Center.

Hawkins, D. (1970). Foreword. In Elementary Science Study (Ed.), *The ESS reader*. Newton, MA: Education Development Center.

Hawkins, F. P. (1986). *The logic of action: Young children at work*. Boulder, CO: Colorado Associated University Press. (Original work published 1969)

Kamara, A. I. (1971). Cognitive development among school age Themne children of Sierra Leone (Unpublished doctoral dissertation). University of Illinois at Urbana-Champaign.

Morrison, P. (1970). The curricular triangle and its style. In Elementary Science Study (Ed.), *The ESS reader*. Newton, MA: Education Development Center.

National Research Council. (1999). *How people learn: Bridging research and practice*. Washington, DC: National Academies Press.

11

A Story in Parts

Avi D. Lessing

If you say a word often enough it becomes you.

—Anna Deavere Smith

You don't have to take a side. Write into all sides. Write into the contradictions.

—Bill Ayers

The first day of my teaching career I forgot to put on an undershirt and deodorant. After my first class, circles of sweat formed under my arms. At lunch I hurried down to the school bookstore to buy a new shirt. I only had $4. The woman behind the counter threw up her hands and tossed me a bright yellow gym shirt, with a narrow rectangular white box in the center in which to write your name.

Becoming a teacher was especially exhausting at first. I was split in two: One of me was struggling to act the part, while another me was safely and smugly tucked off to the side, smirking. I couldn't stop performing and I couldn't stop being the audience.

Not that that feeling was unfamiliar. I cannot easily recall a time I've simply lived without watching myself live. Even now as I type, I watch myself type.

My father, my Pap, compared everything to fiction. He'd say to my brother and me, "Jesus Christ, I feel like I'm in a Kafka fable," and we'd look up at Water Tower Place, on Michigan Avenue, and think, how is this building like Kafka? What is Kafka?

My Pap sees his life through art, fiction, and music, because they feel more pressing and immediate than the reality. As I write these words I can hear him correcting me. "Nothing is real, jongen ["kid" in Dutch]. Not our lives, nor our fictions. For me, what matters most is beauty." Or maybe: "Art for me brings me back to life in a more intensified way." Pap is an iconoclast. As soon as you offer what he might say or do, he'll change his tack and say something different. "Beauty is illusory, jongen. Frankly, what matters most at the beginning of each day is a strong cup of coffee." He watches himself too. When we're together, he watches me watch him.

I picture Pap writing me an email saying we must get together to talk about this essay. I see us at the kitchen table sitting down across from each other. He might shuffle the pages and say, "Now, I love what you write about me. It's *complete fiction*, but that doesn't matter as long as your impression of me rings true to you!"

It's sometimes easier to imitate my Pap than be myself.

It's Impossible

Pap told me once: "Van Gogh's last words before he died were, 'It's impossible.'" Pap has been telling me for years that if he's reborn, he hopes it's as a painter. "I love philosophy and music," he tells me, "but painting is something altogether different, jongen. Somehow closer to what's vibrant and incomprehensible. I don't trust words, least of all my own." I ask him if he likes Van Gogh because they're both from Holland. He tells me he likes Van Gogh because of what he does with color.

Now retired from teaching philosophy, Pap will turn 80 next year. "I hate it when people tell me I look young," he told me recently. "I always think *bullshit*. I'm at the very end, jongen." I'm scared about my Pap dying. "That's one thing that's not an illusion, jongen," Pap once told me. "Death." I say nothing. He says, "The illusions are trying to ward off what can't be warded off."

Picasso

I'm the youngest of my dad's four children from two marriages. By the time I was 10, I started feeling embarrassed that he was older than the other children's dads. Also, Pap listened to classical music, watched foreign films, and often talked about the shortcomings of life. I was memorizing the stats of the Chicago Cubs' utility infielder. I was trying to get into a group of friends. We had little to say to each other.

The Serious One

A lot changed for me, and my relationship with my Pap, after my junior year in high school, when I returned from a teen-sponsored trip to

Israel. Until then, high school had been pretty miserable. I had ruled out whole swaths of experiences as unlikely to happen for me. Among them: excelling academically, experiencing athletic success, possessing good looks, having a girlfriend, hooking up with a girl, lying down next to a girl, having a girl look at me. In my mind, I was permanently ugly.

Whether I was happy or miserable, I couldn't tell why. That's one of the reasons I'm so interested in what my students are thinking and feeling beyond the subject matter, since it may matter more than anything I have to teach them, since it's often an untold story.

Before my trip to Israel, my friends at home liked me because I made them laugh. I did imitations of them that were caricatures. I was a caricature too. While I was making everyone laugh, my friends were getting girls, or so it felt to me.

After that summer in Israel, my group of friends became smaller but closer, my interests widened, and I stopped thinking I was so damn ugly. Maybe it was as simple as my huge gums receding. Or perhaps, I stopped being so embarrassed by my Pap, and myself.

We started having real conversations in the car, at the kitchen table, on the porch. I was reading books he suggested. We could talk about ideas; we could even talk about girls. The night before I left for Israel, there was a great storm. He said, "Do you want to have a talk on the porch?" After he lit his cigar and we had settled in, he said, "You're never going to get the girl, if you play the clown." I took his advice. I played the serious one. I got the girl.

Something to Drink

Later on the porch, he said to me, "Do you want to know what the Holocaust is?" He showed me a picture that spilled past the binding and covered two pages of an old *Life* magazine book. Dead bodies stacked on top of dead bodies. He went inside after that. "Want anything?" he asked me with his hand gripping the door. "Something to drink?"

A Backdrop of Death

When you're 17 and you burst out crying, it's a lot like a wet dream: you don't know what's happening to you.

In the Children's Memorial of the Holocaust Museum in Jerusalem, they recited in Hebrew and in English the names of the 1.5 million children who were murdered in concentration camps. I listened to names, not daring to move, waiting. I looked down at my hands. They didn't look real. Each name uttered an eternal confusion.

The catastrophe that should've taken Pap but didn't.

This was a lot to take for a boy who grew up in the suburbs.

Not without some embarrassment, I was sobbing and waving away the other patrons. And as I watched myself slide down the wall, bringing my knees into my chest, I promised from that day forward I would love my Pap wholeheartedly, a promise that I keep breaking and remaking.

Two days later, in a Bedouin Camp near Masada, I cuddled up against the unimaginably beautiful Shelby Kibam. I asked, "Can I kiss you," and she didn't say yes or no but nodded. I felt like I was watching my life being saved.

In an oral history collection about my family's time in hiding, my Pap said, "I only feel safe in the arms of a woman."

Just Phrases

I recently vacationed with my brother Uri's family in the Outer Banks. Most of our interactions consisted of imitations of our Pap: on the beach, in the car, at the restaurant. No context, just phrases. Uri would say, "Jesus Christ, jongen, this beach feels like something out of a Fellini film." I'd return with, "Listen, jongen, when I go on a plane, I'm *expecting* it to crash." We would laugh and give each other pointers—suggestions to change a word or two here or there.

At the end of the week, our goodbyes were forced. With our *own* words, we could manage only, "That was fun," and "Let's do it again next year." Maybe we should've said goodbye using lines from Pap. I could've said to my brother: "I mean, Jesus Christ, jongen, I don't believe in goodbyes. I hardly believe in hellos." And then my brother could've called me from Maine and said, "Isn't it amazing, jongen, one moment you're together, and then the next you've disappeared. As if it never happened in the first place!"

Jewish

On October 23, 1942, just as the sun came up, my Oma and Opa took the whole family out of their house in Delft, in southern Holland, and into hiding. She told each of her children, "Don't tell anyone you're Jewish, or they'll kill you." My father had just turned 7 years old. His brothers were 10 and 5. The family dyed their hair blond, changed their names, went into hiding, and never lived in their house again.

I think my parents gave us Hebrew names because my Pap didn't want us to hide ever again.

Jewish, ii

When I was a kid, my Pap would nudge my ribcage. "See that man over there," pointing way down the beach. "Jewish." Also objects, activities, and food took on an either/or quality. A symphony orchestra concert: *Jewish*. A baseball game: *Not Jewish*. Jell-O, Michigan, and all physical labor: *not Jewish*. Liverwurst, being vaguely irritated at all times, and bemoaning gas prices: *Jewish*.

Just in Case

When I was 25, my dad dropped me off at the train in the burbs to go back to Chicago. As the train left the station, he started running alongside it while turning the pages of a fashion magazine. It looked like performance art. He became smaller and smaller until I couldn't tell whether he was running or standing still. I turned my head forward and stared out the window.

That was my Pap saying I love you. Just in case one of us never reappeared again.

Pre-emptive Psychoanalytic Dialogue

"Listen, jongen, don't psychoanalyze me in your essay, that's all I ask."
"I'm not, I'm psychoanalyzing myself."
"Ah then, go right ahead."
His laugh is equal parts enthusiasm and disinterest.

Oma

For the 3 years that the family was in hiding, Pap's mother (my Oma) kept splitting people up and changing their locations. In May 1944, the S.S. questioned her on a train while she was shuttling between her three sons. They didn't believe that she was an American (she had her cousin's American passport) and she was sent to Westerbork and then to Bergen-Belsen. On the train going there, she ate every scrap of paper in her purse that gave the names or addresses of her family. She saved the family's lives. I've heard this story so many times, it's as if it happened to me.

Porch

"You see, jongen, Bergen-Belsen wasn't a death camp, but everyone died there." When he said that, something changed about my father's face.

Like a sculptor had set him apart and made his face permanently unshakable. Like his soul was plastered on his skin and nowhere else.

The wind blew down the street, through the trees, and toward us. He rose abruptly. He gripped the handle of the door tightly, turned, and asked me if I wanted something to drink. I told him, "Yes, please," as if we had just met. By the time he came back outside, I had already put away the *Life* magazine book.

Oma, ii

"Do you know the story of how Oma made it back to Holland?" he asked. "Let me tell you: She maintained that she was American because she had her cousin Susan's passport and spoke excellent English. After months at Bergen-Belsen, the Nazis eventually exchanged her for prisoners in Switzerland. She ended up in Morocco and somehow had made her way back to Holland. When she walked up to the house where we were staying, your Uncle Eddie was on the porch reading. This was almost a year after we had been liberated; we thought she was probably dead. Eddie said, 'Who are you?' And your Oma said, 'Don't you recognize me? I'm your mother.' I jumped the entire second-floor staircase all at once. I'll never forget what she said next: 'I never want to see another German, Hollander, or Jew ever again.' That's when we made our preparations to come to America."

"Well," Pap said, "how about a liverwurst sandwich?" Pap is always leaving experiences abruptly, drawing lines where no lines can be drawn.

Success

Out of 100 families in Delft, my Pap's family was the only one to survive intact. "And I'm not telling you this, jongen, to suggest that we were smart or good or any bullshit like that," he says to me on the porch swing. "We were lucky. People are always talking about life in terms of *achievement*. Well, you got tenure. *That's good.* You're married. *Great!* You got a divorce, *well, that's bad.* You survived the Holocaust? *Now that's really great.* Can you believe it, jongen? Even our survival can now be quantified."

The Past

My Pap and I wrote letters back and forth throughout college. I like to think of us as that last generation of people who put pen to paper without a hint of irony or nostalgia. The lag time in-between letters gave our relationship a literary quality. The silence between letters deepened our connection further.

Pap isn't one for chitchat. I sometimes wonder whether he enjoys being with his family, or whether we represent tedious obligation. As his son, I sometimes feel I have to prove our conversations are worth it, or he'll go away.

The physical distance of college removed those obstacles. In letters, I would relay thoughts I had never said out loud before, let alone written down, the ones kids *want* to tell their fathers, but don't. I think their honesty surprised my Pap.

Those letters broke through the awkwardness between us. My mom, who's a therapist, once told me in college: "The years he wasn't so great as a father to you correspond to the years that he was a boy in hiding, when his life was in turmoil and he didn't really have a father himself." I know Pap rejects these facile explanations. He's always saying, "Listen, jongen, you're going to have to talk with your mother if you want psychological explanations about my life."

The Past, ii

He's rarely spoken with me about the war, maybe less than 10 times my whole life and never as an explanation for anything else. I'm pretty convinced he'll disapprove of an essay like this. He'd say, "Jesus Christ, that was seventy years ago. Not sure this is relevant in an essay about you and me; it certainly has nothing to do with *Bill Ayers*." Or: "Listen, I reject all psychological explanations *in the first place* but about the Shoah, I am adamant. It cannot be explained." Or, if I emailed it to him: "Sorry, I decided *not* to read your essay. Not my cup of tea."

He did read a recent draft of this essay. I was in his kitchen doing dishes. "I liked it, jongen. Lots to talk about. I think it's fairly accurate."

We have never talked about it and probably never will.

I tell stories about my Pap because I want him to love me in a way that is probably not possible anymore. Instead, I imitate him. I process things I can't explain in my own words. Processing is a concept Pap loathes. Unlike him, I want psychological explanations for my life.

Going Out to Breakfast

When I was in junior high, my mom would arrange for my dad to take me out to breakfast before school so we could become closer. I looked forward to eating bacon and hash browns, but not to those long, empty pauses. While I was going through bar-mitzvah season, he was reading Spinoza. Instead of reading Spinoza, I thought about my sports teams. It was my way of blocking out the unfurling, inexplicable, lawless existence that spread out before me. But the thing that scared me the most was Pap, or if not him directly, the things he thought about, or maybe more than either of those things it was the vibe he gave off: The world is dangerous. From the ages of 10 to 16 I stayed away from him, and he stayed away from me.

Performance

At the University of Colorado, I took a philosophy elective called Matters of Life and Death, taught by a dying professor named Gary Stahl. Gary invited my Pap to give a talk about Elie Wiesel's *Night*.

I said to him over the phone, "So you're going to talk about your experience, right?"

"No," he said. "I'm going to give a talk about Wiesel. About how the dead should be silent."

His actual talk is hard to describe. It was a mixture of scholarship, personal story, and philosophical conjecture. I looked up afterward and all the students looked like they had weathered a storm. "You have to scare the shit out of people to give them a sense of what it was like. You have to make it into a performance for anyone to grasp the reality." I nodded. "Well," he said, "shall we have something to eat?"

A Stone

During that talk, my Pap said, "What I've done with the past is buried it inside of me like a stone. I've built a little fence around it to protect myself and my children."

I've never felt as protected as he imagined.

When I was 6 years old, Pap took me with him to a Jewish overnight camp where he was lecturing. One night, he left me alone for a few hours (he thought I had fallen asleep). I thought about death for the first time, how I would die, and then never live again. I remember how itchy the brown blanket felt on my little body. I was 6 years old.

After that, I had a recurring nightmare. In it, my dad mounted the stairs toward my room. I'd wake up panicked and turn on the radio, frantically turning the dial for some sports talk to soothe me.

I wasn't afraid of Pap. I was afraid of what he was afraid of.

Separateness

There's a kind of permanent distance that settles in with your parents once you have kids of your own. For the past 5 years, Pap and I haven't talked nearly as often or as personally as we used to. Recently, he came to the house to break the fast for Yom Kippur. We barely spoke, but not out of any discord. I could feel him reaching for something deeper in me, and he could see me reaching for the laundry to fold.

Imitations

I imitate my Pap while he is in the room. He's embodying his presence and I'm embodying a simulacrum of him. The reproduction is a safe way of coming up against his danger, against the idea that a self exists in any intact way. All of this epitomized by something Franz Kafka told his closest friends: "What do I have in common with the Jews? I hardly have anything in common with myself." A story Pap told me.

Fiction

One night, we're having dinner at my parents' house, and Pap calls me out to the porch. "Jongen, I have to tell you what happened to me at Writer's Theater tonight! It was intermission and I was smoking my pipe on the veranda. I was thinking about one of the actor's performances. I said out loud, 'Too Jewish,' and then I realized *I was doing an imitation of you imitating me*. Then, I looked up at the sky and said, "I'm a 77-year-old man who has no *fucking* idea who he is." We laugh and hug after he tells me the story, relating most when who we are is up for interpretation. "Dinner!" my mom calls and we scurry back into the house, into the familiarity of being little more than strangers.

12

Powered by Hope

Joel Westheimer

Let me explain something Ayers' readers all know:
Bill's not only an author but a master of prose
he is a painter of ideas, a sayer of truth
to power, to policy, and even to youth
a philosopher, yes, but not the kind that wears tweed
he's the kind that every teacher and activist needs
he's the kind that takes the unreachable goal
and makes it seem obvious, creative and bold

Ayers talks to everyone from all social strata
his home is a meeting place for people that matter
he welcomes all, the famous and not
his kitchen always serves up a great melting pot
of ideas—that's why he's always engaged
he's both brimming with joy and raging with rage
he knows what we're up against, he knows better than most
but despair gets no hostage when you're powered by hope.

In his book *Teaching the Personal and Political: Essays on Hope and Justice*, Bill Ayers (2004) writes that teaching is "always improvisational, grounded in acts of attention and witness [and] powered by hope" (p. viii). That phrase, "powered by hope," stuck with me, and not long after I read it, I used an amateur attempt at poetry to introduce Bill to an audience of 450 artists, teachers, scholars, and writers. I chose poetry because, like much of Bill's writing and activism, poetry is personal, rife with emotion, commitment, beauty, and imagination. Adrienne Rich writes that poetry begins in terror and ends in possibility. I suspect that, for many of us, teaching is the same: terror on one side, possibility on the other, with hope the connective thread between them.

Before becoming a professor of education, I taught 6th, 7th, and 8th grades in the New York City public schools. Like many idealistic new teachers, I entered the profession committed to nothing less than instilling in young people the confidence, knowledge, and skills required to change the world. I wanted my students to treat one another with respect, to challenge injustice when they saw it, and to learn that they were powerful, that they could make a difference and, in the process, find deep meaning in their social and professional lives.

Archeem (a pseudonym), an African American student in my 7th-grade social studies class, thought otherwise. For my first 6 months in the classroom, Archeem and I were at loggerheads. He was not good at what Denise Clark Pope (2003) calls "doing school." He was a C student. And I was not yet a skilled teacher. I assumed that by offering Archeem something beyond the superficiality of rote memorization and regurgitation, he would work hard, learn more, and enjoy school. Archeem and many of his classmates, on the other hand, figured that I was a newbie who should be challenged.

My first mistake? I figured that as a teacher, I got to dream up the background material for a script that would then unfold within the humane and educative conditions I had put in motion. New teachers often believe they get to write the script, set the stage, and raise the curtain. But students know something that only later becomes evident to the adult in the room: The play has already started. I was entering in Act III. In Acts I and II, the plot was established, the parts cast, the good-guys and bad-guys already chosen, the narrative arc long since determined. There were "smart" students and "dumb" ones. There were class clowns and teacher's pets. Kids know how school works long before they enter their first classroom. They see television cartoons about school; they see movies about school; they've heard other children talk about school; they have older siblings who've gone to school. Our culture has already dictated that school entails a timeless, existential battle between the tasks and rules adults impose, on the one side, and students' efforts to preserve their own souls without getting thrown out, on the other. They wouldn't describe it that way, but that's the gist of it.

Let me give an example about the difficult-to-break narratives already in place before we've even stepped foot in the school building. Ask any child what happens when a substitute teacher comes to the classroom. What do they say? Mayhem—children move the desks around, change their names, and inform the substitute teacher that their "real" teacher allows them to wander around the room whenever they want and to eat their lunch at 9:15 A.M. In short, they make the life of the substitute a temporary hell. Substitute teachers are clueless and have no idea how to teach, goes the script. Socrates himself could arrive in a 5th-grade classroom for a day. It wouldn't matter. The play is already in motion.

Narratives, however, *can* be rewritten. It takes time, patience, and creativity. Back in my first year of teaching, I guessed (having read his school file) that in Archeem's internalized narrative, school was mostly about humiliation. It was the teacher's job to catch him out not knowing things, and Archeem's job to try to avoid those encounters. I imagined that he recognized the usefulness of gaining some of the skills and knowledge being taught in school, but that in a larger sense the connection between what went on in school and in his life outside of school was tenuous at best. In those first few months, neither Archeem nor I knew this yet, but we were both going to find our way outside the dominant narrative of school.

What Archeem Taught Me About Teaching

After a week of classes in which we had discussed the Civil Rights Movement, racism, and prejudice in America, all of my students were duly outraged at the injustices perpetrated against Black people throughout history. Students couldn't believe the folly of thinking that someone's intelligence, skills, or rights could be judged by the color of their skin. They sat riveted by excerpts from *Eyes on the Prize* and speeches by Martin Luther King, Jr., and Malcolm X. I quickly became aware that although the students were quick to criticize a kind of racism that was already widely reviled in the United States and elsewhere, they failed to carry that critique or moral commitment to any other sphere. I witnessed African American students calling Hispanic students "spic." I saw Archeem and his friend Hunter yell "faggot" at a student who didn't share their athletic prowess in dodge ball. When I asked students whether they thought people were still prejudged for superfluous reasons, they didn't know. I knew something was not working, and I had an idea.

Two weeks earlier, various cities had been observing Gay Pride Week. It was highly controversial, even in New York, and certainly in New York City public schools. Despite the explosive nature of the debate (this was the mid-1980s), our school principal agreed when an "out" gay teacher asked to use the second-floor glass display case for posters and newspaper articles about Gay Pride. But 4 days after the teacher spent a great deal of his own time on the display, someone or some group of students smashed in the glass with a chair. The teacher and the principal decided to leave it that way for the time being.

I spoke to José, the school janitor whom I had gotten to know (always make friends with your school janitor—one of the great lessons of urban public school teaching). I asked José if he would arrive during the beginning of my next social studies class with a ladder and insist that he had to fix a ceiling light, which inexplicably would require a power drill and his other noisiest possible tools. He did, and as soon as class started there was no hearing what anyone was saying. I asked students to grab their chairs and to carry them downstairs to the large second-floor hallway where we set up in a circle around the display case with the smashed glass to continue our discussion about racism in America.

I continued to lead the discussion, waiting for what I was not sure would happen. But something happened, and it happened because of Archeem. He had been leaning back in his chair looking characteristically uninterested in the conversation when he suddenly rocked forward and raised his hand.

I nodded to Archeem, not sure what was going to happen next.

"It's like that," Archeem said, pointing to the broken glass. All the students in the circle swung their heads straight to the center of the broken glass.

"Like what?" I asked, hoping I was masking my nervous anticipation of his response.

"Racism is like when you hate someone just because of something about them that you don't even know nothing about." [I am reporting this from the journal I kept in those days, and I'm fairly certain that's about how he said it.] Silence followed. Here was this 13-year-old, tough, African American boy somehow, indirectly, standing up for gay people, and perhaps more important, identifying a contemporary example of prejudice and connecting it to a widely agreed moral standard that called prejudice wrong.

The other students nodded and a discussion ensued about the connection between different kinds of prejudice. Several times in the discussion, students referred to Archeem's contribution [I'm drawing on memory and sketchy journal entries, so these are not exact quotations]:

"What Archeem said made me realize all the different ways human beings diss each other." (Latosha said this, and I recall her having been on both the giving and receiving ends of more than her share of disrespectful taunts.)

"Do you think the way southern White people felt about Black people was like how some of us think about gay people?" said another student.

"No, it's not the same—being gay isn't natural."

"Isn't that what they said about Blacks being free?"

"No, it's not the same because gay people are disgusting!" [laughter]

We hadn't reached a progressive teacher's nirvana by any means, but

the conversation had started. In the weeks that followed, students continued to refer to this conversation. Two of them wrote a note to the teacher
who had created the Gay Pride display apologizing on behalf of "whom-
ever was too chicken to apologize for themselves."

It became evident to both me and my students that teaching about
slavery (racism is bad) or teaching about World War II (Hitler was evil)
was too easy. The historical lessons were fine. But the more important message didn't stick. Although schools habitually avoid controversial issues, engaging controversial issues may be exactly what is called
for. Teaching about injustice might best be achieved through explicit
challenges to widespread cultural assumptions rather than through
re-examination of historical issues that, by virtue of time, have become
unassailable. It is relatively common for good teachers to demonstrate
to students the potential tyranny of opinion over facts in landmark historical controversies (e.g., the idea that people whose skin is black are
not as intelligent or deserving of rights as those whose skin is white).
Less clear, however, is whether such lessons give students the skills they
need to critically analyze contemporary problems and injustices. Rather,
students need to examine issues on which their own perspectives and
positions can be challenged. Indeed, that there are not, as of yet, clear
"answers" (widespread cultural agreement) to the questions raised, specifically makes those issues useful. Back then, having students examine
whether gay men should be allowed to serve in the U.S. military, for
example, became a more useful issue for discussion and critique than
whether African American men should be allowed to serve. The former (at least until this decade) forces difficult analysis and consideration
of a variety of viewpoints, while the latter, piggybacking on already-
established widespread agreement, fails to do so.

I received two complaints from parents who said they did not want
their children discussing gay rights in school. I didn't care. And luckily
my principal didn't care. I had stumbled on one possible, albeit idiosyn-
cratic, way to teach critical thinking. But that was not the only lesson I
drew from this experience. From that day on, not unfailingly, but regularly, Archeem's attitude toward both school and me changed. There
were no miracles, but Archeem seemed to have grown a little bit taller.
He began to raise his hand. He participated in discussions. I told other
teachers about what Archeem had said and they asked him about it too.
When a school assembly included a neighborhood community organizer talking about public housing, Archeem asked me how you get a job
like that working with people in the neighborhood. It seemed, in some
small way, I no longer fit the role of the teacher trying to catch him not

knowing things. And, as you can tell from my recollections, Archeem became more than a thorn in my novice teacher's side. We had changed the narrative.

Powered by Hope

My teacher education students sometimes get annoyed with me for pointing out all the problems with schooling in North America. They learn that in the past 2 decades, education goals, broadly speaking, have become increasingly technocratic, individualistic, and narrowly focused on job training. As teachers about to enter the profession, they do not want to assume that too many of the lessons that inspire hope have been put on the back burner. They recognize that there are many wonderful teachers doing wonderful work, but they worry that the kinds of radical lessons in participation and democratic action that give meaning to teaching and learning tend to be opportunistic rather than systematic—based on an individual teacher's courage rather than on programmatic muscle— and episodic rather than consistent and enduring. At the same time (and I think not unrelatedly), reported rates of depression and alienation among young people have skyrocketed.

Educators face many obstacles to improving schooling. Today, we trust teachers less and less, and standardized tests more and more. Reform policies at the highest levels are made without any evidence that they will work. And students are treated alternately as blank slates waiting to be trained, as clients waiting to be served, or as consumers waiting to buy. In some schools, the entire school day is reduced to almost nothing but test preparation in only two subject areas: math and literacy. We prescribe medications to a shockingly high percentage of students to make them attentive and "normal." In a phenomenon reminiscent of Garrison Keillor's Lake Wobegon where all children are above average, some schools have now deemed the majority of students "not normal."

Meanwhile, elaborate reward and punishment systems are instituted to keep students engaged. It sometimes seems that in the quest to improve students' focus and interest, the only thing we are not trying is to actually make the curriculum interesting and worth focusing on.

In the face of these conditions, it would seem easy to lose hope. I would like to suggest two reasons why we don't have to. First, overall reform trends *never* dictate what is possible in individual classrooms. In the end, it is the teacher who is with students day in and day out. And we all know that teachers, especially those powered by hope and possibility, can and do make tremendous differences in children's lives. Second, as

Vaclav Havel (2004) observed, hope is not the same as choosing struggles that are headed only for success: "Hope . . . is not the conviction
that something will turn out well," he wrote, "but the certainty that
something makes sense, regardless of how it turns out" (p. 82). Hope requires, as the late historian Howard Zinn (1980/2010) eloquently wrote,
the ability "to hold out, even in times of pessimism, the possibility of
surprise" (p. 634). The singer-songwriter-activist Holly Near (1990)
expressed this artfully in her anthem to the many social change movements that have existed for as long as there have been things to improve.
Change does not always happen at broadband speeds, but knowing one
is part of a timeless march toward good goals makes much of what
we do worthwhile. In her song "The Great Peace March," Near sings:
"Believe it or not / as daring as it may seem / it is not an empty dream /
to walk in a powerful path / neither the first nor the last." If I could hope
for one certainty in anyone's arc as an educator, it would be this: the
knowledge that—whether in the face of successes or setbacks—we are
walking in a powerful and worthwhile path.

Here's how I ended that introductory poem:

> on campus or off, it really don't matter
> a well-thought-out lecture, or just idle chatter
> he'll quote a great poem, or cite a great verse
> he'll share a page from the best book or worst
> one minute he will offer a suggestion or two-y
> to someone who's editing a collection on Dewey
> the next he'll answer a call on his phone
> to talk about the latest movie by Oliver Stone
> ever a teacher and ever a learner
> Bill Ayers' stove doesn't have a back burner
> so hold on to your hats, and please stay in your chairs
> and prepare to be wowed by Bill's breath of fresh Ayers.

Note

The author would like to thank Barbara and Michal Leckie for thoughtful
feedback on a draft of this chapter.

References

Ayers, W. (2004). *Teaching the personal and the political: Essays on hope and
justice*. New York, NY: Teachers College Press.

Clark Pope, D. (2003). *Doing school: How we are creating a generation of stressed-out, materialistic, and miseducated students*. New Haven, CT: Yale University Press.

Havel, V. (2004). An orientation of the heart. In P. Loeb (Ed.), *The impossible will take a little while: A citizen's guide to hope in a time of fear* (pp. 83–89). New York, NY: Basic Books.

Near, H. (1990). The great peace march. On *Singer in the storm* [CD]. Hawthorne, CA: Chameleon Music Group.

Zinn, H. (2010). *A people's history of the United States: 1492–present*. New York, NY: Harper & Row. (Original work published 1980)

13

What Doctoral Studies and Dissertations Can Be

William H. Schubert

Prologue:

I learned a great deal from over 2 decades of working with Bill Ayers—as we learned together from and with well over 100 doctoral students whose dissertations one of us chaired and for which the other served as a committee member. This is my version of a fictionalized example of the kind of doctoral experience we tried to create.

Characters:

Faculty Member (FM): Most likely me, Bill Schubert, or Bill Ayers, or Bill Watkins, but most probably a fictionalized composite of the three of us and more. After all, we are each named *Bill,* so to call the faculty member *Bill* would seem to fit, although I just settled for FM.
Potential Student (PS): No particular student; rather, a fictionalized composite of hundreds of doctoral students with whom we worked in Curriculum Studies at the University of Illinois at Chicago for the past quarter of a century or more. Without giving away too much of the plot, PS is later transformed into AS, Actual Student.

Setting:

Faculty office in a college of education in a big urban university, strewn with papers and books, most of which can be found easily by the professor, and no one else. [Conference begins]

Counter Act I: Inter-view

Faculty Member (FM): Welcome. You have come from afar.

Potential Student (PS): Yes, thanks for agreeing to meet with me.

FM: My pleasure. . . . What's on your mind?

PS: I am interested in doing a PhD here, and I decided to visit, because I think doing a PhD is a huge commitment.

FM: It is. I agree. Why here?

PS: I have been teaching and doing social justice work for about a decade and think now may be a good time to start a PhD in curriculum studies. I like teaching a lot and would like to share what I have learned with others.

FM: Teaching and social justice work can provide good background for a PhD in curriculum studies. Why are you considering curriculum studies?

PS: Frankly, I am interested in many areas, and can't decide which to pursue—literature, philosophy, psychology, history, cultural studies, media studies . . . on and on. When I read the FAQs for your program, I thought that pursuit of a doctorate in curriculum studies could enable me to study any of these.

FM: I can relate—that is why I decided to go into curriculum studies.

PS: Anyway, I have been reading in curriculum studies for the past year or so . . . actually, I feel as if I have been reading in this area almost since I began reading.

FM: (taken aback) What?!

PS: I have read enough to know that if there is a central curriculum question that all of the contending camps in the field embrace, it is what you have called the *what's worthwhile* question. All of my life I have been trying to figure this out, and I have begun to realize that it cannot be fully answered; it's always in the process of being answered again and again in different situations and hopefully at deeper and broader levels.

FM: I'd say you are off to a good start . . . you are passing the test.

PS: What test?

FM: It's my informal test of interest in and aptitude for doing curriculum studies. Some of my closest colleagues and I enjoy meeting with prospective students, not only because we feel that we are helping them, but also because the conversation and sharing helps us grow, too. This becomes a mainstay of the program itself. Being in a mentor–student relationship is not best referred to as an act of service—it is really an act of solidarity. We are curricula for one another. One can have only a limited number of experiences. Sharing experiences, insights, ideas, and commitments broadens and deepens our perspective.

PS: That resonates well with me. It fits my social justice interests. We need to learn from others. I have learned much from my students over the years. Through them and their stories I have had experiences that enrich me greatly.

FM: My colleague, Bill Ayers, often refers to Jane Addams as an exemplar who acted in solidarity with, not just in service to, the many diverse participants at Hull House. I feel strongly that students and mentors can learn much from each other if they are open to it. In fact, I think we should look at ourselves as curricula for others. It helps us realize that we are influencing through our being.

PS: I think so, too, and as a literature teacher, I have tried to engage in solidarity of learning with students to see characters and events in literature, fictional though they may be, as curricula for those who read about them.

FM: I like that!

PS: Do you mean I could study that . . . or I should say continue studying that?

FM: You already said that you have learned from your preliminary forays into curriculum studies literature that the basic curriculum question is: What's worthwhile? Well, seeing characters and events in literature as curricula seems very worthwhile to you. And it seems that you have found it to be worthwhile for your students, as well. Right?

PS: (with surprise) Are you saying that I could pursue this via the PhD program in curriculum studies here?

FM: It sounds like an important topic to me. Why do you wonder?

PS: Well, I have been taking my interest in doctoral studies seriously and have spoken with faculty members in other programs. Most of them gave no indication that such a topic could be the organizing center for my own curriculum in doctoral studies.

FM: Correct me if I am wrong here, but it seems that this already has been the organizing center for your curriculum for some time.

PS: (reflectively) Hmmm, maybe it has been. If I look at my practice as a literature teacher and then deduce what my curriculum assumptions were, then I would have some of the basic structures of my curriculum theory. I never did like planning. I mean, writing lesson plans.

FM: Wait. You want to go into the field of curriculum studies and you don't like to plan?

PS: I did not say I didn't like to plan; I said I did not like to write
lesson plans. The latter is so simplistic that it debases the idea of
planning—as in being a *planful* (is that a word?) human being and
therefore a prepared educator. Very different.

FM: I agree, and am just testing you. One of the reasons I went into
curriculum studies before it was called *curriculum studies* is that I
detested making lesson plans, too. That was in the day when teachers
were supposed to write behavioral objectives for every move they
made. What an insult to intelligence and emotion that was! Today, it
is even worse: Every move is also monitored through accountability
surveillances. Anyway, in my teaching day, I thought that if I got
a PhD in curriculum and then rose to professor-hood, I could then
debunk lesson plans and have them removed from existence.

PS: Did you?

FM: Well, I have written a lot about their ridiculousness. However, as
it turns out, I learned that professors and scholars do not make
curriculum policy. Where were we . . . oh yes, how I think you
currently do curriculum theory.

PS: Yes, I can look at my practice and find the theoretical assumptions
that undergird it.

FM: I agree; however, I think you are overlooking another factor.

PS: What?

FM: That you do curriculum theory in the process of living.

PS: How so?

FM: By asking *what's worthwhile* as much as you breathe.

PS: What?

FM: Yes. Don't you?

PS: What?

FM: Ask what's worthwhile as you encounter situations.

PS: I guess I do. I wonder it.

FM: And what resources do you tap to try to answer that question?

PS: The whole repertoire of experience that I have—that I am.

FM: Does that include what you have read?

PS: Well, sure.

FM: Even the fiction? The fictional characters and events? The ones you
try to convey to your students as being as real as the persons and
direct experiences they encounter?

PS: Oh . . . yes.

FM: And why do you try to convince them of this benefit of literature?

PS: Because doing so has helped me . . . and I think helped the students,
too.

FM: Tell me about it.

PS: Well, as I look back to before I was a schoolteacher, I think my
reading helped me compose my life. I tried to learn by reading
all sorts of things—some professional literature, but mostly
good novels, stories, poetry, plays, philosophy, history, social
commentaries, layman's accounts of science—and additionally by
experiencing lots of art, music, and conversation with others. All of
these inspired me to live more fully, and that living helped me relate
better with students.

FM: Yes, that was my experience, too. A good teacher—a growing
person whatever the job or profession—needs to cultivate a
curriculum for his or her continuing growth.

PS: And movies, too, and even TV, and concerts and videogames, and
so much more—the characters and events from all of these sources
are swirling within me. I cannot even remember most of them or
recall them explicitly. Yet, in the situational moment, a unique
combination of them merges with the conscious me to imagine and
form action . . . sometimes in solidarity with others.

FM: So, that is what you can pursue with us in doctoral study.

PS: What?

FM: Find some part of this repertoire to pursue and explore in greater
depth. Maybe it would entail autobiographically trying to portray
what happens as situational exigencies make relevant characters and
events well up to meet the occasion. Or, maybe it is to interview your
students or former students to see how the fictional characters and
events that you shared with them, or that they found on their own,
have welled up to meet needs of occasions for them. I encourage
you to read more and ponder deeply what is worthwhile for you to
contribute as a scholar.

PS: Do you mean that is what I could do?

FM: From my point of view, that is what is worth doing.

PS: So, what should I do next?

FM: Well there is a traditional application form to complete. You need
at least three letters of recommendation from scholars who attest
to your credibility and ability to do scholarly work. You have to
write a goal statement that serves as evidence for being able to write
well and to have something to say. Of course, we look at places
you studied, your majors in previous degree and nondegree work,
grades, and GRE scores. We look for experience in education, and,
if possible, some experience with publication or presentation at
scholarly conferences.

PS: Oh, regarding the last point, since I started reading the literature of curriculum studies, I actually proposed presentations at three conferences in the past 2 years.

FM: The fact that you presented at three conferences is valuable. You might even include in your application package one or more of the papers presented. This shows scholarly experience, which we call for during the program. When it comes time for jobs in academe, every applicant has a dissertation, but not as many have presentations or publications.

PS: Oh, I have had a book published based on my teaching experience, although it is with a popular press and is really just stories—no footnotes.

FM: Many scholars crave a book with a popular press—something actually read.

PS: What about poems? I had a few published.

FM: Worth including in your package.

PS: Really?

FM: Yes. Now, I suggest that you reflect on what we discussed. Sleep on it. Try to select the place that best fits your needs, interests, and aspirations. Talk with my colleagues, especially Bill and Bill. Keep me posted. I wish you the best.

Counter Act II: Doctoral Studies Courses

Actual Student (AS): Hello again.

FM: Why, hello. I see that you have accepted our invitation to study here. Since we talked, and I thought we had a good bit in common, I volunteered to be your program adviser. Welcome! I look forward to working with you.

AS: I thank you for agreeing to advise me. I have been reading your work.

FM: I am glad that you have, and I want you to read writings of others on our faculty, too—especially Bill and Bill. Remember that the assignment of a program adviser is only our best guess of a good fit for a mentoring relationship. So, if you meet someone who fits better, please do not hesitate to ask for a change of adviser.

AS: Okay. For now, though, how should I get started?

FM: You see that there are some basic courses—some courses in foundations of curriculum, and basic orientations to research. Begin by taking those, and as you do be sure to keep your burgeoning dissertation topic in mind. These advanced introductory (sounds oxymoron-ish, I know) courses are designed to show the array of topics within the field, so you have a better basis for deciding the next phases of your curriculum about curriculum studies.

AS: So, there are only a few required courses and the rest are electives?

FM: Yes, we have strived to keep it that way so that the students have a chance to set goals for study within the realm of curriculum studies and pursue those goals. Even though I don't like the language of goals much, we want to engage students in the process of developing their own curriculum. It would, in fact, be ironic not to do so—especially for students who are working on doctorates *in curriculum*.

AS: Refreshing. I mean, it is a huge departure from the usual *one-size-fits-all* menu in most doctoral programs.

FM: Well [looking at the form AS hands FM], I see that you have registered for all of the overview courses in the first semester. Good. Since you want to be a full-time student, I have been investigating possibilities for a graduate assistantship or other funding to help you along.

AS: Thank you. Okay. I'm enthused.

Counter Act III: Electives and Independent Study

FM: It has been a pleasure to share emails with you as you reflected on your required courses this semester. Faculty members with whom you've studied have told me how much they have appreciated your work and class participation.

AS: Thanks, I have a list of those I'd like to study with or read. However, I can find only a few classes that they offer.

FM: Well, try a couple of classes and consider taking independent studies. The essence of what's often called the British model of PhD work is independent study. Lectures and tutorials are available, while the main thrust is to study. Find a carrel in the library or I guess today you can do that with Google Scholar at home or anywhere, and study, study, study.

AS: I am anxious to get started.

FM: Onward!

Counter Act IV: Preliminary Exam

[three semesters and a summer later]

AS: Thanks for all of the communication and feedback. I have now completed my coursework. I especially liked doing the independent studies. I appreciated, too, your contacts with the English Department, since I wanted to take classes there, given my background in literature, even though I am not majoring in it for the PhD.

FM: It is great to see how you have developed your curriculum of curriculum studies as you theorize and experience it. I have learned a lot from interacting with you during the process—one of the perks of mentoring is being mentored by the mentee, too.

AS: Tell me about the next steps. I need to know more about the preliminary exam and dissertation.

FM: The preliminary exam is actually divided into two parts here. The first part is the written prelim, which is roughly equivalent to what is labeled the *comprehensive* or *qualifying* exam at other universities; however, it is not a sit-down event nor is it standardized such that all students get the same questions. We continue with the individualized ethos of the program into the exam.

AS: When can I start on these questions and who evaluates my responses to them?

FM: You select a faculty member who knows your journey through the program thus far, and you ask that person to chair, if they have time. Two others are selected on the basis of perspectives you would like to have on what you write.

AS: Would you have time to chair?

FM: I'd be glad to.

AS: When could I get the questions?

FM: How about now?

AS: What?!

FM: (turning to computer, and after a few minutes) We will need to ask the other two professors to adapt the questions, but since I have worked with both many times before, I can give the questions to you in a way that will be likely to be approved so you can ponder them. Here are they are:

1. As you reflect on your experience in the program (through courses, independent study, research projects, conferences), what are three to five major ideas you have developed or refined that continue to guide your inquiry into curriculum studies? How are these ideas related to one another and how are they embodied within you in ways that meaningfully contribute to your work? You may illustrate this relative to your emergent dissertation idea.

2. You have indicated that you are interested in contributing to the knowledge and understanding of curriculum studies by

studying how literary characters and events become embodied in human beings and give meaning and worth to their lives and contributions in the world. How could this be researched from three different orientations to inquiry? What are the major characteristics, strengths, and limitations of each? Which or what eclectic combination of these orientations is likely to guide your inquiry into this topic?

3. What dimension of the above topic do you want to pursue for the dissertation, and what is one aspect of it that you need to clarify in order to do so? Strive to clarify it, while realizing that with increased clarification comes increased confusion—but at a more sophisticated level.

Try to confine your responses to 10 double-spaced pages for each question, and provide a common bibliography.

AS: That is a big order. Yet, it does seem worthwhile to ponder and to write. How long do I have?

FM: Take as long as you need. The ideas and their expression are the important thing, not the time it takes.

AS: Thanks. What is the other part of the preliminary exam?

FM: An oral exam based on a written dissertation proposal or prospectus.

AS: What does that entail?

FM: Let's address that after you have done the written, which is enough to focus on for now. In many cases the written will serve as a basis for some of the proposal.

Counter Act V: Dissertation Proposal

AS: I appreciate the feedback from all three of you on my written prelim, and I am relieved to have passed.

FM: You did exceptionally well. Congratulations. Now, let's move on to discussion of the dissertation and its proposal. I want to debrief you on a few things, for starters.

AS: Debrief?

FM: Yes. What I am about to say counteracts much that you may have heard about what a dissertation is. Let's talk about that.

AS: I'm bracing myself.

FM: You may have heard that you start with a research question or problem. That is a bit too brittle and presumptuous. Remember, if you ask a question that sounds empirical, you must answer it with empirical findings. So, we think it is better to begin with a *phenomenon of interest.* Too many of the most important questions or problems cannot be answered, except superficially, so we want to avoid that, if possible. We hope you will dig deeper and find contradictions, write into those contradictions, instead of seeking the facade of clarity.

AS: In a way that is a relief. I have long thought that the great questions and mysteries of life are unanswerable, and it provides a sense of ease to know that I can portray moving deeper into them without being expected to resolve them—that would be a charade, anyway.

FM: Yes, you contribute to knowledge by showing the complexity of what is studied. Then, you have doubtless heard of the necessity of a review of the literature section and a theoretical framework?

AS: Yes, and I have heard many laments from students who try to figure out what a theoretical framework is, as well as how much literature to review. They do seemingly endless computer searches.

FM: Don't do a thumbnail sketch of a thousand little studies that have key words in their title that match with key words in your title. They are likely not much alike. We recommend that you ask yourself: What is the *intellectual conversation* that brought you to the place where you can propose this particular phenomenon of inquiry? Think of all of the literary—broadly conceived—influences on your perspective. What shaped the ever-changing phenomenon that you want to study? This also could, of course, include the persons and situations of your lived experience. These too contribute to the perspective that you have—better, the perspective that you *are*. Actually, I think of this process of theorizing and the continual creation of the fluid structures that guide your life as a theory—a living theory—the most important kind.

AS: So I *am* an evolving theory?! I hadn't thought of it that way before.

FM: We all are. And what we do in the world is the practice—praxis, too, since it is always politically oriented.

AS: So, as I live my dissertation—I am trying to grasp this—I have more questions. One is about how to limit it. Others talk about limiting the topic so it is manageable. What do you think?

FM: One of the mysteries of powerful inquiry is that it cannot be reined in, can't be well-managed or controlled. It must run new courses—a curriculum metaphor—sometimes many at once. Of course, you cannot do and should not try to do all of the possibilities that you entertain. Pick a portion, all the while realizing that this is a dimension of a larger and longer line of inquiry that will grow in surprising ways throughout your career.

AS: What about research orientation, methodology, or methods? There are so many forms and variations. How do I select one?

FM: It is not enough to select and apply, despite what many say. First, think carefully about what you want to study. Then, eclectically create, don't merely select, a method that uniquely fits what you want to do. The method you create is almost as important a contribution as the perspectives or knowledge you advance in the field. Substance and method of inquiry are almost inseparable. You can separate them for analysis; however, in practice they are one process.

AS: I have some work to do!

FM: Yes, though it's far from odious. Instead, I hope it is invigorating and inspiring.

AS: It is. I want to get started.

FM: I hope you will find this experience to be an act of creating extended variations on you and your contributions to the curriculum field and to a more just world. I know some would see this as pie-in-the-sky elevation of what graduate study is. Large or small, and small can be large, that's where I am convinced we need to set our sights— and our cites! I am glad you have selected your five dissertation committee members, too. It is a group that will provide varied perspectives to challenge your ideas and at the same time will work together well—an all-too-rare combination.

AS: I am glad to be able to keep all this in mind. I don't want it to just be a study that half a dozen people read. I hope it can be a book or articles in journals.

FM: Work with the image of a book. Think of chapters. After you think your way through the phenomenon of inquiry, the conversation that led to it, the theory that you are becoming, and the method of inquiry you are eclectically creating to explore the phenomenon, think of how the exploration and perspectives that it yields can be portrayed. This invokes consideration of diverse modes of representation. If your image is a book, don't write a traditional dissertation and then convert it into a book. Write a book and send it to a publisher.

AS: Onward! (leaving office)

Counter Act VI: Dissertation and Onward!

[in a conference room, after many conferences, readings, edits, revisions, a final draft, and directly after a final oral exam]

FM: Now is the time for you and your guests to leave the room while we deliberate; it's a tradition. Stay nearby and we will call you back to share our recommendations.

AS: Thank you. (exits nervously)

FM: (after 10 minutes or so) Is Dr. AS in the hall?! Congratulations! Jubilation!

[more revision . . . graduation . . .]

Epilogue

Communication and collaboration continues as the student becomes a professor or moves into some other dimension of educational contribution and continued mutual learning.

One of the best jobs I can imagine! Thanks, Bill, for sharing it and helping to create it.

14

Diving into Life and Writing into Contradiction

Ming Fang He

I have known professor William Ayers since I was a junior faculty member at Georgia Southern University. I was introduced to his pioneering work on activist teacher research, which became one of the most significant sources of inspiration for my own inquiry into teaching, learning, and life in-between cultures, languages, identities, and powers in the U.S. South. Since 2003, Professor Ayers has been invited to speak on Georgia Southern's campus, served on many of our doctoral students' dissertation committees as an external expert, provided inspiring comments as a discussant on various conference presentations of our faculty members and doctoral students, and inspired many faculty members and graduate students to become agents for positive educational and societal change in Georgia.

Inspired by Professor Ayers, I have been working with my doctoral students, a group of multiethnic researchers, to explore creative ways to liberate dissertation writing by diving into life and writing into contradiction in schools, families, and communities in the U.S. South. We explore multiple forms of dissertation inquiry and diverse representations, with a particular focus on cultural, linguistic, and political poetics of personal, community, and historical narrative. We invigorate explorations on forms of inquiry that challenge traditional ways of engaging in, interpreting, and writing about research, and embed inquiry in school, neighborhood, and community life to transform research into social and educational change. We engage in activist-oriented research and writing, transcend inquiry boundaries, raise challenging questions, *transgress* (hooks, 1994) orthodoxy and dogma, and research silenced narratives of under-represented or disenfranchised individuals and groups with hearts and minds (Ayers, 2004a, 2004b, 2006; He & Ayers, 2009) to build a long-term and heartfelt participatory movement to promote cultural, linguistic, and ecological diversity and the flourishing plurality of humanity (Schubert, 2009).

Ayers proposes applying Edward Said's ideas on the role of the intellectual to the the work of educational research, namely that the intellectual must open spaces "to raise embarrassing questions, to confront orthodoxy and dogma (rather than to produce them)" (Said, 1994, p. 12, quoted in Ayers, 2006, p. 85). Ayers believes that the core of educational inquiries "must be human knowledge and human freedom, both enlightenment and emancipation" (p. 87). What we are after is "research for social justice, research to resist harm and redress grievances, research with the explicit goals of promoting a more balanced, fair, and equitable social order" (p. 88). With this unfaltering goal, we "join one another to imagine and build a participatory movement for justice, a public space for the enactment of democratic dreams" (p. 96). We use the following guiding questions suggested by Ayers (2006) as we dive into life and write into contradiction:

- What are the issues that marginalized or disadvantaged people speak of with excitement, anger, fear, or hope?
- How can I enter a dialogue in which I will learn from a specific community itself about problems and obstacles its members face?
- What endogenous experiences do people already have that can point the way toward solutions?
- What is missing from the "official story" that will make the problems of the oppressed more understandable?
- What current proposed policies serve the privileged and the powerful, and how are they made to appear inevitable?
- How can the public space for discussion, problem posing, and problem solving be expanded? (p. 88)

We not only question whose knowledge should be considered valid and how experience should be interpreted, theorized, and represented, but also confront issues of equity, equality, social justice, and societal change through research and action (He & Ayers, 2009; He & Phillion, 2008; He & Ross, 2012). We perceive inquiry and writing as a form of liberatory or radical democratic practice (e.g., Ayers, Hunt, & Quinn, 1998; Freire, 1970; Grande, 2004; hooks, 2003, 2010; Walker, 1967/1983, 1997). We search for autobiographical and cultural roots of inquiries; bring personal, professional, and cultural experience to research; let participants name research problems and define research questions; immerse ourselves in the lives of participants in various cultural milieus as we collect stories, oral histories, or other forms of data;

and make meaning of inquiries in relationship with participants with various cultural and linguistic backgrounds.

For instance, Angela Haynes, in "Quiet Awakening: Spinning Yarns from Granny's Table in the New Rural South" (2007), explores her lived experience as a first-generation doctoral student who negates the truths of a rural southern upbringing steeped in issues of race, class, and gender. She explores the impact of place, class, race, multiple realities, and contested in-between space on southern female identities and the education of oppressed and repressed women in the South. Family members are main characters in the stories. Using critical theory as a theoretical framework and oral history as research methodology, Angela collects generational stories and memories from her Granny's table and fictionalizes characters to better understand complex lives that allow subjugation of, and by, people who cling to family, land, and their way of life. She explores life in the South from her vantage point as a lower-class, White female caught between the reality of place and the promise of education. Yarns spun from her Granny's table reveal a contested way of life stifled in an ever-changing new rural South and raise questions about southern legacy and heritage, one of the most complex, controversial, and significant issues lived by teachers, administrators, parents, and students in the region. Through her inquiries, Angela calls for an education that evokes a wake-up call for people in rural communities to act for change.

Wynnetta Scott-Simmons, in "Self, Others, and Jump Rope Communities: Triumphs of African American Women" (2008), explores the lives of four young African American women as they leave their culturally insular surroundings, Jump Rope Communities, to seek access to the codes of power and registers of language in all-White, all-girl, elite private schools during the late 1960s and early 1970s. Building on the works of critical race theory, critical literacy, and Black feminist thought, Wynnetta explores various forms of cultural literacy such as musical, artistic, and oral literacy in African American communities. To capture the memories, perceptions, and lived experiences of these women 30 years later, she collects stories of their journeys into a world of divergences—divergent language codes; divergent social, cultural, and economic stratifications; and divergent linguistic expectations, behaviors, and dispositions. Wynnetta recognizes that in the face of segregation and resegregation, these women have experienced marginalization due to race, class, gender, language, socioeconomic status, the preponderance of middle-class White female teachers, and low educational expectations. Starting from a historical inquiry into the benefits and challenges of segregation, integration, and the impact of the Civil Rights Movement, Wynnetta studies the spirit of togetherness, the establishment of unifying goals, and the synergy on which the Jump Rope Community thrives.

Michel Mitchell Pantin, in "Nappy Roots, Split Ends, and New Growth: An Autobiographical Narrative Inquiry into the Experiences of A Black Female Educator, No Lye" (Mitchell, 2009), explores the ways that race, gender, class, culture, and place shaped who she was and how she became who she is as a Black woman educator. Michel uses Black women's hair metaphors to comb through the phases of her life as a mobile urban youth growing up in the U.S. South. She transgresses methodological boundaries to fictionalize characters, events, settings, and time to protect herself and characters in her life while capturing the complexities of Black girlhood and providing necessary spaces for recurring themes of resilience, strength, and determination embedded in her stories. Michel was born in the midst of the hip-hop era and grew up during the "I'm Black and I'm Proud" movement in Atlanta, Georgia. Her childhood world was steeped in African American culture (e.g., strong faith, family-oriented, and education as the passport to anywhere her mind could conceive). Michel's world became tangled and matted as her mother married a Caucasian and moved her family to rural south Georgia. Face-to-face with racism, class privilege, and White privilege, Michel finds herself negotiating her identities between two worlds: one as a descendant of America's Black under(represented)class and one as a member of America's Black middle class. Living in-between worlds, pursuing radical doctoral studies, and teaching in an urban school district complicate who she is personally and professionally, and provoke the researcher to question the skin she speaks, the life she lives, and the place where she works, although she recognizes that she is her work and her work is her.

Sonia Janis, in "Are You Mixed? A War Bride's Granddaughter's Narrative of Lives In-Between Contested Race, Gender, Class and Power" (Carlyle, 2010), explores the spaces in-between race and place from her perspective as an educator who is multiracial. As she reflects on her experiences as a 7th-grade student through her position as a public school administrator, she recognizes that the complexity of situating herself in predetermined demographic categories is uncovered as interactions in-between those categories transpire with misconnections and miscommunications. Sonia explores her *rememory* (Morrison, 1990, 1992, 2008) of lives in two distinct regions of the United States: the Midwest and the South. The shifting contexts complicate the interactions that she lives in-between race and place, and teaches her to embrace differences, contradictions, and complexities in schools, neighborhoods, and communities. Part of the challenge of her inquiry is to transgress *monocultures of the mind* (Shiva, 1993), to hear, to make meaning of, and to honor the differences, contradictions, and complexities of lives in-between. The power of this line of inquiry lies in its narrative possibilities to capture the contradictions and paradoxes of lives in-between race and place, "to honor the subtleties, fluidities, and complexities of such experience, and to cultivate understanding towards individual . . . experience and the multicultural/multiracial contexts that shape and are shaped by such experience" (He, 2003, p. xvii). Through her inquiry, Sonia challenges educators, teachers, administrators, and policymakers to view the educational experience of students with multiracial, multicultural, and multilingual backgrounds by shattering predetermined categories and stereotyped classifications, and looking into unknown and fluid realms of the "in-betweenness" of their lives.

Cynthia Mikell, in "Reaping What You Sow: Black Traditions, Black Women and Curriculum of Freedom" (2011), explores southern cultures, Black traditions, and Black women with a focus on the life journey of one Black woman educator through racial, sexual, class, and cultural oppression to womanhood. To protect herself and the characters in her life, she transcends methodological boundaries to fictionalize stories that parallel real-life events. She creates a composite character to tell key life events and experiences, using novellas and seasonal metaphors in her writing. Each novella begins with a prelude that introduces time, place, and setting, and ends with an interlude that summarizes and theorizes the novella. The main character's life is broken down into specific seasons: early childhood, teen years, and adulthood (relationships, teaching career, military, and doctoral candidate). Raised in a segregated rural community that valued education, schooled in a system that subverted or downplayed Black accomplishments in U.S. history, and working in an urban school, Cynthia lives in-between two worlds: one as a Black teacher who understands the struggles of her ancestors, and has witnessed or experienced suppressions, repressions, and oppressions; and the other as a Black woman who teaches younger generations of Black children who know little about Black struggles, history, and heritages. Although she fictionalizes most of the characters in her stories to protect people in her life and in history, Cynthia still feels vulnerable for herself and others. Most of her life has been shrouded in denial and secrecy—an ingrained southern trait that she still finds difficult to change or shake off.

Patsy Faulkner, in "A Curriculum of Place: Who Are We? Southerners Beneath the Red Clay and the Black Dirt?" (2012), explores the South as a place where race, class, and gender are interconnected to language, culture, identity, education, and religion to develop southern identities. Patsy uses the persona of a fictionalized composite character, Ida Dunmore Good, to tell her autobiographical stories blended with the stories of friends, relatives, and acquaintances from her childhood to her adult life as an educator. Patsy illuminates how people resist changes in their received or inherited consciousness. In most instances, meaningful social change, which takes place over time, is more evolutionary than revolutionary. Identities are *ever-changing* (He, 2003; Moya & Hames-Garcia, 2000) with *non-irrevocable* (Freire, 2004) situations and contexts in life. We constantly *improvise* (Bateson, 1989; He, 2003) who we were and how we become who we are. Critical self-examinations and reflections—spiritually, emotionally, ethically, logically, honestly—help evoke changes within oneself and others. Nevertheless, self-examinations and reflections are not enough. One must act upon changes and put changes into one's daily *walkings* (Horton & Freire, 1990). The *human element* must be preserved without being essentialized, standardized, or profited from (Nussbaum, 2010; Schubert, 2009). People must make deliberate, compassionate, and critically conscious personal connections with one another to develop the sense of interconnectedness and interrelatedness, to *cultivate* (Nussbaum, 1997) the *highest* human *potential* (Walker, 1997), and to build the highest levels of social justice, equality, and equity for a better human condition for all.

Stacey Mabray, in "Rainbow in the Clouds: Oral Histories of Black Homosexual Male Graduates' Experience of Schooling in Augusta, Georgia" (2012), explores the oral histories of four Black homosexual male graduates' experiences of schooling in Butler High School in Augusta, GA. Adrian Harris, Marlon Pugh, Horace Lovett, and Michael Robinson, four participants in Stacey's dissertation inquiry, narrate their successful stories of completing high school while experiencing the intersectionality of their identities: Black, homosexual, and male in the U.S. South. Stacey examines the challenges and obstacles that her participants face as they navigate their way through high school while living complex and contested identities as Black, gay males in the South. Stacey begins and ends her dissertation with two letters. The first letter (prologue) is an attempt to put into words the researcher's grave personal and professional sorrow for her misunderstanding, when she was a novice teacher, of a student's open expression of his homosexual desires toward a heterosexual male student. Stacey tells the "misunderstood" and "mistreated" Black male homosexual student: "I cannot rewrite the past, but I can script the future. Before meeting you, I lived an existence unaware. You woke me from a 30-year slumber under the southern magnolias to begin my journey of discovery.

You brought me into consciousness. Please accept my work as an apology. Thank you for being a rainbow in my cloud, wherever you are." The second letter (epilogue) is the cathartic resolution found through the investigation of the narratives of four young men who were also ignored "others." Stacey Mabray uses the words from her participants to create a letter to rainbow brothers in order to "break the silence and stop the death." Because she weaves rainbow metaphors throughout the dissertation, the narratives and insights of these young men are dubbed "rainbows in the clouds."

The inquiries we engage in, the skins we speak, the lives we live, and the places we work complicate our lives, multiply our sense of belonging and displacement, and demand that we dive courageously into life and write creatively into tensions, contradictions, and complexities with equity, equality, social justice, and human freedom as explicit goals. Diving into life and writing into contradiction thrives on passionate involvement, brave commitment, and unfaltering advocacy for disenfranchised, under-represented, and invisible groups and individuals against all forms of adversities, injustices, and suppressions (Ayers, 2004a, 2004b, 2006). It calls for educational researchers to "research with a heart" (He & Ayers, 2009); to advocate for individuals, groups, families, tribes, communities, and societies that are often at controversy, underrepresented, misrepresented, or excluded in the official narrative (Ayers, 2004a, 2004b, 2006); and to work as allies with schools, communities, and tribes to create a culture of resistance, to build up courage, and to use exile space in-between the contested places (He, 2010, p. 471) to develop creative strategies to "transgress orthodoxies and enact educational and social change that fosters equity, equality, freedom, and social justice" (He, Scott-Simmons, Haynes, & Tennial, 2010, p. 220). We are called to build a participatory movement to promote a more balanced and equitable human condition through personal and political acts of teaching, inquiring, and living (Ayers, 2004a, 2004b) in an increasingly diversified and contested world.

References

Ayers, W. (2004a). *Teaching the personal and the political: Essays on hope and justice.* New York, NY: Teachers College Press.

Ayers, W. (2004b). *Teaching toward freedom: Moral commitment and ethical action in the classroom.* Boston, MA: Beacon Press.

Ayers, W. (2006). Trudge toward freedom: Educational research in the public interest. In G. Ladson-Billings & W. F. Tate (Eds.), *Education research in the public interest: Social justice, action and policy* (pp. 81–97). New York, NY: Teachers College Press.

Ayers, W., Hunt, J. A., & Quinn, T. (Eds.). (1998). *Teaching for social justice: A democracy and education reader*. New York, NY: Free Press.

Bateson, M. C. (1989). *Composing a life*. New York, NY: The Atlantic Monthly Press.

Carlyle, S. E. J. (2010). *Are you mixed? A war bride's granddaughter's narrative of lives in-between contested race, gender, class and power* (Unpublished doctoral dissertation). Georgia Southern University, Statesboro.

Faulkner, P. D. (2012, April). *A curriculum of place: Who are we? Southerners beneath the red clay and the black dirt?* (Unpublished doctoral dissertation). Georgia Southern University, Statesboro.

Freire, P. (1970). *Pedagogy of the oppressed*. Baltimore, MD: Penguin Books.

Freire, P. (2004). *Pedagogy of indignation*. Boulder, CO: Paradigm.

Grande, S. (2004). *Red pedagogy: Native American social and political thought*. Lanham, MD: Rowman & Littlefield.

Haynes, A. M. (2007). *Quiet awakening: Spinning yarns from granny's table in the new rural South* (Unpublished doctoral dissertation). Georgia Southern University, Statesboro.

He, M. F. (2003). *A river forever flowing: Cross-cultural lives and identities in the multicultural landscape*. Greenwich, CT: Information Age.

He, M. F. (2010). Exile pedagogy: Teaching and living in-between. In J. A. Sandlin, B. D. Schultz, & J. Burdick (Eds.), *Handbook of public pedagogy: Education and learning beyond schooling* (pp. 469–482). New York, NY: Routledge.

He, M. F., & Ayers, W. (2009). Research with a heart: Activist practitioner inquiry. In R. Milner (Ed.), *Diversity and education: Teachers, teaching, and teacher education* (pp. 195–216). Springfield, IL: Charles C. Thomas.

He, M. F., & Phillion, J. (Eds.). (2008). *Personal-passionate-participatory inquiry into social justice in education*. Greenwich, CT: Information Age.

He, M. F., & Ross, S. (2012). Narrative of curriculum in the South: Lives in-between contested race, gender, class, and power. *Journal of Curriculum Theorizing, 28*(3), 1–9.

He, M. F., Scott-Simmons, W., Haynes, A. M., & Tennial, D. M. (2010). Teaching creatively in-between contested contradictions and complexities in the U.S. South. In C. J. Craig & L. F. Deretchin (Eds.), *Cultivating curious and creative minds: The role of teachers and teacher educators* (Teacher education yearbook XVIII, pp. 218–251). Lanham, MD: Scarecrow Education/ Rowman & Littlefield.

hooks, b. (1994). *Teaching to transgress: Education as the practice of freedom*. New York, NY: Routledge.

hooks, b. (2003). *Teaching community: A pedagogy of hope*. New York, NY: Routledge.

hooks, b. (2010). *Teaching critical thinking: Practical wisdom*. New York, NY: Routledge.

Horton, M., & Freire, P. (1990). *We make the road by walking: Conversations on education and social change*. Philadelphia, PA: Temple University Press.

Mabray, S. N. (2012, April). *Rainbow in the clouds: Oral histories of Black homosexual male graduates' experience of schooling in Augusta, Georgia* (Unpublished doctoral dissertation). Georgia Southern University, Statesboro.

Mikell, C. (2011). *Reaping what you sow: Black traditions, Black women, and curriculum of freedom* (Unpublished doctoral dissertation). Georgia Southern University, Statesboro.

Mitchell, M. L. (2009). *Nappy roots, split ends, and new growth: An autobiographical inquiry of the experience of a Black female educator, no lye* (Unpublished doctoral dissertation). Georgia Southern University, Statesboro.

Morrison, T. (1990). The site of memory. In R. Ferguson, M. Gever, T. Minh-Ha, & C. West (Eds.), *Out there: Marginalization and contemporary cultures* (pp. 299–305). New York, NY: New Museum of Contemporary Art and Massachusetts Institute of Technology.

Morrison, T. (1992). *Playing in the dark: Whiteness and the literary imagination.* New York, NY: Vintage.

Morrison, T. (2008). *What moves at the margins.* Jackson, MS: University of Mississippi Press.

Moya, P. M. L., & Hames-Garcia, M. R. (Eds.). (2000). *Reclaiming identity: Realist theory and the predicament of postmodernism.* Berkeley: University of California Press.

Nussbaum, M. C. (1997). *Cultivating humanity: A classical defense of reform in liberal education.* Cambridge, MA: Harvard University Press.

Nussbaum, M. C. (2010). *Not for profit: Why democracy needs the humanities.* Princeton, NJ: Princeton University Press.

Schubert, W. H. (2009). *Love, justice, and education: John Dewey and the Utopians.* Charlotte, NC: Information Age.

Scott-Simmons, W. (2008). Self, others, and jump rope communities: Triumphs of African American women. (Unpublished doctoral dissertation). Georgia Southern University, Statesboro.

Shiva, V. (1993). *Monocultures of the mind: Perspectives on biodiversity and biotechnology.* Atlantic Highlands, NJ: Zed Books.

Walker, A. (1983). *In search of our mothers' gardens.* Orlando, FL: Harcourt. (Original work published 1967)

Walker, A. (1997). *Anything we love can be saved: A writer's activism.* New York, NY: Random House.

15

Child-Centered Schools and Society-Centered Schools

Progressive Education, Testing, and "E-valuation"

Craig Kridel

That the curriculum should be appropriate to the needs and interests of the learners has been among the most misunderstood issues of education, both by those who have supported it and by those who have opposed it.

—Hilda Taba, *Curriculum Development: Theory and Practice*, 1962

Bill Ayers has been described as a progressive educator, a depiction that he gladly accepts yet one that proves somewhat complicated and troublesome. The disparate nature of progressive education may, indeed, cause such a moniker to be viewed as a compliment or criticism, certainly today as well as back in the 1930s, 1960s, and 1980s. For Bill, who has written so eloquently about the injustices of labeling and who also approaches academic life with grace and good cheer, such descriptions come and go. He embraces them all in his quest for classroom experimentation and nondogmatic approaches to schooling. Yet, ironically, Ayers's career represents an important yet forgotten strand of progressivism from the 1930s, defined not by John Dewey but by a group of obscure Eight Year Study educators whose conceptual dilemmas offer many insights for contemporary education reform. As Ayers recently has been mislabeled and simplistically portrayed, so have many of these progressive educators from the 1930s and 1940s.

With all the various definitions of the term "progressive education," one seemingly basic theme continues to emerge: Progressive education is based on the interests of the child. Either in the first verse or in later choruses, such child-centered stanzas inevitably and typically evolve into refrains of "learning by doing," "teaching the whole child," and "fostering creative expression," which have served to characterize "the movement" for decades and continue to do so today. These conceptions also have been criticized through the years—notably by William Bagley, Arthur Bestor, E. D. Hirsch, and others who felt progressive education had eliminated academic standards and fostered a generation of self-indulgent children who could no longer read or, now, who can no longer think.

A focus on the interests of the child is certainly idiomatic of the writings of Bill Ayers, and so much of his work encourages teachers to learn more about their students and themselves as a way to help the process of negotiating and generating interest in the curriculum. Yet, ultimately, Bill's work and career serve to complicate, as he would hope, and implicitly refute certain perceived misconceptions of progressive education. In essence, his ever-evolving beliefs and quest for knowledge—his "being with adventurous company"—serve to display not unbridled child-centeredness but, rather, attention to student interests guided and forged by a conception of social needs, justice, and engagement. This "essential tension" between interests/needs and a social vision (proving much more sophisticated than the typical child-centered and society-centered distinction) offers insights into contemporary school reform while also inviting today's educators to revisit one of the many interesting and poignant educational debates of American education during the mid-20th century: the conception of needs.

Defining Progressive Education: *A State Devoutly Wished*

Lawrence Cremin (1961) warned against formulating any capsule definition of progressive education, maintaining that no common description existed or could exist due, in part, to the character of the movement, which necessitated diversity and differences. In fact, at the 1938 annual Progressive Education Association (PEA) meeting, a committee reported on its efforts to define the term, and while a statement was produced, nearly the entire group objected, explaining that progressive education is not a definition but "a spirit" (Alberty, 1938). Self-proclamation further complicates any clear description of the term. In essence, then or now, anyone can announce him- or herself as a progressive, thus aligning with the beloved John Dewey. Both Ralph Tyler, the developer of the seemingly un-progressive Tyler Rationale, and Ben Wood, the founder of the Cooperative Testing Service (CTS), which led to the current high-stakes testing movement, maintained that they were progressives whose work was guided by the writings of Dewey. Any conception of progressive education is more practical than precise, and such oddities are expected from a comprehensive term and loosely organized group of educators where mere self-declaration leads to membership. Yet, the breadth of progressive education, crossing decades of practice with only some commonalities and even less clarity, unfortunately has caused contemporary educators to simplify and obscure a scholarly, thoughtful group of educators whose greatest accomplishment was their ability to critique one another's ideas.

This has resulted, alas, in progressive education being reduced to longstanding dichotomies between child-centered and society-centered educators or, more recently, between administrative and pedagogical progressives (albeit certainly a legitimate distinction). Such descriptors, while merely caricatures, have been used as a way to simplify the concept, not for clarification but as a way to discredit its intent in the same manner that Arthur Bestor selected the most simpleminded forms of life adjustment programs to criticize and mock. Further, some culprits are not traditional critics who object to "soft pedagogy" and the permissiveness of youth, but rather, educational and curricular historians and theorists who perpetuate a reductionist narrative by relying on simplistic classifications and "soft-headed" and flawed descriptions. Ironically, the dynamic educational contradictions that helped to define the PEA during the 1930s have been glossed over by detractors and admirers alike, as the term has now become, for some, a merit badge that can be displayed at conferences on social change and, for others, an intentionally misrepresented perspective to ridicule as a way to support educational standards and competencies.

I have now come to question, if not outright dismiss, these historical dichotomies since, I believe, the concepts were not fully embraced even by the PEA leadership. During the past few years, I have been researching a documentary film commissioned by the PEA for the 1939 World's Fair where the organization sought to introduce and popularize, in essence to the world, its conception of progressive education (Kridel, 2012b). The documentary focuses on the Hessian Hills School, a venue that by all appearances would have been identified as a child-centered, learning-by-doing school with its informal atmosphere and benevolent teachers sitting among the children. Yet, the film's featured teacher, Rupert Hampton, had just arrived from the Highlander Folk School where he had worked closely with Myles Horton. In fact, Hampton was one of the five original signers, in 1934, of the Charter of Incorporation for Highlander and was engaged in much social and cultural activism while also being a caring and kind educator. Many of the angelic-looking children in the "soft pedagogy," child-centered Hessian Hills School lived in Red Hill (in Croton-on-Hudson, NY, outside of New York City), an area of liberals, socialists, anarchists, and communists and home to Robert Minor, Upton Sinclair, Floyd Dell, Max Eastman, Stuart Chase, and others. The school's director, Elizabeth Moos, just months before the filming of the documentary, shifted her already-Leftist position by officially joining the Communist Party. Images, assumptions, generalizations, ambiguities, and dichotomies begin disintegrating the "child-centered classification" as the real-life details of this school become known. In essence, the Hessian Hills School defies and embraces these perceived educational contradictions of our contemporary conceptions of progressive education.

From researching this documentary film and my experience during the past 20 years of reading documents and memoirs of many Eight Year Study progressive educators, along with my recent 250 interviews with students and teachers from the 1940s Secondary School Study (what became known as the Black High School Study), I do not see a dichotomy between child-centered and society-centered schools, or a bifurcation between pedagogical and administrative progressives (Kridel, 2012a). However, I know that I could easily construct a scaffold to show such differences, and I am indeed selecting my subjects carefully, as did Bestor. Rather, I see certain educators—albeit not all—who attended PEA conferences, read common educational and political–cultural writings and were actively involved in academic and intellectual pursuits, developed classrooms focused on the interests *and needs* of their students, and engaged in activities that sought to better society and their immediate locale in a variety of ways—much like the Bill Ayers of today. While many educators throughout the United States could be so described, what brought together this group as (Eight Year Study) progressive educators was their belief in a fundamental, common purpose—building communities that embraced democracy as a way of life: They trusted the ability of teachers to address and resolve complex issues, believed in democracy as a guiding social ideal, and maintained faith in thoughtful inquiry to create ways of making education more significant for students and teachers. These progressives, loosely conceived, articulated common purposes and lived lives filled with conceptual dilemmas as they willingly confronted the tension and contradictions within their professional careers. They were guided by common educational, political, and cultural beliefs—not by a set of classifications, rallying cries, or simplistic slogans and flags.

Implicit in the misperceptions of progressive education, especially by some contemporary educators, is another aspect of this simpleminded classification system that dismisses these (Eight Year Study) progressive educators as scholars and learners. I detect, at times, a "transference of arrogance" by curriculum scholars and educational historians who seem to believe that their intellectual and research abilities surpass those of yesterday's classroom teachers and researchers. This certainly was not the case with the many progressive school staff members of the 1930s that I have studied. While Rupert Hampton is seen in the documentary film as a kind, avuncular teacher walking about the classroom posing simple, open-ended questions to the children, he also was recognized as a gifted organist—having studied sacred music at Union Theological Seminary—and a noted ethnomusicologist and music educator who engaged in groundbreaking research. Eight Year Study social studies teacher Margaret Willis prepared an exemplary master's thesis on imperialism in Korea for a degree in history at Columbia University and later would become a recognized photographer (specializing in the Mideast and Egypt) with a New York City agent selling her prints. While maintaining careers as school administrators, E. R. Smith remained active as a noted mathematician, V. T. Thayer continued to write about Locke and Kant in professional journals, and Caroline Zachry obtained certification at the New York Psychoanalytic Institute. While I believe they saw themselves as teachers, scholars, and researchers, I truly question whether they defined themselves as child-centered educators.

Further, many of these progressives turned to the field of education from distinguished careers elsewhere: Alice Keliher was a leader in the New York documentary filmmakers collective, Harold Alberty had been a successful lawyer, and Boyd Bode was embarking on what would have been a distinguished career as a philosopher (certainly in the eyes of William James, who wrote a letter of recommendation for him). I have always wondered how such distinguished academics and accomplished scholars and teachers could be viewed, by others, as turning the curriculum over to "the interests of children." Those scholar-teachers whom I have interviewed from this era are overflowing with intellectual gifts—readings, material culture, experiences—that mean so much to them. They wanted, much as Maxine Greene (1979) describes in her essay, "Liberal Education and the Newcomer," to offer the learner—the newcomer—the opportunity to join them in shared intellectual adventures rather than "throwing up their hands" and supporting any interest that the neophyte might suggest.

The Fundamental Contradiction: Education Based on Student Interests and Education Based on Student Needs

My comments are not meant, however, to denigrate the significance of "the interests of the child" and "learning by doing," or to dismiss the essential tension between child-centered and society-centered schools. There certainly is no question that the concept of child-centered schools helped to define the PEA during the early 20th century and to articulate a popular type of education distinct from the then-common institutional, factory-oriented conception of schooling. And the tension with society-centered educators was important to PEA discourse—the legendary "imposition controversy" arose from the assertions and accusations of George Counts (1932) during his 1932 PEA keynote conference address in Baltimore. Contradiction and complexity certainly existed within the organization in what proved important and fruitful among the many criticisms and proclamations.

Student interests became the center of attention for the PEA and were popularized by William H. Kilpatrick, Dewey's self-proclaimed disciple, when, in 1918, he first proposed a curricular concept called "the project method." Kilpatrick's "packaging" may have proven more important than many previously had thought because it gave like-minded educators an identifiable educational method. With the formation of the PEA the next year, in 1919, the loosely affiliated child-centered educators had an organization and discernible method of instruction. Traditional educators (as well as many progressives) took issue with this approach and asked whether all student interests held equal educational significance. Kilpatrick maintained that the interests of the child were legitimate content if the experience represented "a hearty, purposeful act," a requirement that, for Kilpatrick, ruled out what some educators would consider students' "childish impulses" with little educational purpose (Kilpatrick, 1925). Even with experiences defined as "purposeful acts," those who embraced the concept of schools-as-democratic communities questioned the individualism and lack of a broader social view. In time, the PEA would shift the conversation from an emphasis on interests to the importance of "needs" as a way to acknowledge the significance of the learner while also recognizing the importance of society. Identifying student needs, which are both individual and social, rather than focusing on the interests of the child, would provide the structure for determining the curriculum. Eight Year Study educators, as a way to resolve this curricular issue, articulated four sets of (adolescent) needs: personal living, immediate personal–social relationships, social–civic relationships, and economic relationships (Kridel & Bullough, 2007).

Boyd Bode, described by *Time* magazine in 1938 as "progressive education's No. 1 present-day philosopher," criticized the PEA and Eight Year Study staff for their use of *needs*, what he called a weasel word, as the organizing principle for curriculum design. Difficulties arose when considering how the needs of the student and the larger community would be determined. Would this occur independent of the "voice" of students, or by some preconceived designation of the significance of certain knowledge and values, or from some determining societal or psychological structure? In addition to critiquing how needs would be determined, Bode also questioned the most basic definitions of the term, distinguishing between "real needs" and "felt needs" (whims). He thought educators were defining needs by determining what students "lacked" and what they ought to know. Bode resolved the "conception of needs" by maintaining that the defining principle for curriculum construction was not listing "lacks of knowledge" but, instead, determining a social vision (or what he viewed as a philosophy for school in society). Rather than viewing what students did not, but should, know—an absence of knowledge—Bode reconceived determining needs as a way to establish a common vision and a method to ascertain and develop knowledge that brings together a community for discourse—in essence, a basic belief in (cultural) democracy as a way of life. The conception of needs led to a transformation within the progressive education dialogue of the 1930s and 1940s as educators attempted to temper interests with needs.

What arose from this tension proved equally complex and controversial in that Bode and others were asking educators and students to construct a social vision for their communities. The curriculum was not guided by Kilpatrick's call for purposeful activity or Dewey's guidelines of growth and "experience begetting further educational experiences." Rather, a basic concept of cultural democracy and discourse sought to balance both personal and social dimensions of learning for constructing shared social visions. Yet one odd, curious, and somewhat contradictory resolution emerged within these arguments—namely, the use of school evaluation.

The Ultimate Contradiction: Progressive Education and Testing & Evaluation

With the twists and turns of this essay, I now introduce my real contradiction about progressive education (rather than the pseudo-paradox of child- and society-centered schools)—the Eight Year Study progressives' conception of testing and, as they underscored, e-valuation. With their belief in experiential, inquiry-based, and constructivist learning, Eight Year Study progressives readily accepted and used standardized testing. Those teachers whose lives I have studied were true scholars who, in conversation with Lou LaBrant and William Van Til, noted that constantly revising standardized (content-based) tests allowed them to regularly reassess the significance and importance of knowledge to their community, the field, and the students. They were actively involved in research themselves, and approving a content-based test forced them to engage in the difficult process of assessing significance and the use and worth of knowledge as they sought to construct social visions for emerging communities. They never sought to eliminate achievement tests from secondary school programs but, more important, they added other forms of "appraisal instruments." One of the interesting oddities—talk of contradictions!—of the Eight Year Study was the construction of a series of standardized "tests" that were used (and field-tested) in progressive schools and then sold to other school districts throughout the United States. By 1937, 87 test forms had been constructed and were used by 285 schools and by several hundred other teachers outside of those working directly with the Eight Year Study. Ironically, the proceeds from these tests helped to fund the PEA during lean times when the organization lost the support of the Rockefeller Foundation.

The Eight Year Study progressives saw student assessment much differently than the high-stakes testing of today, which commonly is used as a way to privilege or humiliate children. PEA tests *generated* information and permitted teachers to examine the act of learning, to discuss the importance of knowledge, and to learn more about the changing beliefs of students. PEA tests and appraisal instruments ascertained growth, including students' reading habits, beliefs on social issues, abilities to address social problems, interpretive skills, applications of social facts, and many other areas of development. The Interpretation of Literature "test" went much beyond a student's ability to summarize content. Students were asked not only to demonstrate their own understanding of a story but also to recognize another's point of view and to examine the narrative in relation to a philosophy of life and to human motives.

Assessment was quite expansive. Application of Principles in Social Problems addressed issues of race, class, gender, economics, and politics through various scenarios; for example, a high school graduation incident with racial overtones, the graduated income tax, and the tension between industrial profit and workers' health. Students were asked to take a position on a specific problem or hypothetical situation. For example, Exercise No. 5 pertained to social problems of free speech, democracy, and public discourse:

Exercise No. 5: Earl Browder, Communist candidate for President, was scheduled to speak in Tampa, Florida. He was denied the use of the public halls in the city, but he arranged to speak in a small park. As the audience assembled a group of men, some wearing American Legion caps, others wearing police badges, rushed the meeting, tore down the platform, forcibly removed Mr. Browder and dispersed the crowd.

(Check one or more with which you agree [many more statements were posed].)

___ The group should have been prevented from breaking up the meeting.
___ The action of the group was a commendable patriotic act.
___ It was all right to break up the meeting, but it should have been accomplished by a more legitimate method.
___ The group should have been prosecuted.

Reasons [many more were posed]:

___ Violent methods of suppression defeat their purpose.
___ One should not fight undemocratic movements by undemocratic means.
___ When democracy is in danger citizens have a right to use any method to prevent that danger. (Kridel, 1993)

Teachers viewed testing as more than a way of determining the acquisition of facts and began identifying important student traits—constructed personal–social needs—that, if viewed as a goal of instruction, needed to be ascertained. The Scale of Beliefs assessment proved useful for clarifying students' views on social issues, including militarism, nationalism, racialism, democracy, economic individualism, and labor and unemployment.

Test 4.3 A Scale of Beliefs

Our first loyalty is to our own country rather than to humanity throughout the world. [agree; uncertain; disagree]
Unemployment and poverty are inevitable in any social system. [agree; uncertain; disagree]
The government should institute strict regulations making for honest presentation of businesses and products in all advertising. [agree; uncertain; disagree] [many more statements were posed] (Kridel, 1993)

With today's constant objections to standardized testing in mind, it may seem surprising that the assessment and appraisal instruments were not challenged in the more experimental schools in the Eight Year Study. This was, in part, because these educators viewed evaluation as a process by which the *values* of a school community were articulated and ascertained. In essence, "e-valuating"—the drawing out of values—was conceived as first and foremost a philosophical rather than a technical activity. Tests became a way to determine the values of a school and to gather information about students and about the effectiveness of curricular–instructional practices. Ralph Tyler coined the term "comprehensive appraisal" for this approach to evaluation, where instruments were designed to ascertain student development and not merely to determine the acquisition of knowledge and factual learning. For him, evaluation should begin with teachers discussing the purposes and intent of new educational programs. Conversations were never confined to what could be measured. Rather, teachers' hopes for their students became the point of departure for discussion. The process of defining objectives was recursive, requiring cycles of thoughtful questioning and reworking by staff and groups of teachers until what was written could fully capture what was intended. In essence, evaluation was not a form of student testing; rather, appraisal became an opportunity for students and teachers to articulate their values—either child-centered education, society-centered schooling, learning by doing, or articulating and defining student needs. While today's educators have lost the complexities and contradictions of interests and needs, I suspect we also have lost Tyler's meanings of evaluation and objectives, ironically due to the emergence of a narrow conception of student testing promulgated by CTS and ETS and guided by that "progressive" educator, Ben Wood.

For those many contemporary educators who proudly define themselves as progressives, I would ask you to join Bill Ayers who, in his writings, has integrated a child-centered and society-centered perspective that balances students' interests and needs while honoring and embracing thoughtfulness and scholarly adventure. The quest now for committed progressive educators is to reclaim evaluation as an intellectual and community-building activity that permits discourse and conversation among parents, students, administrators, staff, and teachers. Bill Ayers has been engaged in comprehensive appraisal, e-valuation, and thoughtful reflection on those many occasions he has visited and spoken at the University of South Carolina Museum of Education. Through his inspiration, we strive to put aside false dichotomies and to work for schools to become more compassionate, more generous, more humane, and more thoughtful places for teachers and for students.

References

Alberty, H. (1938). *The report of the Committee on Philosophy of Education.* New York, NY: Progressive Education Association.

Counts, G. (1932). *Dare the school build a new social order.* New York, NY: John Day.

Cremin, L. (1961). *The transformation of the schools.* New York, NY: Knopf.

Greene, M. (1979). Liberal education and the newcomer. *Phi Delta Kappan, 60*(9), 633–636.

Kilpatrick, W. H. (1918). The project method. *Teachers College Record, 19*(4), 319–335.

Kilpatrick, W. H. (1925). *Foundations of method.* New York, NY: Macmillan.

Kridel, C. (Ed.-Arrayer). (1993). Eight year study materials [microform]: From the Progressive Education Association's Commission on the Relation of School and College. 2 microfilm reels; 16 mm. Microfilm OCLC #40071984

Kridel, C. (2012a). The secondary school study web exhibitions: Progressive education in the Black high school, 1940–1948. Retrieved from the Museum of Education, University of South Carolina, website: www.ed.sc.edu/museum/second_study.html

Kridel, C. (2012b). *Towards an understanding of progressive education and "school": Lee Dick's 1939 documentary film on the Hessian Hills School.* Sleepy Hollow, NY: The Rockefeller Archive Center. Retrieved from www.rockarch.org/publications/resrep/kridel1.pdf

Kridel, C., & Bullough, R. V., Jr. (2007). *Stories of the Eight Year Study: Rethinking schooling in America.* Albany: State University of New York Press.

Taba, H. (1962). *Curriculum development: Theory and practice.* New York, NY: Harcourt, Brace & World.

16

Tony at the Red Line Tap

Fred Klonsky

Chapter 1: In which Tony and I discuss spirituality

"Where you been, Klonsky?" said Marty.

"He fell into the black hole of school reform," mumbled Tony.

"True that," I replied.

Turning to Marty, I asked, "Can I get a Paulaner Salvator Doppel Bock?"

Marty answered, "Can't you always?"

"Did you get arrested yesterday?" asked Tony. "Or ticketed?"

"Neither. I was teaching my weekly class of kindergarteners and first-graders how to play 'You Are My Sunshine' on the uke."

"I love that song. My mother always sang that to me when I went to bed as a kid."

I furrowed my brow. "It's kind of hard for me to visualize that image."

"Yes. Well. I need to talk to you about my theory about the mayor."

My brow got even more furrowed.

"I think you guys are missing the broader picture."

"And what might that be?"

"I'm thinking that the mayor is a very spiritual guy."

"What the hell are you talking about, Tony?"

"It's like my cousin Ram Dass always says."

"Uh. Your cousin is Richard Alpert, the guru who dropped acid with Timothy Leary in San Francisco in the 1960s?"

"No. My cousin is Richard Rosengarten, the guru who dropped acid with Benny Shapiro in Rogers Park about six months ago."

"Okay. I'm trying to wrap my head around this."

"Good. That's what cousin Ram Dass would want. Turn off your mind, relax, and float downstream. I'm thinking that the mayor is trying to get Chicago more spiritual. And cousin Ram Dass would say that in order to get closer to the Godhead, you have to relieve yourself of your earthly possessions. Y'know, like John Lennon sang: 'Imagine no possessions. I wonder if you can?'"

"Oy."

"And that is what the mayor wants for the city. He is ridding us of all possessions. Bridges. Roads. Midway. Parking meters. Public schools."

"To make the city more spiritual," I said skeptically.

"Imagine no possessions, man. I wonder if you can?"

"Tony? You're crazy."

"Not me. Mayor Rahm Dass, man."

Chapter 2: In which Tony and I discuss state contracts

It was a dark and stormy night.

It seemed like Chicago hadn't had a day without rain for weeks.

"Good for the ducks," my mom used to say.

"What'll you have, Freddy?" Marty asks.

"Hmmm. How about a cold bottle of Lindemans Gueuze Cuvée René" I said.

"I was guessing that's what you would be asking for so I happen to have one right here." She reached down into the cooler.

"Do you *ever* go home?" I said to Tony.

"Why? What's at home? A TV? Got that here. Some beer? Got that here."

"What about food. Y'know, the solid kind."

"That's why Marty stocks the Doritos ranch-flavored chips on the clips over there," said Tony.

I just shook my head.

"I heard they might be voting on your pension by Friday."

I shook my head again. This time up and down.

"And I hear they claim they have no money, but the governor is going to spend twelve million dollars on new highway construction."

I nodded my head again.

"What? You're not talking?"

"*That's billion.* Not million. And that's what they have done for half a century," I said. "They take retiree pension money and they spend it on other shit. They won't raise the taxes to pay for this stuff. Then they claim Illinois is broke. And cut our pension."

"It's like my cousin Billy No-nose always used to say," said Tony.

"Billy No-nose?"

"Uh huh. Billy No-nose. He was a consultant."

"A consultant?" I say skeptically.

"Uh huh. He used to be a detective for the CPD for years. Then he became a consultant."

"Consulted for who?"

"A company that the state contracted for highway construction."

I hesitated to ask. I wasn't sure I wanted to know.

"He arranged for the gravel and other filler that they used under the concrete road bed."

"Other filler?" I said.

"Uh huh. So consider yourself lucky. The governor is building his highways using your pension money. He could have hired my cousin No-nose and built his highways using you. Mile after magnificent mile."

Chapter 3: In which Tony and I discuss the dangers of sitting at the table

"Richie Imperial Porter, Marty."

"Comin' right up, Klonsky."

"Damn. Look who decided to drop by," said Tony as I saddled up to the bar.

"Why do we say *saddled up* when we sit at a bar?" I asked. "We don't say that we saddled up to a table."

"Why are roads *closed*, but bridges are *out*?" asked Tony.

"It's not like my union president demanded to *saddle up* to the table for pension negotiations."

"That's okay," said Tony. "I try and stay away from tables anyway."

"I kind of noticed," I said. "Bars are definitely your *oeuvre*."

"That kind of reminds me something my cousin Francois always says."

"C'mon Tony. You don't have a cousin named Francois."

"No. I do. He's from Baton Rouge."

"Baton Rouge?"

"Louisiana."

"I know where Baton Rouge is."

"Yep. Old cousin Francois. He goes by the name Tex."

"Christ, Tony. That is the oldest joke in the book—he goes by the name Tex because he doesn't want to be called Louise."

"No," said Tony. "He goes by the name Tex because he wears a white Stetson hat and Tony Lama cowboy boots. And so everybody in Baton Rouge calls him Tex. And you can always find him *saddling up* to a bar."

"And why not a table?"

"Haven't you ever seen a western movie, man? Bad things always happen at a table. There's always some bad guy with a drawn gun hidden under the table. A bad guy like Dan Duryea. Did you ever see the movie *Winchester '73*? They're playing poker and the next thing you know—*boom*—somebody is pulling the trigger. That can never happen at a bar."

"So what does your cousin Francois—I mean Tex—always say?"

"Never eat at a place called Mom's. Never play cards with a man named Doc. And never lie down with a woman who's got more troubles than you."

"I thought that was Nelson Algren."

"Oh. Well, did Nelson Algren say, 'Never ask for a seat at the table'?"

"I don't think so."

"Well, that's from my cousin Tex. And trust me. It's good advice."

Chapter 4: In which Tony and I discuss unions

"Jeez, it's cold," I said to nobody in particular.

Marty looked over from the cash register.

"Know what, honey," I said. "Give me some of your Paulaner Brauhaus Hefeweizen from Shanghai."

"No problem," said Marty. "If you say 'please' and don't call me 'honey.'"

"Yes m'am," I said and winked.

"Don't wink," she said.

"Okay," I mumbled.

Tony turned halfway from his stool. "Where you been hiding?"

"Let's skip the small talk, Tony. I'm pissed. They're getting rid of the rat."

"Who's they. And what rat?"

"Scabby. That big inflatable rat you see on picket lines? The labor big shots think it presents too intimidating an image and they want to get rid of it."

"How 'bout that," said Tony.

"And I just saw yesterday that union membership is the lowest it has been since the Depression. Do they think maybe the union leaders' go-along tactics have something to do with that?"

"My cousin Tony has a joke about that."

"Tony? You have a cousin Tony?"

"Sure. You think I'm the only Tony in the world?"

"How does the family know which cousin Tony they're talking about?"

"Easy. He's the Tony that works for a living. Construction. One of those *broken nose, don't mess with me guys*. Bleeds union blood. Kind of like you. If Tony's on a picket line, you don't want to be no scab, if you know what I'm saying."

I say, "Well, the union suits want a more *business-friendly relationship* with management and Scabby represents too confrontational an image. What would cousin Tony say to that?"

"Tony would ask, 'What's the difference between a boss and a bag of shit?'"

"Okay. What's the difference between a boss and a bag of shit?"

"The bag."

Chapter 5: In which Tony and I discuss Chicago's history and its future

I hadn't been by the Red Line in a while. Anne and I had taken a road trip out to the northwest and then out to Block Island.

I walked into the dark tap room late on a sultry Chicago August afternoon. The air outside smelled of the coming storm. The air inside smelled of old beer.

"Give me a cold IPA," I said to Marty.

"You have something in mind?"

"Bartender's choice," I said.

"I haven't seen you or Tony much lately"

Tony was nursing some shit beer and he barely looked up.

"Hey, I been working," he mumbled.

"Right," I snickered.

"It's not like I never held a job. You think my mother delivered me while sitting on this bar stool?"

"No. But I don't think she gave birth to you with a beer bottle in your hand. And it's been in your grip since I've known you. You and a job? Just the scams your cousins get you involved in."

Tony always got a smile on his face when you mentioned his cousins. He is a true family man.

"What you don't know is that things in Chicago are different now than back in the day."

"Oh, back when Chicago was a workingman's paradise?"

"I ain't sayin' that Chicago was a working man's paradise. But there were plenty of good union jobs. The fact is, Klonsky, I had some good jobs. And my buddies did, too."

Tony tossed back his head and emptied the inch of brew left in the bottle and then lifted his bottle toward Marty as if he was making a toast.

I finished mine as well.

"Hey, Marty. Can we get another? I'm about to hear a story."

Laughing, Marty called back, "Let me get you two and save a couple cold. Tony can take a while once he gets started telling his life story."

"Listen, Klonsky. Back in the day every Chicago neighborhood had four things: a church, a school, a bar, and a factory. When I graduated from Waller in 1973 I got a job at Rock-Ola over on the West Side. They made juke boxes and vending machines. I worked on the third floor pop machine line.

"My buddy Billy Mack went to work at Schwinn bicycles over by North Avenue and Pulaski.

"I dated Mary who lived over by the Lathrop. She graduated from Amundsen. She went to work at Stewart-Warner making auto parts. Stewart-Warner was a block from her home. She just had to roll out of bed and she'd be on the line making stuff. After work the two of us would head for the bar across the street. On the corner of George and Leavitt, I think. Or to The Slammer across from the police station over by Belmont. That was some rough joint."

"There was a factory at George and Leavitt? Those are condos now," I said.

"That's what I'm talkin' about.

"Mary and me, we dated for a couple of years. We'd used phony IDs 'cause we was under age. On Friday nights we headed over to the F & Z on Milwaukee Avenue and California to hear some country bands.

"One night there was a band covering Johnny Cash's 'Folsom Prison Blues.' They used the N word in the line, 'I shot a man in Reno just to watch him die.' A fight broke out. Actually, I may have thrown the first punch, but I don't exactly remember. Although I know Mary kicked some butt. She was never one to put up with that shit about people.

"I had another buddy. Jaime. He grew up on the East Side over by the mills. Went to work at South Works as soon as he graduated from South Shore. That was back when they was just beginning to hire Mexicans and Black people into skilled jobs. And they was hiring women too. Skilled jobs I'm talkin' about."

"Where are you taking me with this history lesson, Tony?"

"Don't rush me, Klonsky. I'm developing my point. See. You think everything started the day before yesterday. That's the thing about you Californians. No sense of history. You're from LA. To you, a McDonald's with a Mansard roof and a single drive-thru lane should be protected as a historical site. But Chicago has history.

"Take the schools, Klonsky. You are all active in the school shit now. Right? But there's a lot you weren't around for. I was here for the boycott back in '63. Old man Daley wanted to keep the schools segregated. So they put up these trailers. Black folks called them Willis Wagons after Benjamin Willis who was Daley's school boss. They kept adding these trailers, putting them on the playgrounds of schools. It was just to keep the attendance districts all-Black and all-White."

I turned to Marty. "I think I'm ready for the next one."

"Told you." Marty shrugged.

"I'm just sayin'. Chicago was a working-class town since before it burned down."

"Now? Not so much," I said. "I read just the other day. Three hundred thousand Black people have moved away in the past ten years. Gone. Not just from Chicago. From all around here. Gone because the jobs are gone. Working-class jobs. Union jobs. Good paying jobs that they weren't even allowed to have until the 1960s and 1970s."

Tony nodded. "Now it's service jobs. Minimum-wage jobs."

"You were talking about schools," I reminded Tony.

"I still am. It's like my cousin Billy always says, 'He not busy being born is busy dying.'"

"That was Bob Dylan," I corrected.

"Right. Cousin Bobby. I forget there for a second."

"Bob Dylan's not your cousin."

"If you say so. I'm just making the point that the city has changed. The schools are gonna change. For good or for bad."

I lifted my head to look at Tony. "But who is gonna decide how? And who is gonna decide who the change is good for?"

"Food for thought, my friend. And speaking of food, may I buy you dinner?" Tony looked over to Marty. "Hey, Marty. Got any of those potato chips I like?"

"Nah. We don't carry them anymore. They got bought by a snack mega-conglomerate out of LA," said Marty.

Illustration by Ryan Alexander-Tanner

Part III

THE HARMONY OF BALANCE

In this final part, we return to the primal contradiction we discussed in the introduction: chaos and structure, feminine energy and masculine energy. It is the contradiction represented by the ancient symbol of yin and yang. The generative power of these energies in balance is the source of all things, as nothing exists without its opposite. Such is their interdependence that in truth they are one and the same; the opposite of a profound truth is another profound truth. To hold them both in balance is the highest aim of human understanding.

Bill Ayers has demonstrated in his life and in his work that there is one way to get there: by diving into the contradictions. Through the actions of his younger years, he became for the nation a symbol of (for many, the worst of) what fire energy's hot anger can inspire. For those who know him, personally and/or through his writings, he is a model of the cooling, healing power of water energy. Not to say that these are stages of Bill's life. He is as fiery and passionate today as he ever was in standing up for justice, but he also, like water, finds the lowest point of common ground with others, softening the rough edges with forgiveness.

The essays in this part reflect this balancing of energies, when the heat and passion of fire are tempered by the cooling flow of water. This is not numbness, not the absence of feeling. As you'll see, the authors in this part feel the anger that the current educational and political landscape calls out of any emotionally alive person (just take a look at a couple of the titles!). That rage is experienced in full, then, as it cools, it is allowed to flow naturally into meaningful action in the world. Through the union of fire and water energy, the writers of these chapters dive into and reconcile some of the most powerful contradictions in teaching: the contradictions within.

In "Black Education for Human Freedom," Joyce E. King provides both wise counsel and a call to action to the African American community. She begins, though, with an invitation to explore a highly contradictory, and deeply painful, aspect of our human history. She explains that only by coming to terms with slavery will we gain the understanding that will allow us to feel the family connections uniting the whole of the African Diaspora.

Gloria Ladson-Billings in "When Did Teachers Become the Enemy?" first expresses the anger that educators have experienced in the face of our public vilification. In flowing beyond that emotional reaction, she looks with hope to the qualities of successful teachers of African American students. She presents an honest and realistic picture of the challenges facing teachers, but ultimately affirms her faith in the strength of those who are called to teach.

Her message of hope is echoed by Sonia Nieto in "Working for the Common Good." While looking at the world with similarly open eyes, Nieto also is struck more powerfully by the good that she sees in schools. She shares the stories of particular teachers who embody the characteristics described in the prior chapter, as well as the harmony of contradictions reconciled—in one case even inscribed on the teacher's corporeal body.

The focus shifts again in W. J. T. Mitchell's "Teachable Moments," this time from the outer world to the inner. By narrating his own internal growth as a teacher, the author makes clear just how myriad are the contradictions we face—even before we open the classroom door. However, his honesty and openness also provide a user's guide to diving in, demonstrating how examining each new discrepancy in our person and our practice leads to further growth in a dialectic process.

As is evident from the title, "'It's a Strange World—Some Get Rich and Others Eat Shit and Die,'" David Stovall is not unacquainted with fire energy. But his essay, like Mitchell's, cites Bill Ayers's help in reconciling the inner conflicts of a teacher. As an educator for justice in an unjust world, Stovall has dived into and reconciled, with help from Bill, some of the contradictions of being human and working with other human beings, bringing an uncommon depth and power to his scholarship and activism.

Finally, the last chapter, Rashid Khalidi's "Personal Reflections About Bill Ayers," provides a glimpse of what keeps Bill in balance. We see him as a husband, as a father, and as a friend. Here, we sense, is the wellspring of the cooling waters; here is the life-giving spark. It is a beautiful image on which to close, reminding us that, as much as Bill has given each of us, there is still more to learn, still more to love.

17

Black Education for Human Freedom

Of the African Renaissance and History in the Present

Joyce E. King

> The only question that concerns us here is whether these educated
> persons are actually equipped to face the ordeal before them or
> unconsciously contribute to their own undoing by perpetuating the
> regime of the oppressor.
>
> —Carter G. Woodson, *The Mis-Education of the Negro*, 1933

It is still quite common to hear assertions (by scholars) that as a result of
our enslavement and brutal separation from our African origins, Black
peoples in the Diaspora have experienced a "loss of self," and therefore
any identification with Africa, African values, and cultural practices has
been obliterated. This school of thought persists, misinformed by certain
Euro-centered scholarship as well as the popular imagination nurtured by
White supremacy ideology. African-centered scholarship and the discipline
of Black Studies, however, provide substantial evidence to the contrary
and demonstrate that what Africans in the Diaspora have experienced is
not self-loss but *dislocation* (Asante, 2009). Carter G. Woodson (1933)
attributed the cause to our miseducation. Thus, the educational task is
to *uncover and restore hidden connections* in order to correct distortions
and omissions that can aid in the recuperation and healing of our African
minds, identity, and spirit (Carruthers, 1999). This educational task rests
on four premises:

First Premise: Truthful, equitable, and culturally appropriate
  education is understood to be a basic human right, and not only

is a condition of Black people's individual dignity and collective survival, but also is fundamental to civilization and human freedom for everyone, irrespective of race and culture.

Second Premise: People of African ancestry share broad cultural continuities, and our survival as an ethnic family, our quintessential peoplehood, is at stake in educational and socialization processes.

Third Premise: Black education has been over-studied from deficit (e.g., "loss of self") perspectives that negatively influence various educational practices, including current tests and standards. These practices represent and betray the very same "sin of omission" that characterizes literature and perspectives that deem contemporary Africans—both in the Diaspora and on the Continent—as relatively insignificant in human history until the advent of Western slavery.

Fourth Premise: Formal education has been structured around ideological pedagogical knowledge for the purposes of miseducation in order to elevate and maintain the control and power of dominant groups.

The education struggle in the United States since the 1960s has included establishing Black studies and Africana studies departments in colleges and universities, and spearheading research, knowledge production, and the development of corrective and inclusive curriculum materials for schools at all levels. The implementation of a high-stakes testing regime—for students and teachers under the banner of "quality" education—has sidelined these educational contributions. My colleagues and I have produced groundbreaking research and scholarship on Black education (Goodwin & King, 2010; King, 1996, 2005, 2006; Wynter, 1990) that we have determined are foundational for education for human freedom. Our work includes *Criterion Standards*, such as the eight examples presented below, that can be used in teacher preparation, parent education, curriculum and textbook development, as well as (standards-based) instruction in classrooms and community settings.

- African humanity and civilization are anterior in the recorded history of the world. Classical Africa was a primary influence on European growth, development, and civilization. (#1)
- African diasporan histories begin in Africa with human history, not with the period of enslavement. (#2)
- African people's heritage includes the African presence in Asia, Europe, [and] the Americas, including Canada, the Caribbean,

Mexico, and South America. An accurate history of the experience of people of African descent includes interactions with other groups. (#3)

- African descent people are one people, continental and diasporic. There is a cultural unity across diasporan communities as well as a common experience of domination, disenfranchisement, and social/political/economic inequalities. (#5)
- The Transatlantic "slave trade" is the foundational base for European and American growth and economic development. The enslavement of African peoples and the exploitation of their labor, socioeconomic knowledge, and technical expertise were as important to the economic wealth in the northern colonies and states as in the American South. (#7)
- The appropriation of African and diasporic forms of cultural expression is the basis of much of what has created a distinguishing U.S. cultural character (e.g., art and architecture, cuisine, music, dance, design, invention, education reforms, language, fashion). (#8)
- African people have resisted domination and oppression from the earliest period of enslavement. Resistance by African descent people to racism and oppression continues and has taken many social, political, economic, and cultural forms, including self-determination, spiritual resilience, and agency in education, cultural expression, and community building (e.g., mutual aid societies, benevolent associations, social movements, fraternal lodges, Freedom schools, Kwanzaa, Rites of Passage). (#9)
- The indigenous African worldview is embedded in African language, which is the key needed to unlock the stranglehold of external interpretations of African people's history and culture. The stranglehold includes interpretations of African domestic systems of servitude, spirituality, and governance. (#11) (Goodwin & King, 2010)

African Languages and the African Renaissance

African underdevelopment must be a matter of concern to everybody else in the world . . . the victory of the African Renaissance addresses not only the improvement of the conditions of life of the peoples of Africa but also the extension of the frontiers of human dignity to all humanity.

—Thabo Mbeki, "The African Renaissance, South Africa and the World," 1998

African languages are foundational in the reclamation of African identity and consciousness—for those in the Diaspora and on the continent as well (Maiga, 2005). We are all victimized by dehumanizing concepts and ideas about the inferiority of "blackness," Africa, and the heritage of people of African ancestry, and the superiority of all that is European (and White). For example, in English and other European languages, the idea of "blackness" is fundamentally negative (e.g., "black sheep," "blacklisted," "blackballed," etc.), as compared with what "whiteness" usually means (e.g., pure, goodness, not bad, a "white lie," etc.). However, in the Songhay language (Songhay-Senni),"blackness" is fundamentally positive (e.g., *"wayne bibi"*—"black sun"—when the sun reaches its fullest expansion and highest point of the day; or *"hari bibi"*—"black water"—the most potable, cleanest water in the deepest area of the Niger River that is far from the shore) (Maiga, 2005). Thus, language provides access to a people's culture and worldview perspective.

African languages are foundational for contextualized teaching and learning about people of African descent. Using the indigenous Songhay language term for "slave" makes it possible to interpret and distinguish the African practice of domestic servitude from the institution of chattel slavery. In Songhay-Senni, *"barnya"* means "slave"—or "the one who does not even have a mother," to be more precise (Maiga, 2010). Prior to the arrival of Europeans (or Arabs), lineage-based domestic servitude existed on the African continent (Miller, 1988). People who had lost their "freedom" as a result of being taken captive in war or as punishment for a crime generally no longer had the protection of their clan or lineage—their mother's people (Wynter, 1990).

The historian Basil Davidson (1961) compared this system of lineage-based domestic servitude in Africa with the forms of un-freedom that existed in medieval Europe. He suggested that more research was needed to understand the African experience of "slavery" from the point of view of the African mindset (King, 1992). Might our ancestors who had been kidnapped and made chattel slaves have retained this cultural memory when they sang the spiritual: "Sometimes I feel like a motherless child, a l-o-o-o-n-g way from home"? That there is no indigenous word for "prison" in the Songhay language (and other languages of West Africa) is also instructive. This kind of deciphering analysis and interpretation of African people's experience is possible when continental and Diaspora Africans work together to examine and reconnect our lived experiences—within the terms of our own cultural reality.

Thus, there is a potential for dislocation when we use the European term *Renaissance* (French for "rebirth") uncritically as a reference point and model to inspire and revive the formation of the United States of

Africa envisioned by great Pan-Africanists like Kwame Nkrumah, Sekou Touré, Modibo Keita, W.E.B. Du Bois, Cheikh Anta Diop, Queen Mother Audley Moore, and Marcus Garvey (Mbeki, 1998). Rather than referencing the achievements of the Medici family and Leonardo da Vinci in 14th-century Italy as models of cultural excellence, or the emergence of Western European humanism based on the "stolen legacies" of ancient Greece and Rome, which Aimé Césaire (2001) rightly critiqued, the Pan-African challenge might be better understood within our own African terms and concepts. For example, *Wehem mesut* ("repetition of births") refers to the Renaissance Era of ancient Egypt (Kemet). Another relevant concept is *Alasaal-Tarey* in the Songhay language: "the process through which we understand our origins as human beings in order to serve humanity" (Maiga, 2010). For Diaspora Africans, of course, the 1920s Harlem Renaissance and the Négritude movement it helped to inspire exemplify our tradition of *reconnecting* with our great heritage for African unity. The ancient Nubian Renaissance and the restoration of the Kushite presence in Kemet ("the Black Land") are other examples. I am inspired by the words of Hatshepsut ("Foremost of Noble Women"), the fifth Pharaoh of the 18th Dynasty of Egypt, who said:

I have restored that that which was in ruins.
I have raised up that which was destroyed. . .
     —Inscription on the walls of Djeser-Djeseru, Nile Valley

We are indeed the "first civilizers" of humanity. Recognizing and affirming Africa's anteriority and cultural unity imply neither a perverse form of reverse cultural superiority nor divisive separatism. For as Aimé Césaire observed during the First World Festival of Negro Arts, "If anything, Négritude is more necessary today than ever. It has moral and ethical implications that *should concern everyone*. It must be valid for the whole Negro world" (quoted in Kennedy, 1968, emphasis added).

For the benefit of Africa's people in all Six Regions (North, South, East, West, Central, and the Diaspora) designated by the African Union, and with regard to human freedom from anti-African ideological thought, we turn our attention to both the centrality of culture as well as the role of cultural diversity in our development, which African humanism—"a true humanism . . . made to the measure of the world"—has long recognized (Césaire, 2001). The following Criterion Standard offers a relevant perspective:

Africa's known mineral wealth and other natural resources place it among the world's richest continents. This remains so, in spite of successive periods of foreign occupation, imperialism, enslavement, and colonialism spanning millennia. The corresponding disconnect between African people and their resources is a key contributing factor to the continuing poverty and disempowerment experienced by African nations and African descent people in other countries. And the disconnect of Africa's human and natural resources from diasporic human and economic resources obstructs the self-actualization of each, while enriching the architects of this separation. Access to and control of African resources is central to foreign and domestic policy agendas of the world's industrial nations and is a major factor in limiting Africa's ability to achieve economic and political independence. (#19) (Goodwin & King, 2010)

Therefore, what and how we teach about Africa and people of African descent, in the Diaspora and on the Motherland, needs to be changed to reflect our Pan-African priorities within the context of a "true humanism."

Lest We Forget: The History That Is in the Present

Our ancestors did not wade through rivers of blood so that we might surrender the interpretation of their lives into the hands of others.

—Vincent Harding, *There Is a River*, 1981

In order for us as poor and oppressed people to become a part of a society that is meaningful, the system under which we now exist has to be radically changed.

—Ella J. Baker, 1969

We must recognize, however, that none of us is truly "developed" unless we are all freed from what degrades African people and denies our humanity. In that regard, miseducation, particularly when it comes to teaching and learning about "slavery," has been most harmful.

We start our story not with slavery but with human history in Africa and our humanity as African people. This is what my teacher and friend, the great scholar Asa G. Hilliard, III–Nana Baffour Amankwatia, II, insisted is paramount in our work as educators. At the same time, we do have to remember what slavery was in order to know the truth about what has happened to us and where we go from here. There can be no true African Renaissance without this understanding.

I am a daughter of those enslaved Africans who were kidnapped and brought to the Americas. I remember the stories told in my family about slavery. But for the most part, we experience ourselves, our history, and our identity through lies told to us and about us that make us feel ashamed. Meanwhile, those who perpetrated and benefited from these crimes against us go about feeling superior with their heads held high. In addition to the evidence of humanity's origins in Africa, another magnificent truth is that African people are "one big family." However, that reality is undermined by one of the most pernicious ways that our history has been used to divide African people (and relieve others of historical responsibility): what our textbooks teach us about "slavery." In school we learn from teachers and textbooks that there never would have been any enslavement if "Africans had not sold their *own* brothers and sisters into slavery" (King, 1996). This specious ideological justification for slavery has left a gaping wound in our souls. *Who among us would want to be African when we are taught that is what has been done to us?* Our response as Black intellectuals and Black studies scholars has been to develop contextualized teaching materials that provide a truthful analysis of this historical dynamic. The point is to examine the indigenous African experience of domestic servitude and enslavement before, during, and after Arab and European domination from the perspective of African peoples' mindset as well as that of the enslavers and colonizers (King, 1992, 2005, 2006).

Let me share an experience I had in East Africa—in Nairobi, Kenya, in 1985 when I attended the U.N. Decade of Women conference. In Nairobi I met a student who was attending a play at the university with his aunt, who was about my age. They invited me home with them to meet the rest of the family. After several evenings at their home, they also invited me to go with them to visit their grandfather in Pumwani—one of the poorest sections of the city. When we entered the elder's home, he greeted everyone; he thought I was from somewhere right there in Kenya. The family quickly told him that I was from the United States. Now, this elderly grandfather, living in the biggest so-called "slum" in the city, who had no formal education, and who had not studied African history or Black history, started to weep. Through tears, the old grandfather looked directly at me and said, "Thank God! One of our daughters has come home." He explained how happy he was that one of the "lost ones" had come *home.* "You should feel proud," he said. "Don't ever feel ashamed of what has happened to you because you have a home here."

"One of *our* daughters has come home." With this simple declaration, this ordinary African elder, living among the poorest, most downtrodden, least "educated" people in the great city of Nairobi, expressed the essence of African people's humanity: the uninterrupted, unqualified, and profound importance of our family feeling, the importance of children down through the generations, and an utterly spontaneous affirmation that wherever we have ended up, we are still at home in Africa—where we still *belong* as African people.

What, on the other hand, was slavery that it has made us feel so ashamed in the world that Europeans created and brought us to in the Diaspora? In *The Spirituals and the Blues*, the theologian James Cone (1972) tells us that slavery

> meant being snatched from your homeland in a stinking ship . . . being regarded as property . . . working fifteen to twenty hours a day and being beaten for showing fatigue. . . . It meant being whipped for crying over a fellow slave who had been killed for trying to escape. (p. 21)

We have endured the slave ship that was our ancestors' floating prison; the incarceration of generations in the cotton, rice, tobacco, and indigo fields that produced the wealth of Europe and the Americas; and the 21st-century modern slave ship that the New Orleans Superdome became for our people who were abandoned there during Hurricane Katrina (Rediker, 2007). In the United States today, a cradle-to-prison mass-incarceration policy imprisons a greater proportion of this society's population than that of any other nation, and the rate of imprisonment for Black women is higher than for any other group (Perkinson, 2010). *Will it require a United States of Africa to undo our dispossession and end our oppression?*

Commentary and Reflections

> For I am my mother's daughter and the drums of Africa still beat in my heart. They will not let me rest while there is a single Negro boy or girl without a chance to prove his worth.
>
> —Mary McLeod Bethune, "Faith that Moved a Dump Heap," 1941

In the paper I presented at the Third World Festival of Black Arts (FESMAN) in Dakar, Senegal, the continental Africans with whom I shared the above story seemed to have been moved most deeply by my experience with the elder grandfather in Nairobi who welcomed me home. Their comments expressed some degree of *emotional* relief, saying that I "spoke the truth" and "said what needed to be said." That an African *elder* had spoken such healing words for the pain of what has happened also seemed to offer added cultural validation—or even vindication—for them.

On a slightly different but also emotional note, a Senegalese sister traveling on the flight with me from New York told me of *her* pain as a mother raising her daughter in the United States. She said Black American youngsters used to beat up her daughter in school—traumatizing her with the taunt: "Go back to the jungle." She thanked me for calling attention to the need to educate all of our children about their African heritage.

Another sister at the festival, a former African ambassador in Europe, was also very eager to tell me about the annual *Zomachi* ceremony of "repentance" organized by people in Benin, to acknowledge their part in the "slave routes" (www.idee-benin.com). Although we were speaking in English, when I mentioned how Black children in the United States have been made to feel ashamed of being African and are called names like "jungle bunnies," this world-traveled diplomat, unlike the Senegalese sister, had absolutely no clue about what these racially insulting words meant. (Many continental Africans whom I have met report knowing little about racism in the United States.)

Finally, a Fulani bookseller from the Niger Republic, pointing first to his ear, then to his chest, said my words went *directly* from the ear to the heart. When I asked why, he said, "Your voice." What about my voice? He said, "It's not often that Africans have a chance to hear a woman speak aloud so forcefully and with such confidence and conviction. Women are sometimes shy around men and do not speak up" [*his opinion*]. I told him my mother always said that when you are speaking to people, make sure that your voice really carries. His parting advice: "Keep doing what your mother said." He thanked me again and I thanked him as we said good-bye.

My point in sharing these reflections is that educators need opportunities to give concerted attention to teaching and writing about these sensitive and historically complex issues. This is actually the focus of much of my research and scholarship in collaboration with colleagues in the United States, Mali (Maiga, 2005), Brazil (King et al., 2011), Senegal (Seck, 2005), and other Diaspora contexts. Do we even know the words to use to unlock the stranglehold of the legacy of slavery, colonialism, and historical division and dispossession on our identities and consciousness in our various academic disciplines and social/historical contexts (e.g., Mexico, Turkey, Canada, Jamaica, the U.K., etc.)? How do we address these issues effectively with our children, "other people's children," teachers, parents, the broader public, civic leaders, or policymakers to convey what is wrong with our education and what we need to do to fix it? Can we, as emancipatory educators, construct what J.G.A. Pocock (1989) calls a "public language" that employs a tone and tenor of conscientious accountability for our own wrongs and the paths toward healing, first, ourselves, while we design enough de-ideologized spiritual and psychosocial space for setting right the wrongs done against us through White supremacy racism and colonization (Martín-Baró, 1996)? The challenge becomes more complex across national borders and cultural contexts even among African descent people within our "one big family."

African American scholars (and scholarship) have a certain advantage to offer with regard to this Pan-African agenda and challenge to discover how African people can recover our consciousness and use our knowledge—on our own cultural terms—to build the United States of Africa together. We must work to affirm our similarities and shared concerns in myriad ways, while also exploring important differences in our experiences. Perhaps this is reflected in the Ghanaian Ashanti/Adrinka symbol for unity in diversity: *Funtunfunefu-Denkyemfunefu*—the two-headed crocodile that fights for food eventually going to the same stomach. Our collective history and destiny, and human freedom hang in the precarious balance.

Funtunfunefu-Denkyemfunefu

References

Asante, M. K. (2009). *Erasing racism: The survival of the American nation.* Amherst, NY: Prometheus Books.

Césaire, A. (2001). *Discourse on colonialism.* New York, NY: Monthly Review Press. (Original work published 1972)

Carruthers, J. H. (1999). *Intellectual warfare.* Chicago, IL: Third World Press.

Cone, J. H. (1972). *The spirituals and the blues: An interpretation.* Maryknoll, NY: Orbis Books.

Davidson, B. (1961). *Black mother.* Boston, MA: Little, Brown.

Goodwin, S., & King, J. (2010). *Criterion standards for contextualized teaching & learning about people of African descent.* Rochester, NY/Atlanta, GA: Rochester Teacher Center/Academy for Diaspora Literacy.

Harding, V. (1981). *There is a river: The Black struggle for freedom in America.* Orlando, FL: Harcourt Brace.

Kennedy, E. C. (1968). Aimé Césaire (An interview). *Negro Digest*, pp. 53–61.

King, J. (1992). Diaspora literacy and consciousness in the struggle against miseducation in the Black community. *Journal of Negro Education, 61*(3), 317–340.

King, J. (1996). The Middle Passage revisited: Education for human freedom and the Black studies epistemological critique. In L. H. Da Silva et al. (Eds.), *Novos mapas culturais: Novas perspectivas educacionais [New cultural maps: New education perspectives]* (pp. 75–101). Porto Alegre, Brazil: Editor Sulina.

King, J. (Ed.). (2005). *Black education: A transformative research and action agenda for the new century.* New York, NY: Routledge.

King, J. (2006). "If justice is our objective": Diaspora literacy, heritage knowledge and the praxis of critical studyin' for human freedom. In A. Ball (Ed.), *With more deliberate speed: Achieving equity and excellence in education—Realizing the full potential of Brown v. Board of Education* (National Society for the Study of Education 105th yearbook, Part 2, pp. 337–360). New York, NY: Ballenger.

King, J., Vaughn, M. S., Gonçalves e Silva, P. B., Conceição, R., Rodrigues, T. C., & Oliveira, E. R. (2011). Engaged research/ers, transformative curriculum and diversity policy for teacher education in the Americas: The U.S., Brazil and Belize. In B. Lindsay & W. Blanchard (Eds.), *Universities and global diversity: Preparing educators for tomorrow* (pp. 205–226). New York, NY: Routledge.

Maiga, H. (2005). When the language of education is not the language of culture: The epistemology of systems of knowledge and pedagogy. In J. King (Ed.), *Black education: A transformative research and action agenda for the new century* (pp. 159–182). New York, NY: Routledge.

Maiga, H. (2010). *Balancing written history with oral tradition: The legacy of the Songhay people.* New York, NY: Routledge.

Martín-Baró, I. (1996). *Writings for a liberation psychology.* Cambridge, MA: Harvard University Press.

Mbeki, T. (1998). *The African renaissance, South Africa and the world*. Retrieved from archive.unu.edu/unupress/mbeki.html

Miller, J. C. (1988). *Way of death: Merchant capitalism and the Angolan slave trade, 1830–1830*. Madison: University of Wisconsin Press.

Perkinson, R. (2010). *Texas tough: The rise of America's prison empire*. New York, NY: Metropolitan Books.

Pocock, J. G. A. (1989). *Politics, language & time: Essays on political thought and history*. Chicago, IL: University of Chicago Press.

Rediker, M. (2007). *The slave ship: A human history*. New York, NY: Penguin Books.

Seck, I. (2005). Worldwide conspiracy against Black culture and education. In J. King (Ed.), *Black education: A transformative research and action agenda for the new century* (pp. 285–290). New York, NY: Routledge.

Woodson, C. G. (1933). *The mis-education of the Negro*. Washington, DC: Associated Publishers.

Wynter, S. (1990). *"Do not call us Negroes": How multicultural textbooks perpetuate the ideology of racism*. San Francisco, CA: Aspire Books.

18

When Did Teachers Become the Enemy?

Gloria Ladson-Billings

In a recent Harris Poll of U.S. adults, teachers were tied with scientists as the second most prestigious professionals. Only firefighters ranked higher. The professions listed after teachers were doctors, military officers, nurses, police officers, priests, ministers or clergy, farmers, and engineers. The 10 lowest prestige professions were real estate agents/brokers, actors, bankers, accountants, entertainers, stockbrokers, journalists, union leaders, business executives, and athletes. Now to be clear, the survey was not of the most highly paid professions, because there seems to be something of an inverse relationship between prestige and money in this survey. What puzzles me about the place of teachers on the high-prestige list is the nagging feeling that teachers somehow have become the new enemy. I imagine that the fact that union leaders appear on the low-prestige list has something to do with how we have come to see today's teacher. Now, perhaps I am given to hyperbole, but I'd like to walk through what I see as a brief look at the transformation of the teacher from hero to goat. I attempt to trace this transformation by responding to two contradictory ideas about teaching—that teachers are the source of the problem and that teachers are the solution to the problem.

Teachers as the Source of the Problem

You may recall that in 1983 then-President Ronald Reagan's Commission on Excellence in Education published its report *A Nation at Risk*. We were told in the report that the primary problems with education in our country were the fragmented and weak curriculum, the lack of regular and standard assessments, the limited amount of time on task, and the teaching—particularly teacher preparation and those who select teaching as a profession. Out of the identification of that set of problems we got a more standards-based curriculum (even a scripted one in some cases), constant standardized testing, the elimination of recess, and the paradox of increased teacher preparation requirements in traditional teacher education programs and the limited preparation for those who choose to go into teaching through alternative means.

We regularly hear how the single most important aspect of a student's education is the teacher standing in his or her classroom. And I agree that teachers are extremely important in ensuring the quality of students' education. But in a knowledge economy where information comes from all directions and the ability to access that information is either helped or hindered by external forces, we cannot place the entire onus for educational success on teachers. If teachers are the sole variable, then we must be admitting that we have put all of the best teachers in the suburbs and the worst ones in the cities and rural communities. Were this the case, the simple solution would be relocation! But we know better. We are dealing with an incredible set of complexities. If we look nationally, we can see that our children are living under some of the most stressful conditions imaginable (data from the Children's Defense Fund website: www.childrensdefensefund.org).

- One in two will live in a single-parent family at some point in childhood.
- One in three is born to unmarried parents.
- One in three will be poor at some point in his or her childhood.
- One in three is behind a year or more in school.
- Two in five never complete a single year of college.
- One in seven has a worker in his or her family but is still poor.
- One in eight never graduates from high school.
- One in five was born poor.
- One in five is born to a mother who did not graduate from high school.
- One in seven has no health care.
- One in 24 lives with neither parent.
- One in 139 will die before his or her first birthday.
- One in 1,056 will be killed by a gun before age 20.

How much ownership can the classroom teacher take for a society that has allowed its children to face such steep odds? I believe that teachers have been made to be the problem because they represent the low-hanging fruit. Talking about broad social policy seems too complex, and we have spent decades, indeed centuries, systematically disadvantaging entire groups of students. The easiest target becomes the teacher and the big, bad union.

Have you noticed how the discourse about teachers now runs? It appears something like this: Some fresh-faced, but not very bright, young people set out to teach. We place them in outdated, weak teacher preparation programs where they waste hours learning how to teach instead of learning more subject matter, and once they get out of school they head to districts where the first thing they are asked to do is sign up with the union. After 2 or 3 years, they earn tenure and now they have jobs for life. Because of their seniority they can't be fired, and some other young, enthusiastic, innovative new teachers can't replace them. Does that sound like a familiar narrative? I know it's one I keep hearing. Unfortunately, it is a poor approximation of the truth.

First, the problem of recruiting outstanding teacher candidates is a real one. Today's young people have so many more career choices, and those careers that offer more lucrative remuneration also offer the most attractive pre-professional recruiting options. For example, when students at my own university are admitted into our engineering program, they often receive outstanding financial packages, summer internships, and job placements. Over at the education school, we have few resources to offer prospective students. Our students pay their own way, go to school and work, and/or take out expensive education loans.

Next, the question of tenure is an interesting one. Teachers cannot give themselves tenure. Some administrator has to verify their competence. The job of the union is to ensure that dismissals are not arbitrary or capricious. A failure to "get rid of" a teacher generally reflects a failure to fully document performance. That part of the story seemingly has not made its way into the grand narrative on teachers. Finally, who are these young, energetic teachers that we are depriving of an opportunity to teach in favor of old, washed-up, tenured dinosaurs? They can't be those not-so-bright, weak candidates with which we started the narrative. They must be the crew of alternatively certified teachers with a 6-week preparation program. Unfortunately, their track record is not nearly as good as some are claiming. In Louisiana, they remain at a rate of about 4% compared with traditionally prepared teachers, who stay at a rate of 40%. Neither number is adequate, but the difference between 4 and 40 is startling. And, we also know that if a district constantly hires brand-new teachers, it reduces its upfront costs, because they are hired at the first rung of the salary schedule.

It is also important to point out that no other professional field or industry would dream of pushing its most experienced people out of the door and expect to remain at the top. The best schools in our nation have incredible stability. At one of the successful urban schools I visited years ago, when I was researching successful teachers of African American students, I learned that the average teacher tenure there was 14 years. This new chant of let's do something about "last hired, first fired" is a ploy that attempts to exploit the language of civil rights and make the public believe that teachers and their unions stand in the way of progress.

Teachers are no more the source of the problem than your umbrella is the cause of rain. No made-up story about bad old teachers and good young ones can change the social realities of students' lives. We, as a society, have to make a decision to state a commitment to care for the "least of these" before we can expect our students to reach their full potential, not just as students but as citizens and human beings.

Teachers as the Solution

So, if we cannot place all of the blame at the feet of teachers, does that mean we can position teachers as the solution? I would argue that we cannot, but the same grand narrative that drives the notion of teacher-as-villain is at work when we decide that teachers are the heroes. The place where we most see this narrative at work is in Hollywood. Film depictions of teachers almost always carry the same storyline—the school is horrible, the administrator is horrible, the parents are horrible, and often the kids are horrible, until one spectacular teacher shows up and turns things around. This teacher is a loner and the *only* one who cares in the entire building. This teacher fights the administrator, the parents, and her other colleagues. Often this teacher has received minimal if any teacher preparation. Stories like *Dangerous Minds*, *Music of the Heart*, and *Freedom Writers* are examples of this genre.

In this narrative, we have to see that the good teacher is the exception to the rule. This way we do not disturb the ongoing narrative of teacher inferiority. This narrative posits one lone teacher who is set down in an entirely dysfunctional school. Her colleagues are unprofessional and uncaring. Before she arrived no one exhibited any concern for the students. Her teacher colleagues, parents, and virtually every other adult have abandoned the students. The other teachers think of them as unteachable "savages." Because of her superior morality this teacher is able to do what no other teacher has ever done. She persists where others gave up. She succeeds where others failed. And wait, she not only improves students' academic lives, she improves their home lives. She gets recalcitrant parents to step up to their responsibilities. She challenges drug dealers and gang bangers. She is, in a word, the students' savior!

It is this unrealistic and simplistic portrait of the teacher that is plaguing the profession. If you are not some sort of superhero, then you cannot be seen as a good teacher. And, you certainly cannot be a superhero in concert with other teachers. You distinguish yourself by being "not like the others." I find that characterization especially troubling since it is one that African Americans in our society who are seen as achievers regularly confront. The notion that some of us are special, exceptional, and different from the others demeans the contributions of our families, communities, and cultures in shaping who and how we are. Similarly, the set-apart teacher is used to condemn and discredit her colleagues. Her so-called exceptionality is used to reinforce the belief that others are just lazy or don't care. We quickly forget, however, that the exceptional teacher also had teachers. Someone assisted her along the way. She learned to teach from a combination of experience and careful guidance. Someone else gave her a vision of what it is to be a teacher.

Breaking Through the Prevailing Discourse

In my work on effective teachers of African American students, I learned that there are a number of outstanding teachers whom most of the public never hear about. They are not perfect, but they are the kinds of teachers any of us would be proud to have our own children experience. Although they choose a variety of teaching strategies and approaches, these outstanding teachers appear to have some other beliefs and dispositions in common that make them effective. Martin Haberman (1995) calls them "star teachers." They are identified by a number of qualities, including:

- *Persistence:* They are unwilling to give up on students—even the most oppositional or recalcitrant ones. They believe that in order to get results, you have to stick with it—often for a longer period than others would. Most urban students who have not met with success will tell you that somewhere along the line, someone gave up on them.
- *Protecting Learners and Learning:* Effective teachers recognize that the central enterprise of schooling is teaching and learning, so they avoid activities that detract from that mission. They don't waste time on anything else because they know that what they have to offer students is different from what anyone else in their lives has to offer.

- *Theory into Practice:* Effective teachers never talk about some aspect of education research as "too theoretical." Rather, they ask themselves: How do I put that theoretical idea into practice? If the theory says that punishment does not work but reward does, the effective teacher looks for ways to reward the behaviors she wants to see over and over again. She is testing the theory.

- *Professional–Personal Orientation to Students:* Effective teachers know how to walk the fine line between familiarity and distance. They maintain their identity as the teacher—not the buddy, not the friend, not the pal—but they know how and when to open up and share more personal moments with students. They exhibit a genuine interest in students' lives and are willing to let students in on some of their personal life, not for prurient or exhibitionist purposes, but rather to connect with students in more meaningful ways.

- *Approach to So-Called "At-Risk" Students:* I hesitate to use the term "at-risk" to describe students because it shifts the responsibility to the vulnerable. I began this essay referencing the Commission on Excellence in Education's report *A Nation at Risk*. This brings to mind the question: How is it that we decided it's not the whole nation, but just some people who are at risk? Haberman's point is that effective teachers have a planned strategy for dealing with the academic needs of students who are likely to struggle. They do not wait until students arrive in their classes to begin trying to figure out what to do. Rather they plan scaffolding and bridging strategies so that all students recognize that they are full members of the classroom community from day one. Students are systematically helped along so they can get to grade-level performance.

- *Dealing with Bureaucracy:* All institutions have bureaucracy and all bureaucracies have ways of thwarting the true purpose of the institution. Unsuccessful teachers are thrown by the demands of the bureaucracy. They become frustrated with the paperwork, the policies, and the procedures. Effective teachers make strategic decisions about which part of the bureaucracy they will attend to. They realize that no one can be fully responsive to a bureaucracy, and any attempt to do so takes away from so many other things they need to do.

- *Fallibility:* Effective teachers are not afraid to admit that they make mistakes; by doing so they help students see their humanity. They also signal that they expect students, too, will make mistakes. These teachers help students to use their mistakes as learning experiences rather than punishing students for their mistakes.

- *Emotional and Physical Stamina:* Good teaching requires good mental and physical health. The work is grueling—full days with energetic students, late afternoons and evenings of reviewing students' work and preparing for upcoming lessons—and it is never-ending. Spending 180 days or more a year with large groups of children and youth means being regularly exposed to every germ and disease imaginable. So teachers need to keep themselves in good health with strong immune systems. Effective teachers also have to maintain good mental and emotional health. Working with students can be a rollercoaster ride. Students' life challenges find their way into the classroom, and good teachers are empathetic without losing their main focus.
- *Organizational Ability:* Good teachers know that teaching is a bit of a juggling act. So to keep all of the balls in the air, they have to be organized. They have a sense of how they want to structure learning and activities. While they may appreciate and invite spontaneity, they are not looking to create chaos. Their classrooms are places where students understand the importance of rituals, routines, relationships, and rigor.
- *Effort, Not Ability:* One of the most powerful lessons I learned from outstanding teachers is the need to convey to students (and believe themselves) that the only thing that stands between them and excellence is effort. Effective teachers do not predetermine students' potential; they help students realize that if they are willing to put in more effort they will reap more rewards. Interestingly, this "effort, not ability" perspective is exactly what we see among our international competitors whose students perform at higher levels than our students. Unfortunately, far too many Americans (and this includes teachers) believe that some people are smart and some are not. In places like Japan or Singapore, students learn that "smart" is something you become, not something you already are.

These are qualities I believe any teacher who wants to be a good teacher can learn and cultivate. He does not have to be a superman to be this kind of teacher. Rather, he has to be the kind who wants to be better. He has to be the kind of teacher who defends the profession in school and out. He has to be the kind of person who, when asked what he does for a living, is willing to say, "I do the hardest, most important work of a free society. I teach." He has to be willing to challenge his colleagues to work together to help struggling colleagues. He has to be willing to accept legitimate critique as a means of professional improvement, and he has to stand up against ad hominem attacks against teachers, no matter who levels those attacks.

A few years ago, we watched as Davis Guggenheim's film *Waiting for "Superman"* (2010) made its way onto movie screens across America. It was such a deeply flawed film that I was shocked at how much attention it received. It was filled with internal contradictions and distortions about public schools and the teachers who work in them. It used classic tropes of the poor, disenfranchised students waiting for a prized spot in a charter school. The overall message of the film was that traditional public schools are *all* bad and charter schools are good (even though the filmmaker does admit that only about 1 in 5 charter schools is judged highly effective).

My challenge to public school teachers is to refuse to accept the role of society's enemy. Refuse to be the scapegoat. Refuse to be the problem. Instead, we need teachers to be willing to go on the offensive. They must write their own editorials. They must conduct their own research. They must invite the policymakers into their classrooms so they can see for themselves what it actually takes to teach in urban schools. The job of the teacher is to work together with her colleagues to help the nation wake up and realize that teachers are not the enemy!

References

Guggenheim, D. (Director). (2010). *Waiting for "Superman"* [Motion picture]. United States: Electric Kinney Films.

Haberman, M. (1995). Selecting "star teachers" for children and youth in urban poverty. *Phi Delta Kappan, 76*(10), 777–781.

19

Working for the Common Good
Teachers, Public Education, and the Moral Imperative

Sonia Nieto

> Education can strengthen the capacity to act for the common good and to take risks on behalf of a moral vision, but only insofar as ideas about democracy and morality become part of the lived experience of young people.
>
> —Bill Ayers, *On the Side of the Child: Summerhill Revisited*, 2003

Notwithstanding the noble sentiments above, speaking about "the common good" sounds old-fashioned and out of touch with present-day educational realities. This is the case not because the common good has become an unworthy ideal, but because regardless of how worthy it is, the common good quietly and unceremoniously was abandoned as a shared value as soon as public education was redefined as a marketplace rather than a project of democratic living. Specifically, once the word *choice* entered our public conversation, the phrase *public good* pretty much disappeared (Miner, 2013). This happened in a wholesale way in the 1980s during the Reagan era, although the signs were certainly there before. Declining care for the poor and marginalized, as well as limited taxation for the wealthy have defined this neoconservative era. As a result, the role of public schools has been largely redefined as preparing young people to compete in our globalized world, with little mention of morality or even democracy.

How did we get to this point? It is a question I often think about because, as a young teacher nearly 50 years ago, it never occurred to me that public schools should be about anything other than educating all students to the highest levels possible. As is clear from a careful reading of educational history, all the progressive advances made in education—some long-lasting

Diving In, edited by Isabel Nuñez, Crystal T. Laura, & Rick Ayers. Copyright © 2014 by Teachers College, Columbia University. All rights reserved. Prior to photocopying items for classroom use, please contact the Copyright Clearance Center, Customer Service, 222 Rosewood Dr., Danvers, MA 01923, USA, tel. (978) 750-8400, www.copyright.com.

and others fleeting—have been the result of demands made by marginalized, excluded, and invisible segments of our society, not by the wealthy and privileged. These advances include the struggle for integrated schools, ethnic studies, gender-fair schooling, multicultural education, bilingual education, special education, and others (Nieto, 2005; Spring, 2012).

I do not mean to say that the public schools I attended, or the ones in which I taught, were perfect or that they did a good, or even adequate, job of educating the young people in their charge. In reality, the goal of an excellent and high-quality education, although a cherished national ideal, has remained an elusive reality for many generations (Nieto, 2005). For example, the first school in which I taught—an intermediate school in Brooklyn with a student body of Puerto Rican and African American students—was little more than a warehouse holding onto those students who could survive that bleak and discouraging place. It was a school where the retention rate of teachers (half quit each year) was even worse than that of students; where students supposedly were grouped according to their ability (6-1 to 6-13, for example, with 6-13 supposedly the students most academically challenged and disruptive); where many teachers spent their "prep period" in the teachers' room describing the students in the most negative and disparaging ways; and where young teachers, such as me, were swept up into the discourse of hopelessness and cynicism.

In spite of this context, nobody spoke about schools as a business, and even the most jaded of teachers recognized that the job of educating the next generation was, at least in theory, a noble pursuit. But who talks about these things anymore? The discourse today has become the language of business: We talk about "accountability," the "marketplace," competition, and yearly high-stakes tests for children as well as increasingly inflexible gatekeepers for teachers. Public education has been hijacked by the neoconservative Right, and the struggles in which many of us took part in the 1960s and 1970s sound like little more than Quixotic ventures.

Enter today's public school teachers: Working in a context that seems foreign to those of us who started our teaching careers decades ago, today's teachers face unprecedented surveillance and disrespect. In addition, standardization of all kinds—pedagogical, curricular, and ideological—is rampant. Given this context, what does it mean to teach for the common good? Does the connection between democracy and morality still exist?

The Moral Imperative in Teaching

Despite the current context, countless teachers across the nation find ways to teach with joy, dedication, and creativity. In the remainder of this brief essay, I want to call on a few of the teachers I have interviewed to describe what they see as the moral imperative in teaching. The examples are drawn from my recent book, *Finding Joy in Teaching Students of Diverse Backgrounds: Culturally Responsive and Socially Just Practices in U.S. Schools* (Nieto, 2013), for which I interviewed 22 pre-K–12 public school teachers who are thriving in spite of obstacles and who, just as important, are effective and caring teachers of students of diverse backgrounds.

In contrast to standardization, achievement mandates, and other instrumentalist notions about the purpose of public education, most teachers spend a great deal of time thinking about ethical issues: Who are they teaching and why? What can they do to promote not only academic learning, but also empathy, caring, and civic courage among their students? What role do they play in developing positive and inclusive attitudes in their students about their peers and, as they get older, their fellow citizens? Teachers understand that knowledge and skills are not enough if used only for individual gain.

In their interviews, the teachers described many examples of teaching with a moral perspective. They made it clear that one of the responsibilities they take most seriously is to instill in their students enduring values to help them become moral human beings with consequential lives. These include empathy and responsibility for others, values consistent with an ethic of care (Noddings, 1992; Valenzuela, 1999). For example, John Gunderson, a high school teacher in southern California, like many of the other teachers, bemoaned the exclusive focus on standardized tests that has taken over education. He was passionate in his belief that a single-minded focus on testing does not necessarily result in students leading a moral life. According to John, the purpose of education is "not [to] make them better test takers so they can play Jeopardy later in life but make them thinkers that can really make a difference. I don't want my kids to grow up being good test takers, I want them to be human" (p. 98).

Although they certainly want their students to shine intellectually, these teachers also recognize that trying to understand others who are different from themselves, and demonstrating responsibility for others, are important human values to be nurtured. An example comes from Carmen Tisdale, a teacher at Carver Lyon Elementary School in Columbia, SC. Carmen describes teaching as "hard and heavy because there's so much more to it than a book and a pencil." For her, teaching is a moral commitment because it is "much more than putting information in their heads. You're helping to form people that are going to lead this world and if you look at it that way, you take it more seriously." In fact, she rated helping to develop her students as moral human beings at the top of her list of the reasons she teaches: "I just want them to be good people and if I haven't taught them how to be good people, that's failure to me."

Another example comes from Amber Bechard, a middle school language arts teacher in Plainfield, IL, a community that has experienced a dramatic demographic shift in the past couple of decades. The school now has 32 languages represented in its student body, as well as a great diversity of racial, ethnic, and cultural backgrounds. Working with her colleagues, Amber instills values of responsibility and empathy through the curriculum. For example, after reading the memoir of Aaron Elster (Elster & Miller, 2007), a Holocaust survivor, she engaged the students in doing memoirs of their own. Later, they invited Aaron Elster to do a read-aloud of his memoir. The students took charge of the entire activity, planning the visit and placing posters throughout the school. Amber described what happened when Elster visited the school:

> Three hundred and thirty eighth graders sat in complete silence while this man walked in and [they] went into a standing ovation without being coached. Just on his arrival. Then he spoke to the class and on three occasions, he broke down in tears. (p. 52)

After his talk, 100 students purchased his book, even though they had already heard his story. Amber said, "They valued his story, they valued his message. For eighth graders to value the story of an 87-year-old man who was a 10-year-old escapee from the Polish ghetto, that was amazing" (p. 52). Yet, that was precisely the objective that she and her colleagues had in mind when creating this curriculum. Not only did the students learn Elster's story, but they also learned to think more deeply about their moral responsibility to others. As Amber said, "They left the last day of the school year with their yearbook in one hand and their memoir in the other, and they valued who they were, and they valued their stories" (p. 52). This was true even of the boys, she said, who one might think would not care about such things, or in Amber's words, "fourteen year old boys going off to high school, with their ego in one hand and memoir in the other" (p. 52).

Teaching to educate good people was also evident in comments made by Adam Heenan. A social studies teacher in a large urban high school in Chicago, Adam teaches his largely Latino/a and African American students with a decidedly multicultural and social justice perspective. He described teaching as a way to serve his community, and he talked about the kinds of values he wants to instill in the students, values he himself has developed as a teacher: "Honesty and resilience, dignity,

resourcefulness and consistency: those are the things that have constructed my teacher identity so far."

Adam spoke about the effect of his classes on students, saying, "So
. . . do I think they come away from my classroom being better human beings? Yeah, I think so. I think they're better off because I am here" (p. 50).
He laughed, saying, "That [sounds] so egotistical! But I like to think that
my students come away learning from my class even if they didn't learn
exactly what I had in mind. They come away with a broader worldview"
(p. 50). Adam gave the example of a project on homelessness his students
were doing in his economics class. Besides developing empathy for others,
he also expected them to learn research skills, take responsibility for their
work, and take initiative. In this project, he said, "they have to create
something of value for other people, not just themselves" (p. 51).

Wearing a t-shirt with the bold words I AM A TEACHER embla-
zoned on it, Adam said it reflected the same kind of pride and dignity
demanded by African Americans who wore placards proclaiming I AM A
MAN during the Civil Rights era. I also noticed Adam's tattoos, one on
each arm. When I asked what they meant, he responded that one was the
Greek word for "audacity," and the other the Greek word for "humility."
He explained that while a student at the University of Illinois at Chicago,
Adam had been a student of Bill Ayers. From Bill, he said he had learned
many things, and this particular quote was one that had resonated powerfully with him: "Good teaching requires audacity but demands humility."
This is but one example of the legacy of Bill Ayers, not just for Adam but
also for the many thousands he has touched directly through his teaching
and indirectly through his scholarly work and activism.

Conclusion

Teaching for the common good definitely requires both audacity
and humility, and Adam Heenan, Amber Bechard, John Gunderson, and
Carmen Tisdale are powerful examples of this truth. For them, as for
many other teachers around the country, teaching is an ethical endeavor.
Teachers need to be aware that their actions, attitudes, and practices can
have untold and longstanding repercussions (although these may be un-
intended) for their students' lives. Whether it is about teaching students
responsibility for themselves and for their neighbors, or learning about
students' identities in order to become culturally responsive educators,
the ethical nature of teaching is unmistakable. Although Carmen, Amber,
John, and Adam are extraordinary teachers, they are in many ways no
different from many other caring and compassionate teachers. They care

about their students; engage them in academic, as well as ethical, content; and prepare them to live productive civic lives. In an era when there is so little talk about ethics in education, these teachers stand out as exemplary educators who dare to believe in their students, honor who they are, and teach them to be responsible and moral human beings. This is another important lesson we can learn from Bill Ayers.

References

Ayers, B. (2003). *On the side of the child: Summerhill revisited*. New York, NY: Teachers College Press.

Elster, A., & Miller, J. E. (2007). *I still see her haunting eyes: The holocaust and a hidden child named Aaron*. Peoria, IL: BF Press.

Miner, B. J. (2013). *Lessons from the heartland: A turbulent half-century of public education in an iconic American city*. New York, NY: New Press.

Nieto, S. (2005). Public education in the twentieth century and beyond: High hopes, broken promises, and an uncertain future. *Harvard Educational Review, 75*(1), 57–78.

Nieto, S. (2013). *Finding joy in teaching students of diverse backgrounds: Culturally responsive and socially just practices in U.S. schools*. Portsmouth, NH: Heinemann.

Noddings, N. (1992). *The challenge to care in schools: An alternative approach to education*. New York, NY: Teachers College Press.

Spring, J. (2012). *Deculturalization and the struggle for equality: A brief history of the education of dominated cultures in the United States* (7th ed.). New York, NY: McGraw-Hill.

Valenzuela, A. (1999). *Subtractive schooling: U.S.-Mexican youth and the politics of caring*. New York: State University of New York Press.

20

Teachable Moments

W.J.T. Mitchell

I should begin by admitting that I have never taught in a public school, except for two brief appearances. The first was to teach for 1 hour in my 2nd-grade daughter's poetry class, where I introduced the students to haiku, evidently spawning a host of imitators. The second was a series of visits to elementary public schools in Chicago, most notably Shoesmith School, located across the street from the house where I have lived for 36 years. My aim there was not to teach the students anything, but to learn from them. I was writing a book about the dinosaur as a cultural icon, later published as *The Last Dinosaur Book: The Life and Times of a Cultural Icon* (Mitchell, 1998), and felt that I should do research into the supposed love that young kids have for the big green monsters. I showed lots of slides of dinosaurs in science books and popular culture, including stills from *Jurassic Park* and cartoons by Gary Larson. I didn't teach them anything, but I learned a number of useful things. Kids tend to segregate dinosaurs by gender and food preference (e.g., the predators are seen as male, the herbivores as female), except for one bright little girl who pointed out that not all T-Rexes could be male, or there wouldn't be any baby T-Rexes. I learned that Barney, the dopey kid-show dinosaur, is not fooling anybody in 1st grade. They shouted out in unison: "He's not a *real* dinosaur. He's just some guy in a stupid dinosaur suit." One 1st-grader then volunteered the observation that Barney is "too childish" to be taken seriously: "Only my annoying little brother thinks Barney is cool." When I asked if anyone knew any jokes or rhymes about Barney, I was rewarded with the following parody of the Barney theme song: "I love you, you love me/Barney gave me HIV."

That is the extent of my experience as an elementary school teacher. As a college professor, on the other hand, I have 45 years of experience, teaching first at a state school—Ohio State University, from 1968 to

1977—and then at the University of Chicago from 1977 to the present. There have been plenty of contradictions, most of them unresolved, and a few commitments, some of them partly achieved, in this long career. I don't know how useful my experiences will be to teachers at the precollege level, whom I think of as "on the front lines," "in the trenches," and other dubious military metaphors. The University of Chicago, by contrast, has seemed to me a kind of protected utopian space for teachers. Our students are highly selected, strongly motivated, and generally well prepared. One of their frequent complaints is that not enough is being demanded of them, and they would like longer reading lists! (I know it sounds like I am making this up, but I'm not.)

The contradictions and commitments arose in my first year as a teacher—the highly charged year of 1968—at Ohio State. I regarded the teaching of literature at that time (and still do) as an emancipatory activity, a commitment to the goal of heightened literacy, critical acuity, and expanded human sympathy. I also was committed in some vague way to a concept of emancipatory pedagogy, a democratic classroom that would expand its scope into the larger world, democratizing the elite, stratified institution in which I was teaching, and from there move out into the streets where the events of 1968 would be realized in a second American Revolution, one in which equality, freedom, and democracy would flourish. In other words, I was the same starry-eyed idealist that I am today. The contradictions, however, erupted immediately in my first year of teaching freshman English. One of the students came to my office and asked me straight out what my credentials were, since I had been caught in some factual error in class discussion. I told him that I had a PhD from Johns Hopkins University—thank you—a place known for its high standards and rigorous training. He expressed surprise. "Oh," he said, "I thought you were just another of the green weenies, like the grad students who do most of the teaching around here."

It dawned on me then that this job might be a little more difficult than I had imagined. My degree certified that I was qualified to teach college (although I was wracked with doubt every time I walked into a classroom). I knew that I was not much smarter than the green weenies teaching freshman comp. And in my course on utopian literature (one of my favorite subjects), I had told the students: "This will be an egalitarian classroom. The only difference between me and you is that I will be getting paid to be here, and you will be paying." The moment the words were out of my mouth, I began to feel sure that they were bullshit of some sort, disguised as an attempt at transparency. That "only difference" makes all the difference in the world, and it was completely disingenuous of me to think that it could be waved off so blithely. Time to reset and rethink what I am doing here.

So of course, I went to the other extreme, making sure that the students were well aware of my credentials, making them read the articles that I was publishing as fast as I could to get tenure, and preparing long lectures that would dazzle them with the number of things I knew and they didn't. I took great pleasure in asking big, unanswerable questions ("What was the Renaissance?") and then letting them know that I was not interested in their answers, but expected them to write down and commit to memory the answer I was about to give them—an answer that I had learned myself in a similar way in graduate school. Or I asked picky little questions: "Blake's *Songs of Experience* were published in 1794. What is the significance of that date?" (Answer: the Reign of Terror.) I refrained from demanding explicitly that they read my mind, but that was pretty much all my Socratic method amounted to. As for my goals as a revolutionary educator, I was pretty sure that these students, raised in the suburbs and farms of central Ohio, would never achieve mature anarchist consciousness without being firmly led by someone like me, who was immersed in Norman O. Brown, Herbert Marcuse, R. D. Laing, the Port Huron Statement, and the *Whole Earth Catalog*. As you can see, my commitments themselves were riddled with contradictions. Time to reset and rethink.

I started by trying to listen a bit more carefully to what my students actually were saying, instead of fretting so much over what I was supposed to be teaching them. And a golden "teachable moment" occurred spontaneously one afternoon, when in a Shakespeare class of 40 undergraduates focusing on *Merchant of Venice*, I began to hold forth on anti-Semitism. One of my students, a farm lad, raised his hand and asked: "What is anti-Semitism?" When I patiently explained that it had to do with ungrounded, irrational prejudices against Jews, one student objected: "It seems to me that Shylock is just paranoid. He is the one who is insisting on a deadly contract." At which point an Israeli student burst out: "You'd be paranoid too if someone spit on your gabardine," echoing Shylock's complaint about the contemptuous treatment he endured from Christian gentlemen. And so we were off to the races in a debate that is, by nature, endless and endlessly illuminating. The subsequent discussion ranged over the many types of racism and prejudice, and the way that literature engages with a world of social and emotional conflict. I don't recall any conclusions, but I do recall feeling that it was the best class of the term, and what a privilege it was for me to be presiding over an amazing, unforgettable moment.

I don't know what the students learned that day, but at the end of the term, one of them wrote on my evaluation form: "If a rocket came through the window and landed in the middle of the classroom, Professor Mitchell would be sure to make it the subject of a lengthy discussion."

I wasn't sure whether this was praise or ridicule, but it did give me an intuition about the way to make "teachable moments" effective: Do not begin by assuming that you know ahead of time what the lesson is that everyone should be learning.

Fortunately, a disciplinary crisis in my own research gave me a way of using my own gaps in learning to some advantage as a teacher. Although I had been, as we say, "trained" as a literary scholar, my research interests were moving toward the visual arts, where I had no credentials whatsoever. So I organized a faculty–student reading group of art historians, philosophers, and literary critics around the subject of literature and the visual arts, or more generally "words and images." (It was called "the Laocoon Group," not primarily referencing the ancient classical sculpture, but the book by the German critic G. E. Lessing on "the limits of painting and poetry.") This group had the effect of making my teaching much more exploratory and tentative, and much less concerned with imparting the knowledge transmitted to me in grad school. I found that there is nothing quite like being out of one's depth as a teacher to bring a certain feeling of excitement, not to mention risk, into a classroom. The best teachable moments, the ones that we remember, are those that occur when the teacher has something to learn along with the students.

So I began moving far out of my depth, into studies of photography, painting, sculpture, cinema, and television; and into theories of imagery and the way images circulate across media, reviving a very ancient discipline known as "iconology." I began to write and teach about the political and psychological use of images, about their role in religion and sacred ritual, and advertising, propaganda, and popular culture, as well as in "art" proper. I invented (or more likely reinvented) a new disciplinary formation called "visual culture," and I began to reread the works of Marshall McLuhan, the founder of media studies in the heroic era of the 1960s.

What this meant for classroom practice was that I rarely taught the same subject in the same way twice; I sought out opportunities for team teaching at every turn; I began to think of freshman courses and PhD seminars as nearly indistinguishable, and found myself teaching classes such as "Violence and Representation"; "The Eye and the Gaze";

"Space, Place, and Landscape"; "The Arts of Memory"; and "Totemism, Fetishism, Idolatry" to highly diverse groups that included students from many different departments and levels of preparation. I am sure that a substantial number of these students would have preferred to have someone who had mastered all the relevant research in these fields. What they found in me instead was an enthusiastic fellow learner who was often only a few pages ahead of them in the reading assignment, and sometimes behind them. The most embarrassingly *unteachable* moment I ever experienced was introducing a freshman class in Greek thought and literature to the wonders of Thucydides's *Peloponnesian War*, and being asked by a bright young girl how this 700-page history comes out in the end. Quick thinking to the rescue: "I don't want to spoil this for you by telling you how it ends."

Fortunately, I teach at the University of Chicago, a place that has an abundance of professors who are the leading experts in their fields and who can be called on when, as always, I find myself out of my depth. Even more fortunately, I have a few colleagues who appreciate our favorite rejoinder when someone asks whether we have read a new book. "Read it? I haven't even taught it yet!"

The contradictions/commitments that I inhabit these days have mainly to do with the significance of the new digital technologies on the classroom experience. I am firmly committed to old media, especially face-to-face discussion and live performance, not to mention frequent writing assignments. But I have tried to find ways to use new media to enhance these traditional modes of learning. I create a discussion board for each course, in which the students can extend the classroom debate after hours. I assign two students to take notes for each session and to post them on the course website under a forum called "Comparing Notes." I often ask the students to write reference articles on key terms and concepts, and to post them on the website. (One interesting wrinkle of this assignment: I always introduce it by telling them that the goal is *not* to be original, but to be reliable and authoritative. This generally stirs up a productive rebellion, since it goes against everything they have been taught elsewhere about "creativity.") When we are dealing with new media, screen-based technologies, and "virtuality," I ask them to come to class prepared to give a "show and tell" performance of the kind they did in 1st grade—showing, not telling, what is new about a new medium. The theory behind these experiments is to affirm the importance of what I would call "lateral learning," in which students learn from one another and regard themselves as producers of knowledge, not mere consumers of the stuff that I know.

For me, then, the dilemma of a teacher's life is captured in Ryan Alexander-Tanner's cover cartoons for Bill Ayers's *To Teach* (2010). Ryan first shows Bill as a teacher standing up, lecturing to a seated student, and then in the next panel shows Bill scrunched into the pupil's chair, the student explaining something to him. That role reversal, so easy to depict, but so difficult to achieve in practice, is precisely the contradictory commitment that haunts every success and failure in my life as a teacher.

References

Ayers, W., & Alexander-Tanner, R. (2010). *To teach: The journey, in comics.* New York, NY: Teachers College Press.

Mitchell, W.J.T. (1998). *The last dinosaur book: The life and times of a cultural icon.* Chicago, IL: University of Chicago Press.

21

"It's a Strange World—Some Get Rich and Others Eat Shit and Die"

Bill Ayers and the Art of Entering Our Contradictions

David Stovall

The title of this short meditation comes from Hunter S. Thompson's (1988) *Generation of Swine (Gonzo Papers, Vol. 2)*. While some may feel the title to be strange, I feel it is fitting to understanding this bizarre moment in public education. I live in a city (Chicago) that has lost 200,000 residents since 2000 (178,000 of them African American), has had 80% of its public housing stock demolished or redeveloped, and is on the verge of closing 49 schools (the largest set of school closings in the history of the United States). For me, Thompson's quote serves as metaphor for a lesson with which Bill challenges students, colleagues, and comrades to engage: Despite the situation, we can never be fearful of writing into the contradictions, especially our own. This challenges us to name the fact that while the few are getting richer, the remainder of us have been left *"to eat shit and die."* For him, these are the spaces that allow us to see our truest selves, no matter how fraught with mistakes and missteps. In my own life and work, these messy, unfinished, tattered, and frayed spaces allow me to understand a critically important aspect of the human condition.

The process of interrogating how I and others have made mistakes and recovered from them allows us to understand the possibility of victory in struggle. Because movements can be co-opted, and individuals can be compromised, the reminder of our human-ness provides the opportunity to reflect and move forward, remaining steadfast in the commitment to build and defend spaces in which young people and families can think and create. However, as students, parents, community members, teachers, organizers, activists, and critical pedagogues, our responsibility to reflect remains imperative. Without our reflection, we risk the chance of rationalizing the disposability of certain students, families, and neighborhoods. If we're not careful, we can provide the rationales for others to *"eat shit and die."*

In the spirit of Bill's challenge, the following two offerings are lessons I've learned from my interactions with him. The first is considerably shorter than the second, but both are reflective of contradictions I've grappled with. In the end, hopefully my experiences will be able to provide some encouragement for those, like myself, who sometimes struggle to make informed decisions.

Don't Take It Personal

Having a university gig as a professor often means that you are traveling in and out of meetings. Sometimes you feel as if you are meeting about the next meeting, but the in-between time can provide brief opportunities to learn things about/from your colleagues. In this particular instance, I was new to the University of Illinois at Chicago and was not enthused about building camaraderie with many of my colleagues. Although I felt I had been aptly prepared for an academic position and to deal with hostile environments, like all things, it is completely different once you're *in* the situation. At this time I hadn't really found the community of folks with whom I would later build lasting relationships. Instead, I was completely disconnected from faculty meetings where people would take the opportunity to run their mouths about issues for which I had little concern.

On this particular day it was cold, and we were making our way over to a building across the street. In this moment I was complaining to Bill about how professor–student intimate relationships were highly problematic. The fact that many such relationships have a highly skewed power dynamic was impetus enough for me to run in the opposite direction. This same rant included a complaint about a student who happened to ask me to consider dating her daughter. After a guest lecture in a colleague's class, one of the students present approached me and said, "I would love for you to meet my daughter—she's interested in similar things and would really like to meet someone like yourself." For me, this was totally out of bounds. Where I was flattered by the sentiment, I was confused as to what emboldened her to feel comfortable enough to make the reference to her daughter. My confusion slowly transitioned to anger as I began to feel cheapened by the entire experience and no longer wanted to be in that situation as a faculty member.

Upon revealing the entire story to Bill and some other colleagues, he looked at me and smiled. While I'm unable to offer a facsimile of the conversation, the following epigraph captures the essence of his reply:

> You know, you're a young guy that is willing to talk about things that a lot of folks are often afraid to talk about (race, justice, housing, gentrification, corruption, collective struggle, revolutions, etc.). That's going to attract a lot of folks to you. But you have to do one thing: don't take it personal—it's not you. Remember, they don't know you. They only know a particular thing about you that they kinda like. You could be the asshole of the universe—they don't know. You can't blame folks for what they don't know. The real work is not taking them up on their offer.

Bill went on to state that he got this lesson from a 70-year-old African American woman whom he was complaining to some years before. She told him that her White male students were so enamored with her and she was trying to figure it out. After taking time to sleep on it, she concluded that her students didn't really *know* her, but instead were clinging to the ideas she brought forward in class. For me, this was a necessary reality check to understand that humility must be central in the work of building community with those working to change our conditions, whether in education or in life in general. Assumptions will get you in trouble only if you are consumed with the idea that whatever you're talking about is the most important thing and takes precedence over everything else. To this day I remain extremely thankful that I got this lesson early on!

Doing the Important Things When No One Is Looking

My second meditation comes from a story with one of my high school students. Over the past 8 years I have been involved with a place called the Greater Lawndale High School for Social Justice (SOJO). In addition to being a university professor I have worked on the design team, local school council, and have taught classes at the school. SOJO was created as part of a larger community struggle (culminating in a 19-day hunger strike) to demand quality education for two communities (one Latino/a, one African American) that historically have been disinvested, marginalized, and isolated. Since the hunger strike and throughout its existence, Bill has stayed close and supported the efforts in the school.

In the junior year of the first graduating class (2007–2008), one of the social studies teachers I was working with created an assignment for students to research someone, either living or deceased, who made an explicit effort to work for justice. If the person was local, they were given an option to interview him or her as part of the paper. Around the same time, one of the students, Rocio (or Ro-Ro as she preferred), was telling me about a book she had come across in the library called *Fugitive Days*. She was really interested in the activities of the Weather Underground and discovered that there was also an Oscar-nominated documentary that had been released. I remembered that during the 2003 Oscars ceremony, I had seen Bill on the red carpet. I sent him a text message asking, "Did I just see you on the red carpet?" He responded with a very simple "yup." Again, for me it was recognition that truth is always the strangest if we pay attention. I told Ro-Ro that the documentary had been nominated for an Oscar. She replied with, "Really . . . did it win?" When I told her no she said, "I thought not—that might've started the revolution right there!"

As we both laughed about it, we continued our conversation. I asked her why she became interested in the Weather Underground. She talked about how their work reminded her of the effort to create SOJO. The Weathermen's commitment to do things differently was parallel to the mothers, grandmothers, teachers, community members, and students who dared to stand up to power while galvanizing a community to support quality education. From there I told her that the writer lives and works in Chicago and that he's still alive. She rolled her eyes and responded with, "I know." After that I told her that I actually worked with him. She said, "No you don't—get outta here, Stovall. You always got something crazy to say." I said, "For real—I know him." She just shook her head. From there I said, "Look—I'll make you a deal. Give me your email and I'll link the two of you. If he's in town he'll come and do the interview. All we have to do is set it up." She said, "You think I'm still in grammar school, don't you? Those tricks don't work, Stovall. I know you're gonna use another email and play like it's really him—get outta here."

From there all I could think was *I hope Bill comes through on this one*. If he doesn't my credibility is shot. To Ro-Ro's credit, she sent me her email. I sent a corresponding email to Bill with Ro-Ro's information so they could be introduced to each other. I saw that he replied and that they were trying to set up an interview.

When I got back to SOJO, Ro-Ro told me, "Stovall, you're playing with me—I know that's you!" When I replied that it wasn't, she twisted her bottom lip and said, "Whatever." From there, I thought the best thing to do would be to let her and Bill communicate on their own without my involvement. I had to travel for a couple of days and knew I would miss class. I told the students and reminded them I would be back the next week.

Because they were deeply into their research projects, the class met in the library. When I walked in, the first thing I noticed was that Bill and Ro-Ro were sitting in a corner talking about his experience with the Weather Underground. They were both comparing it with the hunger strike and what it means to stand for justice. I didn't interrupt their conversation, but I looked over and nodded to her with a big smile. After the class ended she walked over and said, "You still don't know him."

Even though we both laughed about it, the experience meant a lot to me. Here was someone with over 15 books, countless articles, guest op eds, collaborative projects, and international visibility sitting down with *one* student for her research project. Where many would think of themselves as not having the time, this space was more important than filling a lecture hall or signing books. It was engaging in the way we need to engage.

In Parting

While my two ruminations may appear mundane to some, they are critical for me in understanding how to remain humble when the world in many cases rewards you for being narcissistic, obnoxious, and filled with yourself. In the end, the most important work often is done when no one is looking. In grappling with our contradictions, it becomes important to keep our questions and actions centered on working in solidarity with those who couldn't care less whether we were in the most recent *New York Review of Books*. I must remind myself constantly that my individual success is a farce if it comes by way of exploiting the people I work with. I cannot justify rationales for young people and families left to die in the manure of flawed and intentionally destructive educational policies created under the false banners of "choice" and "improvement." Grappling with my contradictions means keeping my feet on the ground. Despite the academic "gig," I must be able to suspend any notion of supposed expertise. Our contradictions rear their ugly heads when we actually believe the unwarranted praise we may get. Bill reminded me to be leery of the façade we may fool ourselves into believing. Instead, a more valued position is one where we are willing to say when things don't go our way or when we are hurt and confused. The ability to humanize ourselves as writers and researchers brings clarity to our work. Removing the veil from our lives allows us to build solidarity with others. I am thankful to Bill for pushing me to understand that this is where we must go in such a strange world in even stranger times.

References

Thompson, H. S. (1988). *Generation of swine (Gonzo papers, volume 2): Tales of shame and degradation in the 80s.* New York, NY: Simon & Schuster.

22

Personal Reflections About Bill Ayers

Rashid Khalidi

In thinking what to write for a book inspired by Bill Ayers's life and work, I asked myself what I could say about Bill's primary concerns—politics and education—that others could not say better. I was certainly not the person to write about Bill and politics. He had already lived a very full political life before Mona and I met him and Bernardine early in 1987, when by chance we were brought together by a former student of his who had taught two of our kids at P.S. 166 in New York City. This was just before our two families moved, by a fortuitous coincidence, from within a few blocks of each other in the same neighborhood on the Upper West Side of Manhattan to a few blocks from each other on the same street in Hyde Park, Chicago. There, over the next decade and a half, our three children and Bill and Bernardine's three kids went to the same school, and we grew to be the closest of friends. We became what really amounted to a large extended family of 10—as we shared several meals a week, Little League coaching duties, and much of our time together.

Politics was naturally one of the basic bonds among the four of us, but each had already gone through quite a few political iterations long before we met. By then we were already pretty much formed in our views: Mona and I mainly as a result of our dozen-plus years of political involvement in Beirut (most of them during conditions of war or extreme conflict); and Bill and Bernardine as a result of their experiences with SDS, the underground Weatherman years, and the time above ground after that. These different political perspectives and experiences made for a good mix and enriched our discussions and interactions. But when we met, our years of peak political activism were behind us. There are many others who know more about the evolution of Bill's political views and who could say more about the topic, central though it was to his life and to our connections with one another.

Nor am I the right person to talk about education, which has been the basic concern of Bill's professional life for the entire time I have known him, and indeed long before that. As anyone reading this volume surely knows, Bill is a master teacher, and pedagogy has always been central to his adult life. I have watched him lecture and teach, I have read his writing on the topic, and I have seen many examples of the shared devotion between him and his students. Although I have been a teacher myself for nearly 40 years, and have learned a lot about my own craft as a teacher from watching and listening to Bill and reading his work, I am not well suited to write about Bill and education. My own discipline, history, is far removed from his. Although much of what he has tried to impart as a teacher is broadly philosophical and entirely transcends disciplinary boundaries (which he despises), there are many others who are more familiar than I with his major contributions to his chosen field.

I finally decided that if there is anything I might be able to contribute to an appreciation of Bill that might provide a fresh perspective, it would involve a few personal reflections, drawn from the quarter of a century during which we have come to know each other, and from the things I have learned from and about him due to that interaction.

One of the underappreciated aspects of Bill's personality is how absolutely calm he always is. Among our volatile and often hot-headed foursome, Bill is by far the most level-headed and balanced, and has the greatest degree of equanimity, no matter how tense or infuriating the circumstances. I sometimes felt that he was overly calm, at moments when by all rights he should have shown a stronger reaction. This bland equanimity in the face of what would have intensely affected any normal person, often exasperates Bernardine (Bill loves to play on that); amuses Mona no end; and arouses my unalloyed admiration. In this, Bill is a perfect foil for Bernardine, Mona, and myself, who are decidedly less calm.

The examples of his sangfroid are legion, but the one that sticks out most in my memory is an experience we shared when the four of us were driving in bright sunshine from Chicago to Minnesota to visit our son in college. Suddenly, a freak snow squall blew up out of nowhere, the car's steering stopped responding, and to my horror our vehicle slid slowly and unavoidably out of control off the highway and into the grassy divider on I-94. In my memory, the entire episode happened in near white-out, complete silence, and very slow motion. Thankfully, no one was hurt, the car was fine, and soon we were on our way again, with me now driving very, very slowly. As best I can recall, none of us said very much at any point during this surreal incident, although I am sure that the others were just as scared as I was. However, Bill could not have been calmer if I had just routinely parked the car on the shoulder in perfect weather. If I have calmed down a little bit over the years, I owe it to the example of Bill. If not, it is in spite of his good influence.

The differences between us in this regard perhaps could best be seen when we coached our eldest two kids as they played together on the same team in the Hyde Park–Kenwood Little League for a couple of years. Bill was a paragon of coaching virtue, composed and cool, and directing our young charges in a completely assured manner, while I was a shade more in the Billy Martin/Lou Piniella mode (without any of the success as manager of these paragons). Thereafter, when I coached for a few years together with Bernardine, I am afraid that neither of us were exactly models of composure, and I shudder to think what the kids we coached picked up from us in terms of standards of baseball behavior. By the end of my decade of coaching, I like to think that not only was I able to impart something useful about baseball to the kids, but that I was behaving a little more calmly. If so, I owed at least some of that calmer affect to Bill's example.

Another way in which Bill is exemplary is his extraordinary work ethic when he is writing. On the numerous occasions over the past 10 years when he has come to stay with us in New York, he immediately has set himself up, usually at our dining room table (which is identical to the famous one on which he supposedly wrote that other fellow's autobiography) or sometimes on the desk in our guest bedroom, and began writing away in longhand, or tapping at his laptop, oblivious to all going on around him. I like to think of myself as an assiduous writer, but I find Bill's ability to simply sit down and write in any environment truly impressive. Like Edward Said, who used to write every single day in the early hours of the morning, Bill has a discipline and tenaciousness in his writing regimen that I find totally admirable and would love to be able to emulate. Here, too, I hope I have learned something from him.

I must admit that my generally unalloyed admiration for Bill, and for Bernardine, initially was somewhat tarnished when they first became grandparents. Their granddaughters were and are adorable, as is their new grandson. And they had always been doting, generous, and tolerant parents, one of their most admirable characteristics and one that influenced our children greatly as well. But frankly, I thought that the totally unrestrained and enthusiastic way they reacted to Dailin and Light after they were born indicated that both of them had completely taken leave of their senses. I will not go into embarrassing detail, especially since as soon as our grandson Tariq was born soon afterward, Mona and I instantaneously were transformed and have since behaved in precisely the same unhinged and enthusiastic way. Here, as in other things, Bill and Bernardine showed us the way.

A much more serious aspect of Bill's demeanor that I have found truly impressive has been his equanimity in the midst of media feeding frenzies. He has had to deal with such ordeals repeatedly in recent years and his calmness has served him exceedingly well. The first time that I had a chance to witness this was when, by some cosmic bad luck, his publisher's media effort around the release of his memoir *Fugitive Days*, describing the Weather Underground's bombings of the Pentagon and other targets, coincided with the attacks of September 11, 2001. Bill had said something in an interview with a *New York Times* reporter that was published on the front page of the Arts section that very morning and that soon afterward was taken entirely out of its original context and placed into that of the traumatic impact of 9/11. Outrageously, Bill thereby was made to appear to favor the atrocities that had just been perpetrated against thousands of innocent people.

Although all of us, his friends and family, were appalled and not a little shaken by the virulence and sheer dishonesty of these hateful outpourings, quite remarkably the despicable behavior of elements of the media and of the bloviators who jumped into the fray to malign him did not appear to faze Bill in any way. Not many people could have managed to deal in such a balanced way with the pure nastiness. Bill simply took it in stride, accepting philosophically not only that he might be forever tarred by the slanders of the gutter-dwellers who had attacked him, but also that the public reception of the memoir he had worked so hard on, and had such high hopes for, was irrevocably sabotaged.

This traumatic experience served Bill well a number of years later when he (and I, to a much lesser extent) was subjected to media mudslinging during Barack Obama's first campaign for president. This began in the spring of 2008, when the Hillary Clinton campaign's master of the dark arts of negative campaigning saw to it that our names were injected into the Democratic primary, in order to use us as a black mark against Obama. The slim basis for this was the indisputable fact that we had known Barack and Michelle Obama socially as neighbors in Hyde Park, where he was our state senator and my colleague at the University of Chicago. This was used by various figures connected to the Clinton campaign to malign Obama by describing him as someone who had associated with questionable characters with dark, indeed implied terrorist, pasts such as ourselves. The impact of all of this on the Democratic primary was limited. But these smears had been duly noted by assiduous Republican opposition researchers, whose principals did not hesitate to resuscitate them during the general election campaign.

Subsequently, Bill was the main target of the famous Obama "palling around with terrorists" accusation by the McCain–Palin campaign and their co-conspirators in Fox News and the rest of the far-Right media. The Obamas' pastor, the Reverend Jeremiah Wright, myself, and a few others were also the targets of some of their poison. Bill's remarkable sense of humor, his calm composure, and his thick skin in the face of the most extraordinary accusations and the most ludicrous slanders enabled him to ride out this tide of vitriol with little apparent effect. Once, when the proliferation of crazy conspiracy theories had reached its height in the Right wing blogosphere with claims that Bill and Barack Obama were so close that it was Bill who had actually ghostwritten Obama's two best-selling books, he was asked by a reporter who had bumped into him at an airport whether these claims were true. Deadpan, and without missing a beat, Bill "admitted" that indeed it was, giving the excited journalist lots of juicy details and sending her scurrying off with her "scoop."

I have always wished I were so quick-witted in dealing with the media, especially when they are in what I call "lemming mode"—that is, all jumping off the same cliff at the same time—as they were during this late phase of the 2008 presidential campaign. The best I could manage in response to the smears directed at me, in much smaller numbers than Bill, was to tell the *Washington Post* that I had nothing to say in response, but would just let "this idiot wind blow over." It doesn't hold a candle to Bill bold-facedly "admitting" authorship of Barack Obama's memoirs!

As anyone who has met him knows, Bill is not only calm, hard-working, relaxed, and funny. What I hope some of these vignettes show is that he is also quite brave. He has the courage of his convictions, as well as the courage to admit where he was wrong in the past. Over the past dozen years, he has stood up without flinching to some of the most vicious currents in American political life, at times at a measure of physical danger to himself. Perhaps worse than those rare moments when he was personally threatened were the seemingly endless stretches when he was being unjustly vilified not just by far-Right media and politicians, but by what sometimes appeared to be the entire American political and media "mainstream." All of this has been amplified by the way in which the Internet and social media produce a snowball effect, as baseless accusations and distortions become hardened "facts," which in turn are the basis for even more debased and fanciful fabrications. This despicable process reached a peak, as I have mentioned, when the publication of *Fugitive Days* happened to coincide with 9/11, and Bill was swept up in the waves of public hysteria following that devastating event. It occurred all over again in 2008 during the presidential campaign. Having endured a fraction of the abuse he faced, I can attest to how hard dealing with this storm of political, media, and Internet slander can be. But Bill's equanimity never faltered, and he imperturbably went on teaching, writing, lecturing, being a good parent, taking care of his grandkids, and just being Bill.

In the end, the real measure of a person, even a respected public intellectual and teacher like Bill Ayers, is not so much his political stances or professional achievements, both of which are highly creditable in Bill's case. It is rather whether people are able to pass on their best personal qualities to their children and grandchildren, and to their students and those whom they have otherwise influenced. The evidence is quite clear in Bill's case. His students are everywhere, are much respected, and respect him deeply; he is sought out by people of several generations as a speaker; and his many books are much read. He and Bernardine have had a powerful effect on our three children, expanding their horizons, teaching and mentoring them, and sharing values with them. Most important, their sons Zayd, Malik, and Chesa, as grown men, have already had ample time to show some of the same attributes of humor, imperturbability, diligence, and courage that Bill himself has always exhibited. That is a superb testament not only to Zayd's, Malik's, and Chesa's sterling qualities as human beings, but also to those of Bill and Bernardine.

About the Contributors

Ryan Alexander-Tanner is a Portland, Oregon-based cartoonist and educator. He is the logo designer for Dave's Killer Bread and the coauthor (with Bill Ayers) and illustrator of *To Teach: The Journey, in Comics*. His educational work is focused on illustration and applying comics to classroom curriculum. You can find him online at: www.ohyesverynice.com.

Alexandra Allweiss is a PhD candidate in curriculum and instruction and educational policy studies at the University of Wisconsin–Madison. Her research interests include comparative and international education, multicultural and social justice education, critical theories, intersectionality in educational experiences, and teacher and community activism in education. Before coming to UW–Madison, she worked as a middle school and high school teacher in Guatemala.

Rick Ayers founded the Communication Arts and Sciences small school at Berkeley High School, known for innovative strategies for academic and social success for a diverse range of students. He is an assistant professor of education at the University of San Francisco in the Urban Education and Social Justice cohort. He is the coauthor, with his brother William Ayers, of *Teaching the Taboo: Courage and Imagination in the Classroom* and is also author of *Great Books for High School Kids* and *A Teacher's Guide to Studs Terkel's Working*. He is a regular blogger on education for the *Huffington Post*.

Patrick Camangian, PhD, is an associate professor in the Department of Teacher Education at the University of San Francisco and has been an English teacher since 1999, continuing in the tradition of teacher-research, applying critical pedagogies in urban schools. His research interests and areas of expertise include critical pedagogy and transformative teaching in urban schools, critical literacy, humanizing education, and urban teacher development.

Bernardine Dohrn, activist, academic, and child advocate, is a clinical professor at Northwestern University School of Law (retired) and founding director of the Children and Family Justice Center. Dohrn was national leader of Students for a Democratic Society and the Weather Underground, and was on the FBI's 10 Most Wanted List. She is coauthor, with Bill Ayers, of *Race Course: Against White Supremacy,* is coeditor of *Sing a Battle Song: Documents of the Weather Underground,* and wrote the introduction to *Letters from Young Activists.* She is author and coeditor of *A Century of Juvenile Justice* and *Resisting Zero Tolerance: A Handbook for Parents, Teachers and Students.*

Hubert M. Dyasi, PhD, is a science teacher educator. He was a visiting scholar at the University of Oxford and at the California Institute of Technology. He has published scholarly science education articles and book chapters, including in *The National Science Education Standards, Inquiry and the National Science Education Standards: A Guide for Teaching and Learning Teaching Science in the 21st Century, Designing Professional Development for Teachers of Science and Mathematics,* and *Principles and Big Ideas of Science Education.* He is a member of several professional societies and the recipient of Outstanding Educator and Distinguished Service to Science Education awards.

Michelle Fine is distinguished professor of critical psychology, women's studies, and urban education at the Graduate Center, CUNY. Over the past decade, Fine has received the 2013 Strickland–Daniels Mentoring Award from Division 35, Psychology of Women of the American Psychological Association; the 2013 APA Award for Distinguished Contributions to Research in Public Policy; the 2012 Henry Murray Award from the Society for Personality and Social Psychology; the 2011 Kurt Lewin Award from SPSSI; the 2010 Social Justice and Higher Education Award from the College and Community Fellowship; the 2011 Beckman Award for mentoring; and the first Morton Deutsch Award (2005). She can be reached at mfine@gc.cuny.edu.

Carl A. Grant is Hoefs–Bascom Professor at the University of Wisconsin–Madison. He has authored or edited 37 books and has written more than 100 journal articles. He was president of the National Association for Multicultural Education (1993–1999), editor of *Review of Education Research* (1996–1999), member of AERA Fellows, and vice president of AERA Curriculum Studies Division B. Dr. Grant received the University of Wisconsin School of Education Distinguished Achievement Award, AERA's Social Justice Award, and AERA's Mentor Award, and is a member of the Kappa Delta Pi Laureate Society. He was a teacher and an administrator in the Chicago Public Schools.

Ming Fang He is professor of curriculum studies at Georgia Southern University. She has taught at the graduate, preservice, and inservice levels in the United States, Canada, Hong Kong, and China. She explores education, inquiry, and life in-between the Eastern, Western, and exile philosophy and curriculum with a particular focus on Confucius, John Dewey, Tsunesaburo Makiguchi, Daisaku Ikeda, Weiming Tu, Martha Nussbaum, and Edward Said. She has written about cross-cultural narrative inquiry of language, culture, and identity in multicultural contexts; cross-cultural teacher education; curriculum studies; activist practitioner inquiry; social justice research; exile curriculum; narratives of curriculum in the U.S. South; and transnational and diasporic studies.

Rashid Khalidi is Edward Said Professor of Arab Studies at Columbia University. He is editor of the *Journal of Palestine Studies*, was president of the Middle East Studies Association, and was an adviser to the Palestinian delegation to the 1991–1993 Arab–Israeli peace negotiations. Khalidi is the author of seven books, including *Brokers of Deceit: How the U.S. Has Undermined Peace in the Middle East, Sowing Crisis: American Dominance and the Cold War in the Middle East, The Iron Cage: The Story of the Palestinian Struggle for Statehood,* and *Palestinian Identity: The Construction of Modern National Consciousness.*

Alice Kim is a cultural organizer, educator, writer, and activist. She teaches and develops curriculum for the gender and women's studies program and Social Justice Initiative at the University of Illinois at Chicago. She was previously the director of The Public Square, a program of the Illinois Humanities Council that creates spaces for public conversations about cultural, political, and social issues. A longtime death penalty and prison abolitionist, Alice is a founding member of the Chicago Torture Justice Memorials, an artist/activist collective seeking justice for Chicago police torture survivors and documenting this shameful history. A humanist, optimistic realist, and pragmatic dreamer, you can find her instigating, building, and conspiring.

Joyce E. King is Benjamin E. Mays Endowed Chair of Urban Teaching, Learning and Leadership, professor of educational policy studies, and affiliated faculty in African American studies at Georgia State University. She holds degrees from Stanford University (PhD in Social Foundations of Education, BA in sociology) and a Harvard Graduate School educational management certificate. Dr. King is president of the American Educational Research Association. Her research and scholarship analyze how dysconsciousness produced by mainstream education resists a critically transformative understanding of race and racial inequity for human freedom. Her most recent book is *Re-membering History in Student and Teacher Learning: An African-centered Culturally Informed Praxis.*

Fred Klonsky is a retired K–12 art teacher. For 30 years he taught in the public schools of Park Ridge, Illinois. For 10 years he was the president of the Park Ridge Education Association, the local union that affiliated with the National Education Association. He is a longtime political activist. As a student at the University of Illinois at Chicago, he studied with William Ayers, although he and Dr. Ayers were friends long before that. Since retiring in 2012 he has been active in the movements that oppose corporate school reform and in defending the pension rights of public employees. He blogs at FredKlonsky.com.

Craig Kridel is E. S. Gambrell Professor of Educational Studies and curator of the Museum of Education at the University of South Carolina. He currently is completing a study of Black progressive high schools from the 1940s. Recent works include *Stories of the Eight Year Study, The Encyclopedia of Curriculum Studies,* and *Classic Edition Sources: Education.* He is a former scholar-in-residence at the Rockefeller Archive Center and visiting fellow, Institute of Education, University of London. His publications have received the AERA Curriculum Studies Book Award, the AACTE Outstanding Writing Award, and the Educational Press Association of America Distinguished Achievement Award.

Gloria Ladson-Billings is Kellner Family Professor of Urban Education in the Department of Curriculum and Instruction at the University of Wisconsin–Madison and the 2005–2006 president of the American Educational Research Association. Ladson-Billings's research examines the pedagogical practices of teachers who are successful with African American students. She also investigates critical race theory applications to education. She is the author of the critically acclaimed book *The Dreamkeepers: Successful Teachers of African American Children, Crossing over to Canaan: The Journey of New Teachers in Diverse Classrooms,* and many journal articles and book chapters. She is the former editor of the *American Educational Research Journal* and a member of several editorial boards.

Crystal T. Laura, PhD, is assistant professor of Educational Leadership at Chicago State University. In her teaching and research, Dr. Laura explores educational leadership and leadership preparation for social justice with the goal of teaching school administrators to recognize, understand, and address the school-to-prison pipeline.

Lisa Yun Lee is director of the School of Art & Art History at the University of Illinois at Chicago. As the previous director of the Hull House Museum, she reinvigorated public programming, developed award-winning preservation programs, and installed a new core exhibition. Lee is also the co-founder of The Public Square at the Illinois Humanities Council, an organization dedicated to creating spaces for dialogue and dissent and for reinvigorating civil society. She has published articles about feminism, museums and diversity, and sustainability. She also writes for *In These Times* magazine. She received her BA in religion from Bryn Mawr College and a PhD in German Studies from Duke University.

Avi D. Lessing teaches high school English at Oak Park and River Forest High School. He recently finished his doctorate in Curriculum Studies at the University of Illinois at Chicago. He is working on a memoir about one day in the life of a teacher. Avi is blessed with a beautiful family: his wife, Bindi, and his children, Raiva and Rafi.

Karla Manning is a doctoral student and university supervisor in Curriculum and Instruction at the University of Wisconsin–Madison. She is a former high school English teacher in the Chicago Public Schools and also has taught ESL in South Africa. Her areas of interest are multicultural teacher education, visual and cultural studies, media literacy, and critical pedagogy. She is a graduate student representative of Division B in the American Educational Research Association. Karla also directed and co-produced the documentary *Black Lights*, which discusses and interrogates the voices and experiences of African American youth in Chicago Public Schools (www.blacklightsthemovie.org). She can be reached at manning.karla@gmail.com.

Erica R. Meiners is the author of several books that chart queer, anti-prison, and educational justice movements, including *Flaunt It! Queers Organizing for Public Education and Justice*, *Right to Be Hostile: Schools, Prisons and the Making of Public Enemies*, the forthcoming *Intimate Labor*, and articles in *AREA Chicago*, *Meridians*, *Academe*, *Social Justice*, *Women's Studies Quarterly*, and *No More Potlucks*. A professor of Gender and Women's Studies and Education at Northeastern Illinois University and a member of her labor union, University Professionals of Illinois, and a science fiction fan and a long-distance runner, Erica also has been a visiting scholar at the Institute for Research on Race and Public Policy (2011–2012) and a Lillian Robinson Scholar at the Simone de Beauvoir Institute in Montreal (2009–2010).

W.J.T. Mitchell is professor of English and art history at the University of Chicago. He is editor of the interdisciplinary journal *Critical Inquiry*, a quarterly devoted to critical theory in the arts and human sciences. A scholar and theorist of media, visual art, and literature, Mitchell is associated with the emergent fields of visual culture and iconology (the study of images across the media). He is known especially for his work on the relations of visual and verbal representations in the context of social and political issues. He has been the recipient of numerous awards, including the Guggenheim Fellowship and the Morey Prize in art history.

Sonia Nieto is professor emerita of language, literacy, and culture, College of Education, University of Massachusetts, Amherst. Her research focuses on multicultural education, teacher education, and educating Latinos, immigrants, and other students of culturally and linguistically diverse backgrounds. She has written numerous journal articles and book chapters and several books on these topics, including most recently *Finding Joy in Teaching Students of Diverse Backgrounds: Culturally Responsive and Socially Justice Practices in U.S. Schools* and the 6th edition of *Affirming Diversity: The Sociopolitical Context of Multicultural Education* (with Patty Bode). She has received many awards for her scholarship, teaching, and advocacy, including four honorary doctorates.

Isabel Nuñez is associate professor in the Center for Policy Studies and Social Justice at Concordia University Chicago. She holds a PhD in curriculum studies from the University of Illinois at Chicago, an MPhil in cultural studies from Birmingham University, England, and a JD from UCLA. She was a classroom teacher in the United States and England, and a newspaper journalist in Japan. She is an associate editor for *Multicultural Perspectives* and a founding member of CReATE (Chicagoland Researchers and Advocates for Transformative Education), a group of volunteer faculty engaged in inquiry and dialogue around policy for Chicago's schools.

Bree Picower is assistant professor at Montclair State University in the College of Education and Human Development. Her book, *Practice What You Teach: Social Justice Education in the Classroom and the Streets,* explores a developmental continuum toward teacher activism. She co-edits *Planning to Change the World: A Planbook for Social Justice Teachers,* which is published by the New York Collective of Radical Educators (NYCoRE) and the Education for Liberation Network. As a core leader of NYCoRE and founding member of the national Teacher Activist Groups network, Bree works to create spaces for educators to sharpen their political analysis and act for educational justice.

Therese Quinn is chair and associate professor of Art History and director of Museum and Exhibition Studies at the University of Illinois at Chicago. During 2009 Quinn was a Fulbright Scholar at the University of Helsinki, Finland, and she writes a bimonthly column for its magazine, *Yliopisto.* She coedits the Teachers College Press Series *Teaching for Social*

Justice and is a co-founder of and participant in Chicagoland Researchers and Advocates for Transformative Education (CReATE). Her most recent books are *Art and Social Justice Education: Culture as Commons, Sexualities in Education: A Reader,* and *Teaching Toward Democracy.*

William H. Schubert is University Scholar and Professor of Curriculum at the University of Illinois at Chicago (retired). His scholarly and pedagogical interests include curriculum studies—specifically, curriculum theory, history, development, design, critique, reconstruction, and study of consequences of the aforementioned. Most fundamentally, the central curriculum question for him is: What is worthwhile and why? How can I inquire about it, pursue, and acquire it—where, when, and who benefits from it, and who does not? More specifically, he is interested in what is worth knowing, needing, doing, being, becoming, overcoming, sharing, and contributing.

David Stovall, PhD, is associate professor of Educational Policy Studies and African American Studies at the University of Illinois at Chicago. Currently his research interests include concepts of social justice in education, the nexus of youth culture, community organizing, and education, and the relationship between housing markets and urban education. He is also a volunteer social studies teacher at the Greater Lawndale High School for Social Justice, where he was a member of the design team.

William H. Watkins was born in Harlem, New York, and raised in south-central Los Angeles. He received a BA in political science, an MEd, and a PhD in Public Policy Analysis–Education. He currently serves as professor and coordinator of the PhD Program, Department of Curriculum and Instruction, College of Education, University of Illinois at Chicago. He authored *The White Architects of Black Education* (2001); was editor and contributor to *The Assault on Public Education* (2012); was editor and contributor to *Black Protest Thought and Education* (2005); and was lead editor and contributor to *Race and Education* (2001). Additionally, Bill has authored over 75 book chapters, articles, and book reviews.

Joel Westheimer is education columnist for CBC Radio's *Ottawa Morning* show and University Research Chair in Democracy and Education at the University of Ottawa. He began his career teaching in the New York City Public School system before obtaining a PhD from Stanford University. Westheimer's recent award-winning book is *Pledging Allegiance: The Politics of Patriotism in America's Schools* (foreword by the late Howard Zinn). He is also author of the critically acclaimed *Among Schoolteachers: Community, Autonomy and Ideology in Teachers' Work.* His third book, *What Kind of Citizen?* will be published in 2014 by Teachers College Press.

Index